WE'VE GOT YOU COVERED

We've Got You
COVERED

Rebooting American Health Care

LIRAN EINAV and
AMY FINKELSTEIN

PORTFOLIO ▪ PENGUIN

PORTFOLIO / PENGUIN
An imprint of Penguin Random House LLC
penguinrandomhouse.com

Most Portfolio books are available at a discount when purchased in quantity for sales promotions or corporate use. Special editions, which include personalized covers, excerpts, and corporate imprints, can be created when purchased in large quantities. For more information, please call (212) 572-2232 or e-mail specialmarkets@penguinrandomhouse.com. Your local bookstore can also assist with discounted bulk purchases using the Penguin Random House corporate Business-to-Business program. For assistance in locating a participating retailer, e-mail B2B@penguinrandomhouse.com.

LIBRARY OF CONGRESS CATALOGING-IN-PUBLICATION DATA
Names: Einav, Liran, author. | Finkelstein, Amy, author.
Title: We've got you covered : rebooting American health care /
Liran Einav and Amy Finkelstein.
Description: [New York] : Portfolio/Penguin, [2023] |
Includes bibliographical references and index. |
Identifiers: LCCN 2023007327 (print) | LCCN 2023007328 (ebook) |
ISBN 9780593421239 (hardcover) | ISBN 9780593421246 (ebook)
Subjects: LCSH: National health insurance—United States. |
Health care reform—United States. | Medical policy—United States.
Classification: LCC RA412.2 .E36 2023 (print) | LCC RA412.2 (ebook) |
DDC 368.4/200973—dc23/eng/20230420
LC record available at https://lccn.loc.gov/2023007327
LC ebook record available at https://lccn.loc.gov/2023007328

Printed in the United States of America
1st Printing

Book design by Jessica Shatan Heslin/Studio Shatan, Inc.

CONTENTS

When asked what she does, Amy likes to say that she studies insurance. Not because it's a great conversation starter. It's not. But because she has learned the hard way that if she admits that she studies health care, she inevitably gets some version of the trillion-dollar question: How can we fix the US health-care system?

The CEOs want to know how to keep their employees' health-care costs down (and their profits up). The folk singers wonder why we can't give everyone excellent health insurance (and all live together in peace and harmony). The doctors insist on airing their grievances about sky-high malpractice costs and endless red tape from insurers (sometimes in the midst of a medical exam).

Even when she's not caught with her pants down, Amy's answer is rarely well received. No one wants to hear that these are hard problems that defy facile solutions. Better to give the conversation-ending answer about working on insurance than try to explain that if she knew "how to fix" US health care, she wouldn't be devoting her professional life to working on this question.

Much of that work has been done in collaboration with Liran. Together, we've spent our academic careers as economists studying the problems that plague US health insurance markets. (It isn't a lie when Amy says she studies insurance, it's just not the most interesting version of the truth.) We've examined the drivers of medical spending in the US, as well as the consequences of specific policies or potential reforms for health insurance coverage, health-care spending, and life or death itself. In our almost two decades of working together, we've tackled some hot-button issues, such as high health-care spending at the end of life and the age at which women should start getting routine mammograms. We've also plumbed the depths of more esoteric topics, such as the market for pet health insurance and the demand for dental insurance.

Whatever we've been working on, we've always been motivated by the big question, the one that always comes up in political campaigns and at cocktail parties: How can public policy best improve US health care? But we've deliberately steered clear of any involvement in those public policy conversations (and those cocktail parties). We preferred to stay within our academic comfort zone and focus on narrower questions that we felt we could answer with scientific rigor. We hoped that our work would someday be useful for the people engaged in the real-world work of designing health-care reform.

Why get involved now? For that, we have Amy's father-in-law to thank, and to blame.

It was the summer of 2019. The Democratic primaries were just getting underway. Bernie Sanders's "Medicare for all" plan was the talk of the town (at least the towns we live in).

So when Amy's father-in-law, Mark, asked her what she thought of

Medicare for all, she was ready with her standard conversation defla-
tor. "'Medicare for all' is a slogan," Amy replied. "It's not a clear policy
proposal. You can't ask me to have an informed view on a slogan."

Mark was not so easily put off. "Fair enough," he replied. "Let me
pose the question differently: What would *you* propose doing about
health insurance coverage?" Amy tried her next line of defense—the
one about it being a difficult problem with no obvious solutions. "I
don't know," she explained. "Health-care reform isn't 'just' a political
problem. It's actually—as President Trump famously said—very complicated. That's why I study it; if there were a clear answer, I'd work on
a different problem."

Amy's father-in-law is persistent. A few days later he came back to
her. "Look," he said, "I know these are hard issues. But come on. . . .
You've been studying them for twenty years. You must be one of the
best placed people to help us understand the options." (Amy's father-
in-law is also generous to a fault.) Mark continued, "Do you *really* have
nothing to say on this topic?"

Ouch.

Health care *is* complicated. But still, Amy couldn't help but feel that
he had a point. After all her years working on US health care, it would
be nice to have at least a few policy insights to share. Amy brought this
up with Liran when they talked the next day.

Our entire collaboration has occurred while living and working on
opposite coasts—Amy at MIT and Liran at Stanford. The Bay State
and the Bay Area. To make this work, we schedule multiple calls every
week. At the start of each one, before we dig into the latest set of com-
putational challenges, estimation issues, or puzzling results, we usually
chitchat for a bit. (Okay, sometimes for more than a bit.) Let off a little
steam about an annoying colleague. Gripe about committee assign-
ments. Trade some professional gossip. The usual academic palaver.

Occasionally, Amy will suggest a crazy new idea for a project we could work on, and Liran will obligingly explain why we shouldn't go there. So it seemed natural to begin her call with Liran that day by describing her conversation with Mark and getting some helpful reassurance that they should stick to the path they were on.

"I kind of feel he's right," she admitted sheepishly at the end of her summary. "We *have* been studying this a long time and we *should* have some sensible views on this." She waited for his inevitable response: yes, it would be nice to solve this problem; it would also be nice to cure cancer, but that's not something they were on track to do.

This time, however, she was in for a surprise. "He's totally right!" Liran exclaimed.

So we started talking. And thinking. And reading. And arguing. Trying to articulate the "right" design for health insurance coverage in the US. Pushing ourselves far outside our comfort zone. (Not the arguing part—that's always been part and parcel of the collaboration.)

At first, our goal was to get only enough clarity to satisfy ourselves, and hopefully also Amy's father-in-law. But the more we looked at current—and even not-so-current—policy proposals to try to articulate a reasonable path forward, the less satisfied we got.

Which got us reading and thinking—and arguing—some more. At some point, we started to realize that no one was coming up with the right answer because no one was asking the right question: What is it that US health insurance policy is trying to accomplish? We have to start there. We must articulate a specific objective before we can engage in an informed discussion of what a sensible policy response might be.

Once we started asking the right question, some of the answers were so startlingly straightforward that it felt negligent not to share them. That's when we realized that it just might take people steeped in health care but who have deliberately remained outside of the political world to offer a fresh perspective and move the conversation in the right direction. That's when we decided we needed to write this book.

Some of what we'll propose comes directly from economics research, including our own. At other times, what we discovered came as a great surprise to us, and caused us to turn our backs on elements of economics orthodoxy that we've written about and lectured on for years.

Some of our answers may seem obvious. Others will surely make you uncomfortable. In the beginning, we were uncomfortable too. But the problems are too big, and too important, to stay within our comfort zone.

There will be something in our proposal to upset everyone. "Entitlements!" we can hear the conservative pundits howl in dismay. "Vouchers!" our liberal neighbors in Cambridge and Palo Alto will cry.

Our promise to you is not to take sides, but rather to leave no stone unturned. We have no ax to grind, no vested interest other than understanding—and elucidating—why and how health-care coverage in the United States can be dramatically improved.

As we develop our argument, we'll include a number of stories, drawn from the experiences of real people. Our training makes us skeptical of such individual anecdotes. Maybe the really egregious stories that get told are just that—egregious outliers rather than indicative of typical experiences. Whenever we're trying to understand something about how the world works, we prefer to rely on a large, deliberately representative sample of anecdotes. Otherwise known as . . . data.

Nonetheless, individual experiences are important for laying bare the real human suffering and tragedies that can be masked by abstract statistics. Our token noneconomist friends also tell us that "real people" find stories more engaging than dense tables of statistics. But you can rest assured that we have taken care throughout to tell an anecdote only to *illustrate* a more general point. They are the window dressings, not the foundation, to our argument.

———

Our answer took us longer—and is longer—than Amy's father-in-law was expecting when he posed his question in the summer of 2019. But we hope that he—and the many people like him who want to better understand what sensible US health insurance policy could look like— will find our answers illuminating, and instructive. Or, at a minimum, thought provoking.

We also hope Mark doesn't ask us another hard question anytime soon.

Breaking Ground

I n the spring of 2020, as an unprecedented global pandemic engulfed the world, the US government grappled with a host of new and unfamiliar challenges. Whether to lock down. When to reopen. Whether to allow indoor dining. Or in-person schooling.

One challenge, however, was sadly familiar: what to do about the glaring gaps in US health insurance coverage. These gaps were not new. But there's nothing quite like a public health emergency to throw long-standing problems with health-care coverage into stark relief.

Here, at least, the government wasn't flying blind. After all, the US had been jury-rigging patches to these coverage problems for over half a century. In the face of a new disease, it quickly took a few pages from its well-worn—if not well-loved—playbook.

One familiar move was to make it easier for low-income Americans to get coverage in times of widespread disaster. New York had done something similar in response to the September 11 terrorist attacks. Other states have adopted a similar strategy when facing other disasters, including Louisiana after Hurricane Katrina and Michigan during the Flint water crisis. In each of these scenarios, the states were able to get special permission from the federal government to expand eligibility for free health insurance coverage further up the income distribution and waive many of the burdensome application requirements that are typically needed to successfully enroll. That's right. In times of designated disasters, the US has institutionalized a mechanism for temporarily expanding coverage. Or at least for trying to expand coverage. Many low-income uninsured Americans do not, in fact, enroll in the free coverage for which they are eligible.

Another well-known maneuver was to try to make it easier for the 150 million Americans whose health insurance comes from their employer to maintain that coverage when they lose their jobs. The federal government had made previous efforts along these lines in the mid-1980s. Now, with the prospect of massive layoffs in the midst of a public health emergency, it went further, giving the newly unemployed more time to file the requisite paperwork to keep the health insurance their employers had previously provided. Looser deadlines are helpful. But the fundamental problem remained. The cost of that insurance, previously paid by their employers, would now have to be paid by the newly unemployed, out of their now-diminished incomes.

Congress also deployed another old chestnut: disease-specific insurance. Confronted with a brand-new disease, it legislated that it would cover the medical costs of treating COVID for the uninsured. This new COVID coverage joined the ranks of a series of existing programs that cover the medical expenses of patients with tuberculosis, breast and cervical cancer, Lou Gehrig's disease, end-stage kidney failure, HIV/AIDS, and sickle cell anemia. Some of these programs, like

COVID coverage, were introduced in the face of a virulent, new infectious disease. Others were created in response to the development of life-saving, but unaffordable, new medical treatments. Still others were the result of effective, sustained lobbying by patients and their families. Like COVID coverage, some only cover treatments related to the specific disease. All end their coverage if the patient recovers.

As our past experiences with disease-specific coverage foretold, COVID coverage fell short of its goal. Many uninsured patients delayed seeking care out of concerns about potentially large medical bills; they weren't aware of the disease-specific coverage, or they worried that if it turned out they had pneumonia rather than COVID, they would get stuck with large medical bills. Other uninsured COVID patients did get care, but nevertheless got billed for that care; they didn't have a record of a definitive COVID diagnosis, or they hadn't filed for coverage within the requisite time window.

John Druschitz experienced many of these problems. Druschitz had been insured his whole life, except for what turned out to be the first month of the pandemic; he had canceled his coverage in anticipation of his upcoming eligibility for Medicare, which would start twenty-three days later, at the beginning of the month of his sixty-fifth birthday. In April 2020, during the first series of lockdowns, he spent five days in the hospital with fever, shortness of breath, and a suspected COVID diagnosis. Because his COVID test came back negative, he wasn't eligible for the new COVID-specific coverage. And although there were other programs that he could have applied for to cover some of his costs, he didn't realize he needed to do so and missed the window in which he would have had to apply. One year later, in April 2021, Druschitz faced over $20,000 in unpaid medical bills, and the hospital that had cared for him was threatening to ratchet up its collection efforts.

Druschitz's story is one of missed opportunity—to apply for the coverage he was eligible for. It is also a story of near misses—for the COVID diagnosis Druschitz needed and for the sixty-fifth birthday that would soon get him covered by Medicare. Such missed opportunities and near misses are also the story of US health policy—the plug-the-leaks, squeaky-wheel-gets-the-grease approach that we have taken for over half a century.

The pandemic produced the latest in a long series of such inadequate health insurance policy "fixes." In doing so, it also showcased what we will argue is the enduring, but unwritten, social norm that the US has been trying—but failing—to fulfill: universal access to essential, basic health care, regardless of a patient's resources. It's time to go back to the drawing board and finally do it right.

———

There is no shortage of proposals for health insurance reform. A steady stream emanates from politicians, think tanks, journalists, academics, practicing physicians, and your uncle Bob. They all miss the point.

They invariably focus on the thirty million* Americans who lack insurance at any given moment. But health insurance problems extend to most of the remaining 90 percent of Americans who currently have insurance. Many live with the constant danger of losing that coverage if they lose their job, give birth, get older, get healthier, get richer, or move. And even if they manage to maintain their insurance, most of the privately and publicly insured Americans can still face enormous medical bills for their "covered" care. Indeed, along with one in three uninsured families, almost one in five insured American families struggle with unpaid medical bills.

*Wherever possible, we will use statistics from 2019 or, if unavailable, as recent as possible up to 2019. We avoid post-2019 numbers because of the potential for them to be distorted by the COVID-19 pandemic.

In other words, the coverage we *do* have is a universal mess. It is nonsensical by design. Or, more accurately, by lack of design. It was never deliberately planned or systematically repaired. It has emerged haphazardly, with different parts created at different times to deal with different issues that got thrust into the limelight. The health-care policy responses to the pandemic were just the latest example of this piecemeal jumble of well-intentioned and ultimately inadequate attempts to provide medical care to those in need.

The conclusion from part I of our book will be inescapable: incremental reform isn't the answer. We can't rely on yet more Band-Aids and partial patches. Our long history of these attempts will make clear that continuing such efforts is nothing more than the triumph of hope over experience, to borrow that famous description of second marriages. The only option is to tear down the current "system" and rebuild it from the ground up. We need to develop a sensible and effective policy, without shackling ourselves to the detritus that already exists.

To do so, we must start by defining the goal: What is the problem that health-care policy should address? We can't engage in design until we are clear on purpose. Focusing on the objective also means asking whether universal coverage is the solution, rather than assuming it is. Part II of the book will tackle this question in depth.

There are many good reasons for government to get involved with health insurance. Because we want to improve people's health and well-being. Because Adam Smith's "invisible hand" can't work its magic in the medical marketplace. Because access to medical care shouldn't depend on income. Because health care is a human right.

We've written extensively and lectured generations of students about many of these arguments. But much to our surprise, when we looked carefully, we discovered a need for universal health care that does not stem from any of these familiar reasons. Rather, the need for universal health care is rooted in our unwritten social contract: access to essential health care, regardless of resources.

Reasonable people may disagree about what our social contract *should* be. (Unreasonable people may disagree too.) Perhaps you firmly believe in the myth of the United States as the land of opportunity, with limitless possibilities for anyone who takes the initiative. You think that handouts to those in need simply discourage the essential frontier spirit of effort, self-reliance, and independence that is the core of our national identity. We have no intention, or ability, to try to influence your values. But we are confident that we can convince you of our description of the *empirical* social contract under which—like it or not—the US operates.

We realize that the existence of such a contract may be hard to believe in a society that also advocates for lifting oneself up by the bootstraps. Yet, as we'll argue, from colonial to modern times, the record is clear: Our country has always tried to provide essential medical care to those who are ill and unable to provide for their own care. In the eighteenth century, this obligation helped propel the brand-new US government to create the world's first national compulsory health insurance. In the twentieth and twenty-first centuries, this same social norm has been the impetus behind much of our history of sporadic and ad hoc insurance reforms that have created insurance coverage for particular groups—or particular diseases—whose plight has become politically salient. It is also behind the vast web of government-funded, government-regulated free or low-fee medical care for the uninsured and underinsured that we will describe.

The pandemic threw our obligations into stark relief. But they have always been there. These obligations are rooted in a universal human instinct to respond to visible, acute disasters. But while our moral impulses are not uniquely American, the ineffective way that we have responded to them is a singularly American tragedy.

Once we recognize that we always have and always will attempt to provide access to medical care to those who are ill and cannot provide it for themselves, the only solution is to formalize that commitment up front with insurance coverage. Alexander Hamilton articulated this argument over two centuries ago. In the last few decades, it has been embraced by American leaders from across the political spectrum as a rationale for universal health insurance coverage. It is neither a liberal nor a conservative argument. It is merely good sense.

Perhaps you'll want to go even further and try to use universal coverage as an instrument for reducing the enormous health differences that exist across Americans of different incomes. Or the appalling disparities in health between Black and White Americans. You feel that health is sacred, occupying a special place in our moral firmament that makes inequality in health particularly abhorrent, and particularly in need of redress.

For you, too, our answer will be once again rooted in empirics rather than ethics. We'll explain that as a practical matter, health insurance policy cannot function as the great equalizer. Indeed, large and persistent health inequality is a pervasive feature in countries around the world, including those with universal health insurance coverage. The main drivers of the disparities in death and disease are not, it turns out, disparities in health insurance, or even in access to medical care. As counterintuitive as it may first seem, the evidence is clear: those who aspire to greater equality in health would be well served to train their sights elsewhere than health insurance.

Whether you are a Democrat or Republican, whether you favor big government or small government, any successful attempt at health insurance reform must grapple with two core, empirical realities: what our social contract is, and what health insurance coverage can—and cannot—accomplish. And whichever side of the ideological divide you fall on, no one can argue that our current approach is what we *should* do. It is incoherent, uncoordinated, inefficient, and unplanned. Or, as the iconic American broadcast journalist Walter Cronkite once remarked, "America's health care system is neither healthy, caring, nor a system."

This has to change. In the third and final part of the book, we'll describe the two key principles of the solution: universal coverage for a basic set of medical services, and the option to buy additional, supplemental coverage in a well-designed market. Beyond this high-level description, we'll draw on decades of economics research, as well as evidence and examples from around the world, to clarify the key design elements.

We'll emphasize that all medical care included in basic coverage must be provided to patients for free. Why free? Because otherwise we'll end up creating cumbersome patches for the inevitable instances in which individuals cannot afford the costs of the medical care we are committed to providing. This may sound obvious, but it is heresy to the economics profession, and to the many countries that have followed economists' advice and tried to make patients pay out of pocket for part of the cost of their universally covered care.

But we'll also insist that basic coverage should be just that: basic. It must cover the medical services that are essential for restoring or maintaining basic human functions. But that's where our commitments end and our choices begin. There is a lot of medical care that is desirable but not essential, and can be left out of basic coverage. The same goes for many nonmedical aspects of care: the ability to see the doctor of your choice at your preferred timing and location, for example, or semiprivate hospital rooms.

Keeping basic coverage basic will keep the cost to the taxpayer down. Yet another key element for controlling government health-care spending will be a budget for publicly funded health care. Remarkably—and absurdly—the US government has never actually had a health-care budget that caps the amount the government can spend on medical care. This also has to change.

Naturally, there will be those who want (and can afford) medical care that is not included in basic coverage. They may also want upgrades to already-covered services, such as quicker access to the doctor or a private hospital room. Here, economics—bolstered by policy experiences at home and abroad—will have a lot to teach us about how to make sure that the market for supplemental coverage functions well.

———

We arrived at this blueprint by using the approach that comes naturally to us from our economics training. We first defined the objective, namely the problem we are trying but failing to solve with our current US health-care policy. Once we were clear on the goal, we then considered how best to achieve that goal, which led us to the key principles and design elements. Nonetheless, once we did this, we were struck—and humbled—to realize that, at a high level, our proposal contains several key components that every high-income country (and all but a few Canadian provinces) has embraced: guaranteed basic coverage that must be delivered within a fixed budget (two things the US currently doesn't have), and the option for people to purchase upgrades. The lack of universal US health insurance may be exceptional. The fix, it turns out, is not.

Focusing on the purpose of universal health insurance clarified not only the essential elements of universal coverage but also the inessential. As a result, we will be silent on many of the policy debates du jour, such as whether we should have "single-payer health care." We won't weigh in on the debates of yester jour either, such as the merits of "managed competition," for those whose memories go back far enough. This is deliberate. There are many such design details, and they can be important, both substantively and politically. But their resolution is not a requirement for fulfilling our social contract.

At this point, the astute reader may remark that one thing that is a requirement for fulfilling our social contract is actually enacting universal health coverage into law. Well spotted. In the epilogue, we'll touch briefly on the inevitable question of how our proposal can be achieved politically. This takes us considerably beyond our realm of expertise—we apparently missed the day in graduate school when they handed out the crystal balls. That said, we'll explain why our reading of the historical record in both the US and abroad suggests that it was not our destiny to be—nor is it our destiny to remain—the only high-income country without universal health-care coverage.

We have therefore intentionally focused on what we *should* do, rather than what some may think we currently *can* do. In this sense, our book is in the spirit of the famous Chicago economist Milton Friedman. He argued that the role for economists in public policy is to develop the best ideas, and keep them alive and ripe in the public imagination until the day when "the politically impossible becomes the politically inevitable."

The US health-care system is long overdue for a reboot. And we have a blueprint for what to build in its place. We've got you covered.

WE'VE GOT YOU COVERED

PART I

IT'S A TEARDOWN

The deep-seated rot in US health insurance coverage

During the Democratic primary for the 2020 US presidential election, a clever *New York Times* article oriented readers to the candidates' different health-care proposals through an extended home renovation analogy, describing the different plans as alternative approaches to renovating a dilapidated old house. One proposal would allow people to stay in the house while some modest repairs were done to patch the roof and repaint. Others would undertake more major repairs to the existing house, perhaps even adding an entire new wing.

As any home contractor knows, however, the most important fork in the road occurs before the renovation stage. Whether to renovate at all, or instead to tear down the existing house and start anew. A major renovation has a lot to recommend itself. A house may need a new roof and a new heating system, and perhaps an entirely new plumbing system and set of appliances as well. But if the foundation is solid and the floor plan makes sense, it can take less time and money to fix the problems than to start from scratch. And it can be convenient to be able to stay in the familiar house while the improvements are made.

It is therefore understandably tempting to try to slot US health insurance into the "fixer-upper" category. It's the natural—and common—reaction among would-be reformers. It was certainly our initial instinct when we started working on this book. Extend coverage to those who still lack formal insurance. Change the laws so that getting sick, getting well, changing jobs, or moving states doesn't come with the risk of losing insurance coverage. Make sure all insurance plans meet some minimum standards. Plug the leaks, patch the holes, throw a new coat of paint on the walls.

It won't work. As we'll describe in part I, the problem is not merely the many broken parts in need of repair. It's that the whole structure—from roof to foundation—is rotten to the core. It has the wrong design. The foundation is cracked. The construction is shoddy. Even the most skilled realtor would find this a challenging listing to sell. And just wait till you see what the home inspection will reveal.

No need to take our word for it that renovation is futile. For more than a half century, we've repeatedly tried that approach. Renovations both big and small. No matter how much we patch it, the old cracks have always reemerged. It's long past time to tear it down and rebuild.

1

Poor Design

The ubiquitous risk of becoming uninsured

We are the only major country on Earth that doesn't guarantee health care to all people as a right," exhorts the progressive politician pushing for universal health insurance coverage. That's Vermont senator Bernie Sanders, speaking in 2015.

The eminent economist likewise laments, "The United States has the unenviable distinction of being the only great industrial nation without compulsory health insurance." That's Irving Fisher, speaking in 1916, a century before Sanders. Fisher was advocating for a bill that would make health insurance coverage mandatory, although with an economist's characteristic modesty, he did concede that his health insurance proposal "is not a panacea. It will not bring the new millennium."

The new millennium came—without Fisher's help or the passage of his bill—and the distinctive American dilemma remained: how to provide health insurance to the millions of Americans who lack coverage. But if the thirty million uninsured Americans were the only—or even the major—problem confronting US health insurance policy, there would be an easy fix. Just extend one of the many existing health insurance programs to cover the uninsured.

That wouldn't cut it. The problems are much bigger, and much deeper, marbled like fat throughout. Consider this: In any given month, about 12 percent of Americans younger than sixty-five are uninsured. But twice that number—one in four—will be uninsured for at least some time over a two-year period.

The very purpose of health insurance is to provide a measure of stability in an uninsured world. Yet, perversely, existing health insurance coverage is itself highly uncertain. Right when you fall ill and need insurance most, you can find yourself suddenly, unexpectedly, uninsured.

This risk of losing coverage doesn't get the attention it should. It gets far fewer headlines, campaign proposals, or even academic analyses than the plight of those who are uninsured at any given moment. In fact, we were ourselves at first surprised by the statistics on insurance uncertainty. So much so that we dug a little further into the data to confirm that the precarious nature of health insurance coverage persisted in the post-Obamacare era. It does.

Salient or not, the uncertain nature of health insurance coverage is key to understanding the deep-rooted rot at the core of our health insurance house. This is not how insurance is supposed to work. But it's how it does "work" for all nonelderly Americans. Kids and adults. The healthy and—unfortunately all too often—the sick. The publicly insured and the privately insured alike.

YOUR TAX DOLLARS AT WORK

Let's start with the precarious insurance of the privately insured. Almost half of the US population—over 150 million people—receive private health insurance through their employers or a family member's employer. That's almost all Americans who have private health insurance.

There's no natural reason why their boss doubles as their insurer. This unusual arrangement arose through an accident of history, a common theme of US health-care policy. During World War II, the federal government imposed wage and price controls to try to prevent inflation. Employers—desperate to attract and retain scarce workers—soon discovered a way to get around the wage ceilings and provide higher compensation. They could offer—and pay for—their workers' health insurance, because these payments weren't counted as "wages."

The practice of excluding employer payments for their employees' health insurance from the definition of employee earnings has remained in place to this day. As a result, any such payments are tax-free. An employee doesn't have to pay income tax on any contributions her employer makes to her workplace-based health insurance premium.

As any international travel aficionado knows, there's real savings to be had from being able to buy things tax-free. The "duty-free" nature of employer-provided health insurance is a large part of the reason that employers are the source of most private health insurance in the US. It's also responsible for a whopping $300 billion a year in forgone tax revenue that the government doesn't collect on wages in the form of employer contributions to health insurance premiums. To put that number in perspective, that's about two fifths of the amount of public spending on K–12 schooling in the United States.

The unintended reliance on the employer as health insurer has a number of unfortunate consequences. For one thing, it's Robin Hood in reverse, providing more of a handout to richer Americans—whose tax rates are higher and who therefore get a much bigger subsidy when something is excluded from their taxable income. For another, workers can end up "locked" into their jobs—and not retiring or changing jobs—simply because of the health insurance their employers provide.

And here's the real kicker: if a worker becomes too sick to work they can . . . wait for it . . . wait for it . . . that's right . . . lose their health insurance. Precisely when they really need it to cover their medical bills.

Kind of a dumb way to set things up, if you think about it.

In the mid-1980s, this absurd state of affairs prompted federal legislation to try to address the problem. It created a legislative patch, known as COBRA coverage, specifically designed to help people maintain their health insurance even after they leave their jobs. It does so by allowing employees to continue their current health insurance coverage for up to eighteen months after having left their employers. Well intentioned no doubt, but ultimately COBRA may be only slightly more useful than snake oil.

We've already alluded to some of the problems with COBRA in the introduction, when we described how the COVID-19 pandemic inspired the government to temporarily strengthen that law. It was moved to do so because, in another recurring theme of US health policy, the patch had a catch.

The real problem is that while COBRA gives the former employee the option to continue to enroll in her former coverage, she must pay the full cost of that coverage. When she was employed, her employer paid for most or all of her health insurance premiums. Now that she's lost her job—and with it her paycheck—she has to pay the full premium herself, which averaged around $12,000 a year in 2019. "Sticker shock" is what one senior benefits consultant termed the typical reaction to the high premiums from COBRA coverage, "at a time when you're financially stressed already."

One New Jersey woman who had worked as a clerk at the same firm for nearly twenty years found herself laid off after she was diagnosed with stage-three ovarian cancer. She died a year later at the age of fifty-two, having stopped her treatments. "It wasn't financially sustainable to keep paying Cobra out of pocket," said her daughter, reflecting on her mother's decision.

It should therefore not be too surprising to learn that, in practice, COBRA coverage for the unemployed is quite rare. Only 130,000 Americans had COBRA coverage in 2017, although more than eleven million adults were unemployed that year. "[COBRA] is well named because of its bite," one journalist quipped.

ISN'T IT IRONIC

While the privately insured risk losing their coverage when they lose their jobs, many people with public health insurance face the opposite problem: they can lose their coverage if they get a job and their income increases. Eligibility for public coverage can also require that people wait until they are sufficiently ill to get coverage; they can then lose that coverage if their health improves. Once again, this creates uncertainties—and glaring gaps—in health insurance coverage.

Some of these gaps are vividly illustrated by an in-depth ethnographic account of a year in the life of four generations of a poor, African-American family in Chicago. Chillingly titled *Mama Might Be Better Off Dead*, the book describes some of the extraordinary challenges faced even by those fortunate enough to be eligible for public health insurance coverage. Although the events take place in the late 1980s, most of the glaring problems it describes persist to this day, despite the series of "landmark" health insurance reforms that subsequently occurred.

At the center of the family is Cora Jackson, also known as "Mama" to her family. We'll get to some of the problems with *her* health insurance coverage in the next chapter. For now, the experiences of her adult son Tommy and of her adult grandson-in-law Robert provide a window into some of the peculiar circumstances in which one can gain—or lose—public health insurance coverage in the United States. Both Tommy and Robert suffer from major health problems that—in a common Catch-22—are eligible for public coverage only once they become sufficiently severe, and only as long as they remain so.

Tommy had worked on and off for years at various jobs—bartender, butcher, exterminator—none of which provided health insurance. His high blood pressure therefore went uninsured—and untreated—until, at age forty-eight, he had a disabling stroke that paralyzed the left side of his body and confined him to a wheelchair. Now officially disabled, he at last became eligible for the public health insurance program that now covers 8.5 million permanently disabled Americans a year. Covers them, that is, after a required two-year waiting period that begins at the onset of their disability.

Robert had known since he was a young man that his kidneys did not function properly. He was periodically incapacitated by bouts of fatigue and swelling in his legs. Yet none of his short-term, minimum-wage jobs provided health insurance. Only once his kidneys were sufficiently impaired did he qualify for public insurance through a program that covers over a quarter of a million patients who have end-stage (but only the end stage) renal disease. By the time Robert was forty, that insurance had already paid for a kidney transplant, which his body had rejected. It was now paying for ongoing dialysis treatment. Every few days, Robert would travel to a dialysis center to be hooked up to a machine that filters his blood for bodily toxins, as well-functioning kidneys would otherwise have done.

In a macabre sense, Robert's failed transplant was a blessing in disguise. Had his transplant been successful and he had recovered kidney function, his insurance coverage would have ended—because he'd no longer have "end-stage" renal disease. This would have left him with a functioning kidney but without insurance to cover the immunosuppressant drugs that he would need to be on for the rest of his life, and that cost thousands of dollars a month.

This "now you have it, now you don't" nature of health insurance coverage is unfortunately closer to the rule than the exception. Tommy's and Robert's precarious coverage came courtesy of specific Medicare programs that are perhaps less well known than the Medicare coverage for the elderly. But uncertainty also pervades the health insurance coverage people get under Medicaid, the public health insurance program for low-income Americans that covered one in five Americans in 2019. Medicaid coverage is often hit or miss because its eligibility requirements are based on factors that frequently change, such as a person's income, where they live, and their health conditions.

Other eligibility pathways are temporary by design, such as pregnancy or recent childbirth. As a result, one in four women who are covered by Medicaid while they are pregnant lose that coverage shortly after giving birth. "The clock is ticking," as one physician described his scrambles to get his patients the medical care they need—including medical care unrelated to childbirth—before their coverage runs out. Some women repeatedly cycle in and out of coverage as they have children. What do they do when they aren't pregnant? "I refuse to get sick," answered one woman who lost coverage six weeks after the birth of her fifth child.

And what about coverage for her kids? Kids can be eligible for Medicaid even when their parents are not, as eligibility typically extends higher up the income distribution for kids than for adults. Income limits on eligibility also tend to be higher for younger kids than for older kids. That means that kids can get kicked off insurance by making the mistake of getting older; a first and sixth birthday are particularly ill advised.

And kids have a way of growing up. At age eighteen, many low-income teenagers lose their coverage, unless they were in foster care, in which case they can stay covered until age twenty-six. Ours is not to reason why.

A pediatric cardiologist, Arthur Garson, told the heartbreaking story of a patient named Ginny who was born with congenital heart disease, whom he had treated since she was five. She died shortly after her nineteenth birthday—when she lost coverage, and with it the prescription drug insurance that paid for her essential medication. As Dr. Garson wrote:

> I think of Ginny often—almost every day. I never could understand how the "system" that had paid to fix her heart, and paid for her medicine, dropped her at nineteen. But that's the way it works. Medicaid (and the State Children's Health Insurance Program) covers children of the poor, like Ginny, but between the ages of nineteen and the Medicare age of sixty-five, the so-called safety net has huge holes—and Ginny fell through.

All told, this Medicaid coverage comes with an annual cost to taxpayers of more than $600 billion. If you—like us—find your mind starting to glaze over as numbers creep into the hundreds of billions, here's one way to wrap your head around the Medicaid price tag: it's about the same as the national defense budget. Once you add Medicare—

the public health insurance program for people who are sixty-five and older and people with disabilities, which covers another one in five Americans—we're looking at almost $1.5 trillion in annual government spending. No wonder a Treasury official has suggested that the right way to think about the federal government is "as a gigantic insurance company with a sideline business in national defense."

Let's hope that our national defense provides better protection than our health insurance. At least the benefits from national defense are automatic. We all enjoy the security and protection it provides, without having to think about it, or sign up for it. The same unfortunately cannot be said of the substantial taxpayer spending on public health insurance.

That's because, in order to be covered, individuals have to first realize which of the alphabet soup of state and federal programs they are eligible for. Then they have to figure out the particular documentation they need to submit for the program they think they may be eligible for, fill out the application, and submit that documentation. And hope that they are in fact eligible for the program they are applying for, and that their application is complete and correct.

Each of these steps creates additional uncertainty. Each of these steps is the unavoidable consequence of a system that doesn't provide for automatic, universal coverage.

The result: many more people are *eligible* for insurance than are *covered* by it.

WHAT YOU DON'T KNOW CAN HURT YOU

Here's a depressing fact: to help achieve universal coverage, the 2010 Affordable Care Act set aside over $60 million a year in government funding to pay for health insurance "navigators." These navigators were paid to get the word out about newly expanded health insurance opportunities, encourage uninsured individuals to apply, and help them complete the necessary application forms.

Liberals were outraged when the navigators' funding was subsequently cut by the Trump administration, and gratified when it was restored by President Biden. But the need for these navigators in the first place points to a fundamental problem, one that simply paying for more navigators can't fix.

Making people eligible for coverage isn't the same as covering them, even when that coverage is available for free. People can't sign up for programs they don't know about, and often have trouble enrolling—or staying enrolled—in the ones that they do learn about. Indeed, in 2019, about eighteen million uninsured Americans—six out of ten uninsured—were in fact eligible for free or heavily discounted health insurance. Some estimates suggest that over one quarter of uninsured parents and as many as three quarters of uninsured children were eligible for but not enrolled in coverage that would be completely free.

Many people simply do not know which of the messy, overlapping patchwork of different health insurance programs they are eligible for. Even within a single program such as Medicaid, eligibility is neither obvious nor easily determined. It depends on a complicated formula that includes factors such as income (which often needs to be low, although what "low" is varies depending on a number of other factors), assets (which may or may not count a car or a home), family size, age, pregnancy, and current health conditions. To add insult to injury, these opaque formulas can vary from year to year and from state to state.

Multiple studies have shown that simply sending letters informing people about the coverage that they are eligible for can boost insurance coverage. But they don't boost coverage by that much—about one to three additional people enrolled for every one hundred people receiving outreach. That's because information is only the first hurdle.

Managing to enroll is another matter altogether. One father, Anthony Putney, described the repeated difficulties he had getting and maintaining Medicaid coverage for his toddler Lily, who suffered from a seizure disorder. In one instance, her coverage was mistakenly terminated after her father, who was a naval officer, received a raise. He spent two months waiting in long lines and meeting with caseworkers before he was finally able to get her coverage reinstated. On another occasion, the navy transferred Putney from New Jersey to Virginia, where it took him over two years to get Lily enrolled in the Virginia Medicaid program. "Once again, these interruptions led to delays in care and vast changes in services for Lily," he wrote, "not to mention the financial stress that affected our entire family."

Enrollment is rarely automatic. Or easy. In Massachusetts, for example, free coverage is available to low-income adults if they successfully complete a six-page "basic" application form, and potentially several supplemental forms as well. These forms contain multiple questions about the applicant's health, employment, and income, as well as details on where they live and their other family members. Those who make it all the way through this enrollment process are all set. Or more accurately, they're all set till next year, when they need to remember to document that they are still eligible, or risk losing coverage.

Staying enrolled is yet another challenge. Many Medicaid recipients lose coverage because they don't even realize that their coverage doesn't continue automatically, and that they have to refile forms—often every year—in order to *maintain* their coverage. The forms to stay enrolled are also lengthy and complex. As one researcher commented, "A 47-page form is daunting for a Ph.D. . . . . It's even more daunting for a low-income family with a lot of stress in their lives."

Ironically, the government can be quite good at automating *disen*-rollment. For years, for example, Texas conducted frequent, automatic income checks for families on Medicaid, disenrolling those who they determined were no longer eligible. Their process resulted in many thousands of children erroneously disenrolled each month.

Often people are not even aware that they have been disenrolled until they try to get medical care. Like the mother in Tennessee who didn't realize her son had been mistakenly disenrolled until she took him to the doctor. Or the mother in Idaho who, right before her son's surgery, discovered that his Medicaid coverage had ended because she had not filed the required annual financial forms on time.

In response, a number of nonprofits have been created to try to help families get or keep the Medicaid coverage they are eligible for. The full-time employees at these well-intentioned organizations work to inform patients of their rights—like which programs they are eligible to enroll in and what they need to do to maintain their eligibility—and try to help them fill out the forms and assemble the documentation needed to obtain and retain their Medicaid coverage. Only in America.

Difficulty in enrolling—or staying enrolled—is the Achilles' heel of attempting to expand coverage by expanding eligibility to specific groups for specific programs. As if the gaps in eligibility weren't enough—gotta be the right age or right income or have the right disease—people often end up uninsured even when they are eligible for formal coverage.

And when they become uninsured, the consequences can be severe. Chief among them: more limited medical care, and greater risk of substantial financial hardship from the large medical bills for the care the uninsured do receive.

WHEN THE RISK BECOMES REALITY

The constant struggles and acute distress of those who are uninsured at any given moment are appalling to witness and shameful to tolerate. Stories abound. The low-income mother in Mississippi who loses her insurance after the birth of each child and has to self-medicate between pregnancies with "Molotov cocktails" of over-the-counter medication. The domestic violence survivor in Illinois who lost access to her husband's veterans' health insurance after her divorce and can no longer afford to treat her lifelong injuries from abuse. The blue-collar worker in Idaho who has been repeatedly injured on the job but, without insurance, resorts to sanding down his own bone spurs rather than seek treatment because, he says, "I can deal with the pain, but I can't deal with not paying the bills." The twentysomething uninsured man in Chicago who cycles in and out of the emergency room for his uncontrolled asthma because he distrusts the "shady" navigators who try to help him sign up for the Medicaid coverage that he is eligible for.

The data also provide clear evidence of the benefits of insurance coverage. Some of that evidence comes from an unusual experiment conducted by the state of Oregon, whose motto translates from Latin as "She flies with her own wings." That's certainly been the case when it comes to Oregon's health policy. In 2008, Oregon conducted a lottery for health insurance. The jackpot: free public health insurance. You heard that right. Right here in the United States, in the twenty-first century, a state literally ran a health insurance lottery.

Oregon heavily advertised its lottery—running ads on the radio, on buses, and on billboards, urging low-income, uninsured adults to put their names down for a chance to win. Over seventy-five thousand people signed up. The state then randomly drew names for the ten thousand health insurance slots it was giving away. Those who were randomly selected got coverage. Many other thousands who had signed up were not selected; they lost the lottery and remained uninsured.

It was just like a clinical trial for a new drug, in which some patients are randomly assigned the new drug and others are assigned an older drug or a sugar pill. Except in this case, Oregon randomly assigned Medicaid to some low-income uninsured adults, and not to others. And while the typical purpose of a clinical trial is to make sure that a new drug is safe and effective before it can be prescribed to patients, here there were no concerns that giving health insurance to the uninsured might be unsafe.

Oregon chose its unusual approach for a more prosaic reason: lack of funds. The state had only enough money to enroll a small fraction of the adults who were eligible for the program. State officials debated and agonized over how to allocate their limited number of slots, and ultimately concluded that the fairest thing to do was to hold a lottery. Comedy host Stephen Colbert promptly lampooned the idea of a state resorting to lottery-ing off health insurance with cracks about "Pick Sicks" and "gambling for health insurance."

The only silver lining to this torrid state of affairs is that it provided researchers (including Amy) with a unique opportunity to study the consequences of being uninsured. That's because the lottery assigned insurance coverage at random—by the luck of the draw. Amy and her collaborators tracked the lottery participants over the next two years. They examined what happened to the low-income adults who were randomly assigned Medicaid coverage and compared this with what happened to those who, also at random, lost the lottery and remained uninsured.

The answer: those who won the lottery were better off—in many respects—than those who lost the lottery. Those who won spent less of their own money on medical care and had less medical debt than those who lost the lottery. Medicaid, in other words, did what health insurance is supposed to do, providing substantial financial protection against medical expenses. Medicaid coverage also increased the use of medical care. The adults who won Medicaid coverage went to the doctor more often, took more prescription drugs, and were more likely to get recommended preventive care, such as mammograms or checks of their cholesterol levels. They were also more likely to visit the emergency room and more likely to have a hospital stay.

The lottery winners also reported themselves to be in better physical and mental health than the lottery losers. Their improved mental health was subsequently confirmed by clinical exams that the research team conducted; these revealed depression rates that were 30 percent lower for those who won the lottery and got insurance coverage. But the exams also showed no difference in physical health measures like hypertension and high cholesterol between the two groups.

A subsequent, much larger study did detect physical health benefits from health insurance coverage. In 2017, researchers worked with the IRS to send out letters to almost *four million* randomly selected uninsured American households, warning them of the financial tax penalty, which was then in effect nationwide, for remaining uninsured. They found that households who got the letter were more likely to have insurance coverage over the next two years, and that the insurance coverage in turn reduced deaths and saved lives.

Or as one Oregon lottery participant wryly concluded his interview with Amy's study team, "No insurance is horrible, insurance is good. Like they needed a study to figure this one out." Fair point. The problems with being uninsured are clear. And we don't need more studies to "prove" it. (Liran might even add, "We didn't really need the one that Amy spent several years of her life on.")

What's also clear: The "problems of the uninsured" are not limited to those who happen to be uninsured at the moment. They lurk for all of us who are under age sixty-five. At any moment, a birthday, a birth, the loss of a job, a raise, a move, or a successful medical treatment could leave any of us uninsured.

———

The astute reader will notice that we slipped in one important caveat about insurance uncertainty—it applies to "all of us who are under age sixty-five." There is an exception to every rule, and the exception to the rule of precarious insurance coverage is Medicare coverage for the elderly. That coverage automatically begins the month you turn sixty-five, and it remains yours, to have and to hold, for richer and for poorer, until death do you part. It's as certain as death and taxes, and in this regard, it is unlike any other form of health insurance in the United States.

That may help explain the enduring appeal of the political catchphrase "Medicare for all," which has been the rallying cry for universal health insurance ever since 1970, when it was used to describe Republican New York senator Jacob Javits's proposal for national health insurance. Visceral but vague—like most useful slogans—"Medicare for all" evokes the notion that if we've managed to get health insurance coverage right for some, it shouldn't be so hard to do so "for all."

But once we describe some of the medical costs that the current "Medicare for some"* doesn't cover, "Medicare for all" will seem much

---

*There are actually two distinct types of insurance that fall under the name Medicare: the original, public insurance that is essentially automatic for the elderly, and a private alternative option that was first introduced in the early 1980s. By 2019, this private alternative had been chosen by over one third of elderly Americans in lieu of the public Medicare option. We follow the common convention of using the term Medicare to refer to the original, public program unless otherwise indicated. We'll come back to the private Medicare option in chapter 13.

less appealing. And once we explain that, even when they manage to hold on to that insurance, most of the privately insured also face important gaps in what their insurance will cover, the decidedly less catchy slogan "[insert your favorite health insurance program here] for all" will also hold little allure.

Shoddy Construction

The incomplete insurance of the insured

The somewhat surreal plotline of the hit TV show *Breaking Bad*—in which the meek high school chemistry teacher Walter White becomes a crystal meth producer—is based on an all-too-real premise. Walter initially gets into the meth business to pay for his cancer treatment. He does have insurance. Private insurance from his employer, in fact. But, like so many insured Americans, his insurance turns out to be highly inadequate.

The very real struggles of the insured to cope with high medical bills don't make for as good a television drama as those of the fictional Walter White. But, as we'll explore in this chapter, these struggles are a pervasive feature—or, more accurately, a bug—of the health-care experiences of those with insurance.

Most US health insurance policies, public and private alike, have important gaps in what medical care they will cover. You wouldn't patch a hole in the roof with rotten wood. And we wouldn't want to extend

the subpar protection of the currently insured to the currently uninsured.

MIND THE GAPS

Consider Medicare. PBS journalist Philip Moeller regularly fields questions about gaps in Medicare coverage in his weekly Ask Phil advice
column. From Barbara, whose sister is in a nursing home following
a "massive stroke," and who has discovered that Medicare will make
her pay over $150 per day for that care if she stays more than twenty
days. Or from Susan, who's already maxed out her annual allotment of
Medicare-covered physical therapy days preparing for back surgery,
and now faces the prospect of having no coverage for the physical therapy she will need to help her get back on her feet after her operation.

Cora Jackson's experiences provide another illustration of some of
Medicare's gaps. Cora is the eponymous Mama in the book *Mama Might
Be Better Off Dead*. We already met her son and her grandson-in-law—
and some of the problems with their health insurance—in the previous chapter. Cora, aged sixty-nine, is coping with high blood pressure,
diabetes, and a host of other chronic conditions. She endures a series
of hospital stays during which more and more of her leg is progres-
sively amputated in response to spreading gangrene.

Her main source of health insurance is Medicare. By law, Medicare
covers only services or supplies that are deemed "medically necessary." At first glance this seems sensible. Why pay for "unnecessary"
expenses? The problem, of course, lies in what Medicare defines as
necessary. For example, one elderly man in Washington State recently
discovered that Medicare will pay for his doctor-prescribed wheelchair
only if it was needed inside his home. Leaving one's home is apparently not deemed "medically necessary."

For Cora, the "medically necessary" requirement means that Medicare won't pay for the transportation this elderly, wheelchair-bound amputee needs to get to her doctor. Not surprisingly, she therefore often misses her appointments. When those missed appointments fail to detect dangerously low levels of blood coagulation, a known risk from one of her medications, and she begins bleeding uncontrollably, Medicare does pay for the ambulance trip and the subsequent hospitalization. Those were now "medically necessary." During the year described by the book, she goes through a series of such crises—and hospitalizations. By the end of that year, she has died.

Medicare's gaps are not limited to such specialized types of care as skilled nursing care, physical therapy, and transportation for amputees. The gaps also extend to plain-vanilla doctor visits and hospital care. Medicare patients are required to pay one fifth of *all* doctors' bills. They must also pay for the first approximately $1,400 of hospital costs each year, as well as for their first three units of blood, which can easily cost the patient $900 in blood money (sorry, couldn't resist).

All told, such gaps leave Medicare patients with large amounts of uncovered medical expenses. In 2016, Medicare enrollees spent, on average, over $5,000 out of their own pockets for their medical care; a quarter of them spent 25 percent or more of their income on that medical care. These gaps are no accident. They reflect a deliberate decision by the government to make Medicare patients pay for some of their medical care. The result: Medicare covers less medical care than many private plans offered by large employers. And that's not even factoring in the specific needs of Medicare's elderly population, such as home care and nursing home care, most of which Medicare also doesn't cover.

Even if we accept, for now, the conventional wisdom that patients should pay some of the cost of their medical care (but hold that thought till chapter 9), the way that Medicare accomplishes this is completely backward. It leaves its "insured" patients exposed to unlimited medical bills. There is no limit to how much Medicare patients may have to pay in doctors' bills. Every time a Medicare patient sees a doctor, they are on the hook for twenty cents of every dollar of their bill. No matter how high those bills get. If a patient's prostate cancer treatment racks up $100,000 in physician charges, he'll have to pay $20,000 of that out of his own pocket.

That's not what well-designed health insurance is supposed to do! Its purpose is to provide financial protection against the medical costs of poor health. The very last thing it should do is leave its patients vulnerable to limitless medical expenses.

As a result of Medicare's poor design, most Medicare enrollees get additional insurance to cover the gaps in their Medicare coverage. Many buy additional private insurance (sometimes called Medigap plans) that explicitly covers some of the gaps in Medicare. Others are eligible for additional coverage through Medicaid, and for all the problems of ascertaining that eligibility and maintaining their coverage that we described in the previous chapter.

The grass is not much greener for those lucky enough to have private insurance. Such plans—like the kind that Walter White might have—also typically require patients to pay a portion of the cost of their medical care. And that portion has been rising over the last few decades.

High-deductible health insurance plans—in which the patient must pay the first couple thousand (or more) dollars of any medical spending for the year—are increasingly common. By 2019, almost one in three workers with employer-provided health insurance were in such plans. The idea is to give patients a bit of "skin in the game" so they don't immediately race to the doctor every time they have a sniffle. Or cancer.

These large deductibles create headaches for hospitals and physicians, who increasingly have to chase their insured patients for what they owe. One journalist memorably described the physician experience. "One moment they're removing a pre-cancerous skin mole. The next, they're haranguing patients to pay what's become a growing portion of the total medical bill."

But the real problems are for the patients who, despite their health insurance, can end up owing large amounts of money for their medical care. This can create a financial burden for even relatively affluent families. When an insurance plan has a $3,000 deductible and a 40 percent coinsurance rate, it doesn't take much for the medical needs of the "insured" to quickly generate overwhelming bills. A 2018 NPR story, for example, described how a married couple with $100,000 a year in earnings and this type of employer-provided health insurance were pushed to the verge of bankruptcy. They had incurred nearly $12,000 in medical debt from the birth of their (healthy) son, and were working five jobs in an unsuccessful effort to pay it off.

Another big source of high out-of-pocket medical expenses for the privately insured is the designation by the insurer that certain doctors and hospitals are "out of network." In this case, the amount the patient has to pay out of her own pocket is typically two to three times higher than it otherwise would be. The idea is to enable insurers to negotiate lower prices with health-care providers in return for "steering" their patients to those providers. And one way to "steer" patients to particular doctors or hospitals is to make the patients pay a lot more when they go to other ones. The problem is that it's the patient's responsibility to check that her provider is "in network." That can be a particular problem for emergency visits—where it may not be top of mind to check that the hospital and its doctors are in network. A number of states have passed laws to try to crack down on so-called surprise billing practices, and the federal government has followed suit. But these laws have not solved the problem. The federal law, for example, tries to crack down particularly hard on surprise bills in the emergency room. But its restrictions don't apply to most ambulance trips, which are a major source of surprise bills for patients who end up in the emergency room.

THE DEBT THAT NEVER DIES

All told, the ubiquitous coverage gaps in both public and private insurance result in astoundingly widespread medical debt. Every year, about one quarter of nonelderly American households report trouble paying their medical bills. In more than half of these households, the person who incurred the bill was insured when treatment began, and often remained insured throughout their treatment. Even among the elderly—all of whom have insurance through Medicare—about 10 percent report that they have unpaid medical debt.

Medical debt is also enormous. In early 2020—before the start of the COVID-19 pandemic—there was $140 billion in unpaid medical bills held by collection agencies. To put that number in perspective, that's more than the amount held by collection agencies for all other consumer debt from nonmedical sources combined. And here's the really shocking part: three fifths of that debt was incurred by households with health insurance. Although Walter White's dramatic response to his cancer diagnosis is surely not typical, the premise that a cancer diagnosis tends to be financially destabilizing even for an insured patient is in fact borne out in the data.

Hospitals frequently resort to suing their patients over unpaid medical bills. Data from Wisconsin hospitals indicate that, in 2018, hospitals filed 1.5 lawsuits per one thousand residents. Many of the patients who are sued have health insurance. An insured mother of three young children in New Mexico was sued for $17,000 in hospital bills that she owed over and above what her insurance had already paid. Many of the hospitals that sue are nonprofit or public hospitals, financed in large part by taxpayer money. And many have "crosses on their top," commented one attorney who provides pro bono help for patients who are sued by hospitals for their unpaid medical debt. "Jesus didn't say you should sue the poor," he added.

If the suit is "successful," the patient is subjected to a forced collection process to cover the original debt, accrued interest, and the hospital's legal costs. This can include garnishment of wages and savings, property liens, and household bankruptcy. In the extreme, hospitals can even have patients arrested and jailed if they fail to show up in court to provide relevant information on how they will pay their bills. But the hospital often wins a pyrrhic victory—after all, patients who can't afford to pay their medical bills often have very little income or assets to garnish. As one billing consultant put it, "The damage to patients' lives is considerable, while the dollars extracted most likely aren't."

In 2014, concerns about the financial and psychological impact of unpaid medical debt—for the insured and uninsured alike—prompted two former debt collection executives, Craig Antico and Jerry Ashton, to start a nonprofit. RIP Medical Debt buys up and forgives patients' medical debt. As of December 2019, they had forgiven over $1 billion in medical debt for over 500,000 individuals and families. Buying up and forgiving debt is cheap, because the debt collectors are so rarely successful.

Indeed, hospitals often sense the futility of debt collection efforts and instead sell off their debt to debt buyers for pennies on the dollar.

(Selling off debt is also a convenient way for hospitals to distance themselves from aggressive debt collection tactics and avoid embarrassing exposés.) These debt buyers then in turn engage in aggressive— indeed, sometimes criminal—harassing tactics to try to make their financial "investment" in medical debt pay off.

The government has made some feeble attempts to regulate the most egregious practices. In 2020, for example, a federal rule made it illegal for debt collectors to call a debtor more than seven times per week. Limiting harassing calls to once a day seems like a useful, if tiny, first step. Until you realize that each doctor's bill (for the surgery, the anesthesia, etc.) can count as a separate medical bill, and hence a separate debt.

To add insult to injury, even after all of the attempts by medical providers and debt collectors to collect payment, most of the enormous amount of medical debt is never repaid. Estimates suggest that about 90 percent of medical debt remains unpaid and ends up on medical providers'—and taxpayers'—bottom lines. But not before a lot of needless effort and suffering has occurred, not to mention damage to patients' credit ratings.

UNAFFORDABLE EXPENSES

There's a reason why most medical debt is never paid off. It's that medical bills are different from most of the other financial shocks that insurance is designed to cushion, such as unemployment, disability, or death. (Yes, we realize it's odd to describe death as a financial setback, but it is for the decedent's family, so bear with us.) The key difference: medical costs don't decrease as income decreases. The cost of treating cancer and heart disease isn't lower for poorer individuals. And their risk of getting these diseases is, if anything, higher, because poverty and poor health often go hand in hand.

By contrast, almost every other kind of insurance protects against the possibility of a financial loss that declines as income declines. Life insurance, disability insurance, and unemployment insurance are designed to replace some of the lost earnings that come with death, disability, or job loss, respectively. The more you earn, the more you risk losing, and therefore the more expensive it is to provide that insurance. Lower-earning individuals can therefore get cheaper insurance, because what the insurance will pay out in the event of a bad outcome is also lower. Even property and casualty insurance has a bit of the same flavor—lower-income households tend to spend less on cars and on houses, and therefore the cost for insuring their car or home is also lower.

Medical costs, however, don't decline as income declines. This is one of the reasons health insurance is frequently—and accurately—described as "unaffordable." The medical bills that need to be insured can be many multiples of the patient's income. And because most health insurance plans require patients to pay some portion of those bills, even the insured can face unaffordable medical bills.

It is presumably for this reason that, as we mentioned earlier, Medicare patients who are "poor enough" can get their substantial cost-sharing requirements paid for by another public health insurance program—Medicaid. But that doesn't help the many patients whose incomes are too high to qualify for Medicaid, but who cannot afford to pay the substantial medical expenses they would face with only Medicare coverage. Cora Jackson was caught in this trap. Her sole source of income, Social Security, provided an annual income of $7,428 in 1988, which would be equivalent to just over $16,000 in 2019. This left her with just a bit too much income to qualify for Medicaid, but not enough income to afford private supplemental coverage or to be able to pay the medical bills not covered by Medicare.

Fortunately, the wise men (yes, they were mostly all men back then) who designed Medicare and Medicaid back in the mid-1960s understood that even a nonpoor individual could become impoverished by her medical bills. From the start, therefore, they created a separate pathway to Medicaid coverage for individuals in certain demographic groups—such as pregnant women, children, or the elderly—whose income was too high to qualify directly for Medicaid, but whose medical bills became sufficiently large relative to their income and financial assets. Each state could then decide whether or not to include this separate pathway—known as the "medically needy" program—as a component of its Medicaid program. To this day, only about two thirds of states have done so.

In the states that have, the medically needy Medicaid program seems like health insurance done right. Insurance protection is most important when medical bills become "too high," eating into resources that are essential for nonmedical needs. What level of medical bills is "too high" obviously depends on one's income. Hence the genius behind the program: no matter how high someone's income is, they can end up medically needy if their medical bills get large enough.

But although it rests on the firm rock of sound economic principles, implementation of the medically needy program is on much shakier ground. The devil is always in the details, and in the case of the medically needy program, those details have resulted in a wholly inadequate set of protections.

The key problem is that enrollees are required to periodically file paperwork to requalify as medically needy. Here too, in principle, there's a logic involved. Just because you had a large medical bill once in your early twenties doesn't mean you are still medically needy in your forties. But, once again, in practice the design is flawed.

Cora Jackson had to requalify every single month. Which meant that her granddaughter Jackie had to track her medical payments each month, and save the receipts, until Cora had paid enough of her own money toward her medical care that month to qualify as medically needy. Jackie would then bring Cora's receipts to the local public aid office, which would take a few days to review her paperwork and then declare Cora medically needy. Only then was Cora eligible for Medicaid coverage for any subsequent medical expenses that month. As a result, Cora often got the additional coverage for only a few days at the end of each month. As Jackie commented, "By the time I get the card, it's time to do it again."

You might think—or at least hope—that with three decades of health-care reforms since Cora's story took place, this design flaw would have been fixed. Alas, it is not so. Many states still require individuals to requalify for medically needy coverage on a monthly basis, and the rest require requalification at least every six months.

The descriptions thus far should leave no doubt that the US health-care house is in dire shape. Insured Americans struggle with important gaps in what their insurance covers, as well as the pervasive risk of losing that coverage. Currently uninsured Americans struggle even more. The natural instinct is to try to make repairs.

But these problems can't be easily patched over. As we will see next, our many attempts to do so have made this painfully clear.

Rebuild, Don't Renovate

The sobering lesson from our health policy history

n July 1965, President Lyndon Johnson flew to Independence, Missouri, for the watershed event in US health policy: the bill-signing ceremony for Medicare and Medicaid. Johnson chose the location—the birthplace of Harry S. Truman—to recognize the former president, who two decades earlier had tried unsuccessfully to enact universal coverage. With President Johnson looking on, eighty-two-year-old Truman was enrolled as Medicare's very first beneficiary.

Medicare and Medicaid weren't the universal coverage that Truman had pushed for. And even for the elderly and the poor who did get coverage, the inadequacy of that coverage quickly became apparent. Only two years later, President Johnson was fielding proposals to expand Medicare benefits to include prescription drugs—which had been omitted from the original legislation for cost reasons—and to expand Medicaid eligibility to low-income children and pregnant women. Medicaid coverage for children and pregnant women would be added in the 1980s, creating some of the problems that we saw in chapter 1 of kids losing coverage as they get older, and moms losing coverage after they give birth. Medicare prescription drug coverage would have to wait until 2006; it was also soon deemed inadequate and quickly prompted additional reforms.

It's an all-too-familiar pattern. Since the advent of modern medicine and modern medical expenses in the mid-twentieth century, our health policy history has consisted of an endless series of patches, repeatedly layered on top of a broken system. Laws create coverage for specific groups: people with particular diseases (at least until they recover), low-income children (until they grow up), patients experiencing an emergency (until they are "stabilized"), hostages and their family members (during their captivity and for a limited time after it), the disabled (after waiting two years), prisoners (until they are released from prison), and the list goes on.

The result, as the historian of medicine Charles Rosenberg describes, is that "policies on the ground seem less a coherent package of ideas and logically related practices than a layered conglomerate of stalemated battles, ad hoc alliances and ideological gradients, more a cumulative sediment of negotiated cease-fires among powerful stakeholders than a self-conscious commitment to data-sanctioned goals."

It's mind-boggling that we haven't had a deliberate national policy for health-care coverage, but have instead let this policy house be haphazardly put together. With different people dropping by on their own, when circumstances permit, to build the walls, install a heating system, or dig the foundation. It's time to build a new house, from scratch.

As real estate agents like to say, "Rebuild, don't renovate!" Home renovation, they warn, can "lead you down a never-ending (and stealthily expensive) home improvement rabbit hole." The risk of expensive—

and unsuccessful—home renovation is so pervasive that it's become a standard trope in television and movies. Think Tom Hanks and Shelley Long in *The Money Pit*. We have yet to see a major motion picture devoted to the dangers of health-care reform. Nevertheless, the same principle applies: sometimes it's best to start over.

We've experienced more than a half century of the renovation approach to US health insurance. In this chapter, we'll describe a few of these attempts in more detail. Although each is individually well intentioned, collectively they underscore the ultimate futility of treating US health insurance policy as a fixer-upper. Patching the patchwork inevitably leaves gaps at the seams. As we'll see, these attempts will also reveal an important motivating force behind US health policy, one that must be front and center in any successful policy solution.

WHO SHALL LIVE

In November 1962, *Life* magazine revealed the existence of a committee in Seattle that had been empowered to grant some individuals a second chance at life. This was no metaphor for rehabilitating criminals or treating substance abuse. It was literally about life or death. A brand-new technology—an artificial kidney—was suddenly offering a possible reprieve from a death sentence for patients whose kidneys had failed. Hailed as a modern miracle, dialysis had the potential to transform what had been a fatal disease into a chronic condition. At least for those who could afford the extremely high cost of dialysis—about $15,000 a year in the early 1960s, which would be over $125,000 a year in 2019 dollars.

Most people couldn't afford that cost. And the hospital in Seattle that had pioneered the new technology couldn't afford to provide it for free

to all afflicted patients. Hence the need for a committee to select people to receive dialysis. Seven "quite ordinary people . . . high-minded,
good-hearted citizens" were brought together to make these decisions.
One was a banker, another a housewife. They served as volunteers. At
the time the article came out, they had already picked five people to be
given the gift of life.

Informally referred to as "the God Committee," they were "in fact
a Life or Death Committee," noted the *Life* story. "With no moral or
ethical guidelines save their own individual consciences, they must
decide, in the words of the ancient Hebrew prayer, 'Who shall live and
who shall die.' . . . They do not much like the job."

The public didn't much like it, either, when they read about it. The
heated criticism and extensive discussions over the ethical issues
posed by such a committee helped launch what would become the
modern field of bioethics. It also sparked extensive policy debates over
whether—and how—the government should provide funding for a
life-threatening illness with an unaffordable medical solution.

Three years later, in the midst of these debates, the landmark Medicare legislation was passed. But Medicare covered only the elderly,
while kidney disease also struck down children, as well as individuals
in the prime of their working lives. As a result, the same year that Medicare was enacted, Washington senator Henry Jackson—whose childhood friend was one of the Seattle patients hoping to be given access to
the miracle cure—proposed a separate federal program to cover medical care for kidney failure. Faced with sustained advocacy efforts and
public pressure, including a dramatic moment in which a patient was
wheeled in and dialyzed in front of a congressional committee, Congress eventually agreed. In 1972, it extended Medicare coverage to patients suffering from end-stage kidney disease, regardless of their age.

We have already encountered this program in chapter 1—Mama's grandson-in-law Robert was covered by it in the late 1980s. It exists to this day; in 2019 it covered over 250,000 people and cost the federal government about $25 billion. And—then and now—the program makes little logical sense. Why cover the expensive dialysis treatments but not the medical care that could have perhaps prevented Robert's kidney disease from progressing to the stage where dialysis was needed? Why cover kidney disease and not the many other expensive, debilitating chronic diseases that affect the nonelderly?

Nonetheless, it turned out to be only the first in what became a series of disease-specific public insurance programs. As if we could get to universal coverage one disease at a time.

There are now also separate public programs created to cover patients with tuberculosis, breast and cervical cancer, sickle cell anemia, Lou Gehrig's disease, HIV/AIDS, and (most recently) COVID. Often these programs are themselves a series of patches. For example, the 2000 federal law that created coverage for breast and cervical cancer treatment for low-income, uninsured women was a patch to an earlier patch from 1990. In the 1980s, Congress was confronted with the spectacle of people who could not afford cancer screening, and were subsequently dying from breast and cervical cancer that would have been treatable if caught earlier. With low screening rates in low-income communities—and decades of research arguing for the importance of screening and early detection—Congress provided funds to pay for free or reduced-cost breast and cervical cancer screening for low-income uninsured women.

Initially, this program seemed to be a huge success. Screenings increased substantially. But this success highlighted the program's flawed conception: The 1990 bill mandated that clinics that received funding for screening must ensure that the women they diagnosed with cancer get treatment. Yet it explicitly prohibited these clinics from using any program funding to *treat* detected cancer. This left the clinics scrambling to find other funds from state programs or private foundations to cover the cost of treating the cancer that the national program now paid to detect.

Powerful advocacy groups—including the National Breast Cancer Coalition and the American Cancer Society—mobilized for change. They argued that it was unethical to diagnose people with a disease without providing them with a means to treat the disease. They organized physicians to testify before Congress about their personal struggles to try to arrange treatment for patients they had diagnosed with breast cancer through the program. They bolstered this testimony with poignant stories of uninsured women with breast cancer who resorted to sharing medications, using water balloons as breast prostheses, and, in some cases, dying for lack of treatment. And they pointed to the disease-specific expansion of Medicaid eligibility for tuberculosis treatment a few years earlier as a precedent to follow.

Eventually the advocates succeeded in creating the second patch. Medicaid eligibility was expanded to cover women with breast or cervical cancer. As long as the cancer is diagnosed at a clinic funded through the original program, in a state that offers this optional Medicaid program. And the woman is the "right" age. And, of course, only if that diagnosis is for breast or cervical cancer. One uninsured woman with late-term breast cancer who qualified for the program—while her mother who was diagnosed with stage-four lung cancer did not—wryly joked that she had "won the cancer lottery." At least until her cancer went into remission and her coverage then ended.

Not all patches are disease specific. But they are all inherently flawed. Even those that come at the personal behest of the commander in chief.

A PERSONALIZED, PRESIDENTIAL PATCH

On March 9, 1978, Julie Beckett gave birth to a healthy baby girl in Cedar Rapids, Iowa. Four months later, baby Katie contracted viral encephalitis, leaving her paralyzed and unable to breathe or swallow on her own.

Julie and her husband, Mark, had private health insurance that covered Katie. When their insurance benefits, which were capped at $1 million, were exhausted, Katie qualified for Medicaid because of her disabilities. But her parents were caught in a bureaucratic trap: Medicaid would cover Katie only if she were institutionalized. Julie and Mark could not take their child home from the hospital if they wanted to maintain her insurance coverage.

In November 1981, when Katie was three years old, her story caught the attention of none other than newly elected president Ronald Reagan. The man who had declared in his January inaugural address that "government is not the solution" was sufficiently moved by Katie's plight that he directed his staff to find a government solution. As a result, the Reagan administration issued a special waiver to the Medicaid rules so that Katie could go home without losing her Medicaid coverage. She made it home in time for Christmas, where she was greeted with a Christmas present from the Reagans—a rag doll—and a card wishing her and her family "the loveliest holiday ever."

The Reagan administration also set up a review board that could waive the rules to allow certain other disabled children like Katie to receive care at home while retaining their Medicaid coverage. Congress got into the game the following year with legislation that gave states the ability to allow Medicaid coverage in Katie Beckett–like circumstances. That created what is now known as the "Katie Beckett waiver." In 2020, eighteen states had this waiver, and a few others had similar programs.

But the customized patch doesn't even fully fix the specific, narrow issue it was designed to address. Despite all the presidential attention and fanfare, the patch was itself frayed around the edges. The Katie Beckett waiver applies only to *children* with long-term disabilities. Once that child turns nineteen, she's typically subject to adult Medicaid rules, and the Katie Beckett waiver for getting covered care outside of an institution no longer applies.

Why did Congress in its infinite wisdom see fit to create this coverage for disabled children but have it last only until adulthood? It may be that, at the time they were making the law, that's all that seemed relevant. Most children as severely disabled as Katie didn't live to adulthood. But medical technology has improved considerably since 1981, and many of the children covered by Katie Beckett waivers are now able to live longer. Long enough, in some cases, to get kicked off Medicaid. Katie herself ended up living to thirty-four, three times longer than her doctors had predicted when, as a toddler, she captured the attention of the Gipper.

Little has changed since President Reagan and Congress failed to anticipate that Katie Beckett might live to adulthood. As recently as the COVID-19 pandemic, Congress enacted special coverage rules for patients with acute COVID, but failed, at least initially, to anticipate— or include coverage for—the potential long-term side effects of COVID.

What an absurd way to "fix" problems with insurance coverage— imperfect patch by imperfect patch, egregious case by egregious case. And yet this incremental patching has remained the underlying approach to expanding insurance coverage in the United States for over half a century. Often, as we have just seen, these patches take the form of highly tailored extensions of insurance coverage for specific contingencies. However, sometimes they also try to fill some of the holes in safety net care for those who still lack insurance.

IN CASE OF EMERGENCY

On May 21, 1974, Frederick Campbell was born in the parking lot outside of Marshall County Hospital in Holly Spring, Mississippi. This isn't a story about contractions progressing too quickly. His mother, Hattie Mae, had made it to the hospital in plenty of time. But the hospital refused to admit her because she didn't have insurance. Even after she gave birth in her neighbor's car, right outside the hospital entrance, the hospital staff would not treat her, or her newborn son. When she subsequently sued the hospital for breaching their common-law duty to her, the court ruled in the hospital's favor.

At that time, hospitals frequently refused to treat uninsured or low-income patients who arrived at the emergency room. In fact, the practice was so well publicized it had its own name: patient dumping. Sometimes, this dumping took the form of refusing to admit patients, such as uninsured pregnant women like Hattie Mae. At other times, hospitals were (too) quick to discharge their uninsured patients. G. R. Lafon, an uninsured fifty-four-year-old laborer with third-degree burns to his sides and back from a grease fire at a local fish fry, was one such case. One hospital sent him on his way after inserting an IV and a catheter. He had to drive for seven more hours, with the IV bottle hanging from the coat hook in the car—and get turned away from yet another hospital—before finally arriving at the county hospital that was legally required to treat him. There, he ultimately received a skin graft and spent nineteen days as an inpatient.

Concerns about patient dumping ultimately produced one of the most famous patches in US health care, a 1986 federal law requiring that hospitals examine and stabilize all patients who come to the emergency room, regardless of their ability to pay. This requirement has been invoked by politicians from across the political spectrum to argue that lack of universal coverage is not, practically, consequential. Republican president George W. Bush was widely pilloried when he commented that "people have access to health care in America. After all, you just go to an emergency room." But Republicans do not have a monopoly on this sentiment. New York Democratic senator, and former Harvard professor, Daniel Patrick Moynihan made a similar remark in the midst of the Clintons' ultimately unsuccessful attempt to enact universal health insurance in the early 1990s. He argued that "we do have universal health coverage actually," and pointed to the fact that no one can be denied needed emergency care. Far from providing access to adequate health care for all Americans, the antidumping law didn't even accomplish its narrower goal of making sure that patients could get medical care in emergency situations. Stories—and evidence—of patient dumping continue to this day.

Once again, the 1986 law was merely the latest in a series of inadequate efforts to prevent patient dumping. Congress had tried to outlaw the practice as early as 1946. At that time its leverage came from the new, large-scale federal program paying for the construction and modernization of hospitals. This program lasted for decades and provided funding for thousands of hospitals. It also provided the government with an opportunity to impose requirements in return for that funding. One of its quid pro quos was that hospitals treat and stabilize any patient with emergency medical conditions.

That requirement proved toothless. There was no clear definition of what constituted an emergency. There were no dedicated enforcement efforts. And there were no financial penalties for violations. A hospital could turn Hattie Mae away without any fear of repercussions.

In response to this failed effort, as well as to patient dumping becoming more frequent as health-care costs rose in the 1970s, many states also passed legislation in the late 1970s and early 1980s to try to end patient dumping. But with little clarity on what constituted an emergency, and few sanctions against hospitals that ignored their common-law responsibility, most state laws were also largely ineffective.

The 1986 federal law was explicitly designed to address the limitations of its predecessors. It required hospitals to provide an "appropriate medical screening examination" to any patient who came to the emergency room—regardless of diagnosis, financial status, or race. If the screening revealed an "emergency medical condition," the hospital was further required to "stabilize" the patient before discharging or transferring her. No longer could hospitals claim that they weren't sure the patient presented with an "emergency." The law also specified substantial financial penalties for hospitals and physicians who violated the requirements. No longer could they violate the law with impunity and expect to skate away scot-free. It might have seemed like progress at the time.

But the problems remained. In fact, they were inevitable. Because, like the previously unsuccessful efforts to prevent patient dumping, the 1986 law—which is still on the books—missed the point: any real solution must do more than simply impose requirements on hospitals for the here and now of the emergency. This has been made abundantly clear by the experiences of physicians and patients in the decades since this latest patch was sewn on.

One issue is that a requirement that the hospital "stabilize" a patient with an emergency medical condition doesn't mean the hospital must actually *treat* the underlying medical issue that precipitated the emergency. Or ensure that the patient get the follow-up care needed to do so. So yes, when a patient suffers severe abdominal pain because of her cancer, or experiences chest pains from her heart disease, the emergency room staff can no longer turn her away. They will stabilize her. But then they'll send her home. They won't actually treat the cancer or the heart disease, just the emergency it happens to produce at that moment. After that, the patient is not their problem—at least until her untreated condition produces the next emergency.

As a result, some patients end up continually returning to the emergency department to be repeatedly, temporarily "stabilized." Some of these so-called frequent fliers are struggling with underlying psychiatric issues that are never addressed and therefore continually land them back in crisis. As one emergency physician described it:

> We're often greeted by familiar faces, people we've met with for three, four, maybe five days in a row. Although these patients have been evaluated and are medically stable for transport, they remain in a persistent state of psychiatric crisis and are stuck in treatment limbo until they receive intensive psychiatric care. As emergency physicians, we are proud to provide an essential service to this highly stigmatized and often marginalized segment of our population, but many of us can't help but feel an ongoing sense of futility and hopelessness for them. While we were trained in providing the care needed for initial stabilization, we don't have the skills to meaningfully treat their underlying psychiatric illness.

Another problem with the patch is that while the hospital is required to stabilize the patient, regardless of her ability to pay, the hospital isn't required to absorb the cost of doing so. Hospitals can—and do—bill uninsured patients for their emergency room care. Getting medical care in an emergency is of course important. But it puts a bit of a damper on things when that life-saving treatment is followed by life-crushing bills. One uninsured man who ended up in the emergency room following a heart attack subsequently received a bill for over $125,000. As he wryly remarked to his son, "If the heart attack did not kill me, this will."

There have been targeted efforts to address this issue. For example, the federal government reimburses hospitals for providing (required) emergency health-care services for uninsured immigrants who would be eligible for Medicaid if they were documented immigrants and had lived in the country for at least five years. This of course does nothing for the vast majority of uninsured patients who use the emergency room but don't qualify for this program.

———

We've treated you to a few specific examples of what is a much larger phenomenon of patches. They typically have a common origin story: a particular problem surfaces, generates public outcry, and prompts (limited) policy action. A 1960 CBS documentary entitled *Harvest of Shame* draws attention to the plight of migrant farmworkers and prompts federal legislation to fund their health care. A young AIDS patient from Indiana successfully draws attention to the tragedy of the AIDS epidemic, and four months after his death, the 1990 Ryan White CARE Act provides federal funding for the health care of low-income uninsured or underinsured HIV/AIDS patients. A global health crisis prompts federal legislation in 1993, providing coverage for tuberculosis treatment to otherwise uninsured low-income patients, at least in the states that opt into the new program. In 2001, a well-organized advocacy group effectively lobbies for expanded public health insurance coverage for patients suffering from ALS, otherwise known as Lou Gehrig's disease. Coverage for ALS is extended further in 2020, after gaining support by Major League Baseball and attention from the viral "Ice Bucket Challenge."

Patching is almost surely a politically easier lift than tearing down and rebuilding from scratch. It's oh so tempting to think that the latest set of patches will do the trick. Come on, one last try. This time, we'll get it right.

Only when we look back on the last seventy years of well-meaning, creative, but ultimately futile incremental attempts to try to provide adequate protection against the medical costs of poor health does it become unavoidably clear that we have no choice but to start over. History teaches us that more patches won't work.

History teaches us something else as well. It tells us why we have all those patches in the first place. If we're going to tear down a dilapidated old house and build a new one, we first have to decide what we want from that house. As we'll explore more in the next part of the book, the patches we've described—as well as other policy responses we'll encounter—reveal our purpose, our deep-seated social commitment to providing essential medical care when confronted with desperately ill patients who are unable to afford that care.

PART II

FORM FOLLOWS FUNCTION

The purpose of health insurance policy

The influential nineteenth-century architect Louis Sullivan is known as the father of the American skyscraper. He's also credited with the phrase "form follows function." His towering (by the standards of the time) steel-framed skyscrapers broke with established architectural form to meet the increasing demand for office space, producing buildings with "an indefinite number of stories of offices piled tier upon tier."

The dictum that design should be guided by purpose—rather than current fashion or historical precedent—is as relevant for health insurance as it is for high-rises. It is imperative that we first clearly define the intended function of US health insurance policy. Form must follow function.

There are many possible motivations for government involvement in health insurance coverage. One is that health care is a basic human right, a key pillar of morality in a modern society;

Franklin D. Roosevelt famously declared it so when he proposed a Second Bill of Rights in 1944. Another is the desire to improve the population's health. Or to redress the shocking differences in health between rich and poor Americans, and between Black and White Americans. Or to fix the problems that Adam Smith's "invisible hand" leaves visible in the medical marketplace.

None of these, however, turn out to be the driving force behind the patchwork of policies we have described. Rather, as we'll argue, these patches were motivated by the universal tendency to eventually act when confronted by people who are desperately ill and unable to access essential medical care. Our history, in other words, reveals an enduring social norm that we have been trying—and failing—to achieve.

The existence of this unwritten social contract may be hard to believe in the face of the many problems with US health care. Patients who cannot afford the medical care they need. Hospitals and doctors who turn away indigent and uninsured patients, or hound them for payment of enormous medical bills.

But these represent the failure to fulfill our obligations, not their absence. Having goals and achieving them are two different things. We've already seen multiple examples of policy efforts to try to make sure that patients have access to essential medical care, regardless of their resources. We'll encounter some more in the next chapter. Such efforts reveal our social contract, our goals, even when these efforts fall short.

We'll also briefly explore some of the leading hypotheses for where this social contract comes from. But we don't have to understand where it comes from—or even agree with it—in order to recognize that it exists. And once we do, we'll argue that universal coverage is the only sensible way to fulfill this social contract. If we are inevitably going to respond when people face acute health problems without the resources to address them, it is better to formalize—and fund—those commitments up front. This is not a new insight. It has been recognized for centuries, and in modern times it has been embraced by liberals and conservatives alike.

Clarifying the function of universal health insurance will also clarify and delineate its limits. Our social contract is to provide a standard of adequacy for health-care needs, not to strive for equality in health or in health care. Separating the issues we are and are not tackling with health insurance policy is essential for good design.

Some readers may of course feel an admirable moral imperative to reduce the shocking health disparities that exist within the US. For them, we'll provide an important cautionary note of empirical realism: health insurance policy is not the place to tackle this problem. Contrary to what the popular rhetoric might suggest, access to medical care is not a primary determinant of health disparities. The evidence here is clear.

Failing to build a health insurance system that recognizes what our social contract requires—and what it does not—is the path to perdition. It's the path we've followed—unsuccessfully—for over half a century. That form has not produced function.

A Universal Commitment

What the insurance of the "uninsured" teaches us

No one in America is actually uninsured when it comes to their health care. That may sound like a bizarre claim, especially from two people writing a book arguing that we should have universal coverage. But hear us out.

As we'll explain in this chapter, there is a surprising—and surprisingly formal—set of public policies designed to provide essential medical care to those who lack formal health insurance. These policies don't work well, as the evidence in part I or any passing familiarity with US health care makes clear. But the existence of this "secret insurance" of the uninsured is essential to understanding what our health-care policy has been trying—and failing—to do.

NO ONE IS ACTUALLY UNINSURED

One in ten Americans lack formal health insurance coverage. But they are not uninsured.

What would being actually uninsured look like? Most people's wedding rings are actually uninsured. Unless you've explicitly purchased private insurance for your ring (and who does that? No one with wedding rings in the price range we're familiar with), you have no backstop if you drop the ring down the drain while washing the dishes, or it slides off your toddler's finger into the unreachable depths of the heating grate when she's playing dress-up. No one other than you will pay to rip apart the plumbing to try to find the ring, provide another ring in its place, or pay for a brand-new one. You're on your own.

Not so for someone without health insurance who needs medical care that they can't afford. They receive a substantial amount of medical care and don't pay for most of it. That's precisely what health insurance is supposed to accomplish.

The evidence from the Oregon health insurance experiment is illuminating here. We already described in chapter 1 how the results from that study made clear that having formal health insurance delivers real benefits. Better protection against expensive medical bills. More access to care. Improved mental health. But it also revealed something striking about the experience of the uninsured: they receive about four fifths of the medical care they would get if they were insured, including primary care, preventive care, prescription drugs, emergency room visits, and hospital admissions. And they pay for only about twenty cents on the dollar for that medical care. If they were actually uninsured, they would pay for all the medical care they receive.

National data corroborate the finding in Oregon that the uninsured pay only a small fraction of the cost of the care they receive. Of course, as we saw in the previous chapters, they are typically billed for their large expenses. But, as we also discussed, those bills ultimately remain mostly unpaid.

The pattern of what medical expenses the uninsured do—and do not—pay for is also telling. For an insured patient, the portion of her medical bills that she pays herself tends to shrink as her medical bills rise. Once those bills get into the thousands of dollars, she is typically paying very little, if anything, out of her own pocket. That's how insurance should function. Its primary purpose is to protect the patient against the risk of truly catastrophic expenses.

And that's also what the experience of the nominally "uninsured" patient looks like. As the bills accumulate, she pays a lower and lower portion of them. Indeed, once the bills have gotten high enough, the uninsured patient is typically paying less out of pocket than a privately insured patient with the same medical bills would pay.

That said, there are good reasons why the uninsured are referred to as such. Their medical bills aren't paid out of an actual insurance policy, one that spells out in advance what medical treatments the policy will and will not pay for, and what share of those treatments it will pay. Nor do the uninsured send their medical bills into a third-party entity that then reimburses their physician or hospital.

But just because the process is different doesn't make their insurance any less real. There are a host of government commitments in place to provide the uninsured with medical care when they cannot pay for it. A vast web of public policy requirements and dedicated public funding to provide them free or heavily discounted medical care. And no, we're not just talking about the emergency room.

To understand how these policies play out, consider a (hopefully instructive) analogy to homeowners who are "uninsured" against flood damage to their homes. Since the early 1970s, the federal government has required homeowners in high-risk areas to purchase flood insurance. It has also heavily subsidized that insurance to try to make it affordable. If this sounds familiar, it's because it is. A similar mandate, with accompanying subsidies, was introduced for health insurance in the 2010 Affordable Care Act, popularly—or unpopularly, depending on what circles you run in—known as Obamacare. Of course, not everyone does what the government tells them they must do. Just as many Americans don't have health insurance—despite the mandate to do so—many homeowners in high-risk flood areas don't have the mandatory flood insurance.

We know what happens when natural disaster strikes the "uninsured" homeowner. We see it play out on the evening news every year during hurricane season. Politicians find it hard to resist the urge to parachute into the stricken area, tour it in a hard hat, and publicly declare a federal disaster, unleashing dedicated federal funding for rebuilding and relocating. That funding—administrated by the Federal Emergency Management Agency (FEMA)—then provides the "uninsured" homeowners in the disaster area with temporary housing and other supplies, as well as with money for their home repairs. Of course, the coverage FEMA provides isn't as comprehensive as a formal homeowner's insurance policy. But whatever they call it on TV, federal disaster relief is insurance for "uninsured" homeowners.

As we'll describe in the rest of this chapter, a similar set of FEMA-like government programs provides health care to those without health insurance. These policies—like FEMA—highlight our societal commitment to not stand by passively when confronted with certain types of crises. They just don't get the same kind of media attention on the nightly news.

THE INSURANCE OF THE "UNINSURED"

When it comes to the medical care of the uninsured, the media tends to focus on the heroic actions of volunteers. The local community that rallies together to raise funds for a child's chemotherapy. The family that launches a GoFundMe campaign to pay for a relative's life-saving surgery. The pop-up health clinics where teams of volunteer clinicians provide a few days of free medical, vision, and dental care in an underserved area.

Stories like these vividly illustrate some of the human costs of the lack of universal health insurance, and at the same time inspire us with examples of individual generosity. One volunteer physician working at a temporary clinic summarized these feelings well. "As we gathered at the end of the day, one of the officials said, 'Isn't it horrible—that we need this?' And another answered, 'Isn't it wonderful—that we have this?' And I said, 'Yes.'"

It would be absurd for us to describe the uninsured as having insurance if such ad hoc and uncoordinated efforts by a small number of individuals and dedicated nonprofits were the primary means by which the uninsured ended up receiving free medical care. That would be like saying Blanche DuBois had a safety net to fall back on because, as she famously explained, "I have always depended on the kindness of strangers."

The kindness of strangers is small potatoes in the grand scheme of the health care that the uninsured receive without paying for. The big potatoes are big, to the tune of over $40 billion a year that is spent on health care *for* the uninsured but not *by* the uninsured. They are also primarily public potatoes—about four fifths is government funded and therefore, of course, government regulated.

What does all this public policy and funding mean in practice for the medical care of the uninsured? Although the emergency room looms large in the public mind, it is only the tip of the iceberg. Yes, every year there are over twelve million visits to the emergency room by uninsured patients. But there are also over fifty million visits to physicians' offices, over ten million visits to community health centers, and over two million hospital admissions. Through a piecemeal slew of policies at the federal, state, and local levels, the government has created a large, complex web of publicly regulated, publicly funded programs that provide free or low-fee health-care options for the uninsured. These include preventive care, care management for chronic health problems, and nonemergency hospital care.

The full extent and reach of the formal, public commitments to "cover" the uninsured shocked us as we started doing research for this book. We were astonished to realize that the problems of the uninsured arise not *because* of a lack of policy attention but *despite* it.

In dollar terms, hospitals are the largest source of safety net care, providing about three fifths of all uncompensated health care. Almost all are required by law to provide some charity care for those who cannot afford to pay, even in nonemergency circumstances. For-profit hospitals are exempt, but these account for only 15 percent of all hospital beds.

The central role for hospitals in providing safety net care is the outgrowth of their origins as charitable, rather than medical, institutions. The first hospitals emerged in eighteenth-century America, before the advent of anything that might resemble modern medical care. We don't mean merely before twenty-first-century medical genomics, or twentieth-century open-heart surgery. We mean the centuries—indeed, millennia—stretching from classical antiquity through the late nineteenth century, in which the physician's main function was to try to produce bodily excretions in order to aid in the restoration of balance in the body's "humors." A time in which the expression "the cure is worse than the disease" was unfortunately often all too accurate.

Aware of medicine's limitations—indeed, perhaps because of them—the nineteenth-century notion of "health care" centered primarily on rest, warmth, and good diet. It therefore centered on the family, particularly the matriarch. Her main instruments were cleanliness, food, and fresh air to maintain health, and basic nursing and medicinal herbs (which she prepared and stored along with the fruit preserves she made for winter nourishment) in times of illness. The original "family practice."

In this environment, the first hospitals emerged to provide food, shelter, and Christian moral teachings to patients who could not be supported by the predominant system of family care. They therefore emerged in the growing cities, which disrupted the traditional family networks that still persisted in the rest of the (still predominantly rural) country. The earliest general hospital in America was Pennsylvania Hospital in Philadelphia, which opened in 1752, followed by New York Hospital in Manhattan in 1791, and the Massachusetts General Hospital in Boston in 1821.

These early hospitals were funded primarily by local philanthropists; there were virtually no paying customers or public financing for hospitals before the late nineteenth century. Their purpose was to provide material and spiritual comfort toward brethren who fell ill without family to care for them. This was seen as an opportunity to practice Christian charity, a word itself derived from *caritas*, Greek for love. As the historian of medicine Charles Rosenberg has explained, American hospitals were created because "there was no other option. Fellow creatures could not be allowed to die in the streets."

This sentiment persists in modern times too. And although, in most respects, the twenty-first-century, high-tech, high-cost hospital bears little resemblance to the nineteenth-century charitable institution, its charitable mission has now been codified into public law and public funding. Nonprofit hospitals—which account for about 70 percent of all hospital beds—receive substantial federal and state tax breaks and in return are required to provide some charity care for indigent patients. Publicly owned and operated hospitals—which account for 15 percent of hospital beds—receive direct government funding to help pay for their operating costs, and in turn are legally required to accept patients regardless of ability to pay. The government also pays all hospitals—regardless of their ownership—more money for treating Medicaid patients if they also treat a large number of uninsured or low-income patients. In other words, rather than pay to cover the uninsured with public insurance, the government instead pays hospitals to cover the hospitals' costs of treating those uninsured patients.

Of course, none of this means that uninsured patients are well taken care of. We've already seen that the uninsured get less medical care, and are saddled with more medical debt, than they would if they were insured. These debts can accrue even when the patient is legally entitled to a hospital's charity care. Part of the problem is that who is eligible for charity care can vary greatly from hospital to hospital. For public hospitals, the requirements for what charity care they must provide differ not only from state to state but also even from county to county within the same state. Nonprofit hospitals tend to have no rules—or even guidance—for their required charity care policies.

Nor is there any mechanism to ensure that patients are made aware of a hospital's charity care policy. Hospitals routinely bill for care regardless of income. In Maryland, for example, the state has gone further than other states and requires *all* hospitals—including for-profit hospitals—to provide free care to patients making below 200 percent of the federal poverty line (about $53,000 for a family of four). Despite this requirement, many hospitals try to collect payments from patients who are eligible for free care. Throughout the country, it's up to the patients to realize that they are eligible for charity care, and then to apply for it. Needless to say, many do not. Others may simply not get medical care because they do not realize they would be eligible for charity care.

There's no doubt that the modern policies designed to get hospitals to provide charity care are poorly designed. They are even more poorly implemented by hospitals looking out for their bottom line. Nonetheless, the existence of extensive government requirements that hospitals provide charity care speaks to our enduring sense of obligation, as Rosenberg put it, to not let "fellow creatures ... die in the streets."

BAND-AIDS INSTEAD OF STITCHES

Outside of the hospital setting, the same societal obligations have spawned a bewildering array of other public programs designed to provide safety net care to the uninsured. One of the biggest is the twelve thousand community health centers that serve low-income uninsured and underinsured patients for no, or very low, fees. Deliberately located where there are few medical providers—often in rural and low-income urban areas—they treat about one in every twelve Americans a year. For those lucky enough to have a clinic nearby—and to know about its services—the clinics offer preventive health care, such as well-child visits and immunizations, and primary care to help patients manage chronic conditions, such as high blood pressure or diabetes. Many also try to offer mental health services. Some manage to offer dental services.

The term *community health center* evokes the image of a small, grassroots local organization that has devised an ersatz clinic in an abandoned storefront, operating with volunteer staff, foundation funding, sticks, and glue. It's a misleading image. These clinics are federally authorized, funded, and regulated by Section 330 of the Public Health

Service Act. Federally Qualified Health Centers to be precise. Not exactly mom-and-pop operations.

They're not exactly thriving operations either. Direct federal funding for these health centers covers only a small share of their total operating costs. They must therefore scramble to stay afloat by cobbling together a medley of funding from an assortment of other sources. Bizarrely, most of these other sources are other federally funded programs. Not even "borrowing from Peter to pay Paul," they're more aptly borrowing from Peter to pay Peter.

There's one pot of federal funding available for Native American patients, another for patients with diseases such HIV/AIDS and tuberculosis, and another for migrant workers. There are also different federal programs that pay for different medical services—prescription drugs, family planning, maternal and child health, lead screenings, breast and cervical cancer screenings, substance abuse, treatment of sickle cell anemia, and the list goes on. Each separate source of federal funding has its own eligibility rules, application processes, and reporting requirements.

Health centers can also apply for in-kind support from the federal government. One program recruits and retains clinicians for the centers through the National Health Service Corps. Another offers prescription drug discounts to their patients. Another provides free vaccines for low-income children. Yet another indemnifies the clinical staff from malpractice suits. It boggles the mind—or at least it boggles *our* minds—to think of these federally created and authorized centers applying to and coordinating among this hodgepodge of federal sources.

And that's just what's on offer from the federal government. State and local governments have their own programs as well. Pharmaceutical companies often donate free or discounted drugs to patients who successfully complete the application process and meet the eligibility requirements for a particular drug. Local nonprofits may lend a hand.

To help navigate this complex maze, there are for-profit consulting firms that earn their living advising these nonprofit centers on how to access available government resources. "A clinic literally could have up to 50 different funding sources, and 50 different reports that must be turned in at different times of the year," said one consultant, explaining her firm's business model. "The system has become so complex that you basically need a whole department to make sure you're following the rules."

In addition to the consultants, clinics often hire full-time staff whose job it is to help patients successfully apply to various programs that can fund specific types of care. But in the end, much of the administrative burden falls on the clinics' physicians. One physician at a community clinic in Philadelphia described her unsuccessful efforts to get her uninsured patient into hospice care for his advanced-stage, inoperable kidney cancer.

> My multiple phone calls failed to find a hospice provider that would accept an uninsured patient. . . .
>
> . . . In the end, all I could offer was medication for his pain. . . . I still remember standing in my living room one night a few days before he died, phone held in one hand, using the other to page through reference books to find instructions on how to adjust the dose of morphine for cancer pain.

Sometimes physicians are able to engineer creative work-arounds. "I learned to prescribe generics off of the $4 Walmart and Target lists and connect uninsured patients with [a federal program designed to make] a list of essential but expensive medicines more affordable at

$15 each—or free for the homeless," explained one physician describing her experience treating patients with asthma in a community health clinic in Chicago. But as she went on to note, "not all doctors knew of these workarounds, and not all patients got the medicines they needed."

It's these sorts of machinations—time consuming, idiosyncratic, and often futile—by publicly funded clinicians and clinic staff (aided by their for-profit consultants) who make you start to question the sanity of this whole endeavor. Surely this is not the best way to provide insurance to the uninsured.

And yet their existence—like that of FEMA—is telling. Like the government programs that are designed to provide hospital and emergency care to the indigent, these publicly funded clinics illustrate the fundamental social contract that the US has always operated by. To try to help patients in great need. But only in certain circumstances. In the next chapter, we'll explore why certain circumstances and not others trigger a sense of social obligation.

Origin Stories

Why this social contract?

The New Testament parable of the Good Samaritan, recounted in the Gospel of Luke, tells the story of a traveler who, on his way from Jerusalem to Jericho, has the misfortune to be attacked by robbers, beaten, and left lying "half-dead" on the road. A priest passes by the unfortunate man, ignores his plight, and continues on his way. So too does a Levite. Finally, the eponymous Good Samaritan shows him compassion. He tends to the poor man's injuries, "sooth[s] his wounds with olive oil and wine and bandage[s] them," and carries him on his donkey to an inn, where he pays the innkeeper to take care of him until he recovers.

In case you are wondering about the moral behind this morality tale of coming to the aid of the injured, here's a hint: over a dozen hospitals in the United States bear the name Good Samaritan. The lesson is clear. It is virtuous to practice altruism and charity toward strangers in need of medical care.

Economists weren't so sure. In a famous 1975 article, the libertarian economist and subsequent Nobel Prize winner James Buchanan coined the term "the Samaritan's dilemma" to explain the troubling repercussions of our instinct for compassion, sympathy, and charity toward those in need. Here's the problem he foresaw: If a traveler can embark on a journey secure in the knowledge that strangers would come to his aid if misfortune befell him, Buchanan conjectured that the traveler would take fewer precautions and expose himself to more danger. He would travel more frequently, make less effort to avoid the more dangerous routes, and be more likely to travel alone and at night. The well-intentioned charity toward unfortunate travelers could thus backfire, creating *more* misfortune among travelers. The issue with the Good Samaritan, in other words, is one of unintended consequences, a perennially popular theme of economists' lunchtime chatter and PhD dissertations alike.

How then to protect ourselves against our own well-intentioned but ultimately misguided charitable instincts? True to his libertarian roots, Buchanan offered no public policy solution. "Modern man has 'gone soft,'" Buchanan lamented,* as he exhorted the reader—in the spirit of Lady Macbeth urging her husband to murder the king—to try to restrain our natural impulses, to "screw [our] courage to the sticking place."

We have yet to see much in the way of compelling evidence for the Buchanan theory that if only public policy and private philanthropy were able to resist the temptation to help those who are sick and eco-

---

*Modern woman, too, judging by the leading example he chooses to illustrate his Samaritan's dilemma: the softhearted mother who cannot bring herself to spank the child who needs discipline, thus encouraging the child to continue to engage in bad behavior. His proposed solution: delegate the disciplining of the child to the (presumed present) nanny, who will be able to do what needs to be done to encourage good behavior!

nomically destitute, many or most of the currently uninsured would realize the need to purchase health insurance. But that doesn't really matter. What *does* matter is that we are clearly not able—or willing—to follow Buchanan's injunction and deny that aid to the sick, to ignore the moral imperative embodied by the actions of the Good Samaritan.

In the rest of the chapter, we'll explore why we cannot resist coming to the aid of the destitute in certain situations, such as medical emergencies or natural disasters, but apparently can in many others, such as when confronted with chronic hunger or poverty. We'll see that our private instincts reflect well-known psychological biases. It's jarring to realize that these biases have been encoded into our public policy.

MORAL EMERGENCIES

From the very dawn of the republic, the federal government actively provided disaster relief in the face of catastrophe. This included relief from both natural calamities, such as droughts, floods, fires, or grasshopper plagues, and man-made ones, such as the Whiskey Rebellion of 1794 or the Minnesota "Indian depredations." During the Great Depression, the concept of federal disaster relief was further extended to include public unemployment insurance for those who were destitute "due to an economic catastrophe over which [they have] no control."

The sociologist and legal scholar Michele Dauber has argued that there is a common thread linking eighteenth-century federal disaster relief to twentieth-century public unemployment insurance. "The plot structure of the disaster narrative is fixed," she wrote, "but the set of plausible occupants for the role of 'disaster' and 'victim' have expanded and contracted over the last two centuries." This theme of responding to what Dauber terms "the plot structure of the disaster narrative" extends to modern US health-care policy.

Thus the end-stage renal disease patient, who is dying because he cannot afford a new, salient, life-saving treatment, gets that treatment covered. But he gets no coverage in the early stages of his kidney failure, when medical management and guidance might be able to prevent the illness from spiraling out of control into a life-critical emergency. And he loses coverage after a successful kidney transplant because the emergency has been staved off, never mind the fact that he will likely struggle to pay for the immunosuppressants he must take for the rest of his life so that his body does not reject the transplanted kidney.

Thus the federal requirement that hospitals stabilize patients in an emergency regardless of their ability to pay, but permits those same patients, once stabilized, to be discharged, with a large bill. And without any resources or plan to treat the underlying health condition that provoked the emergency, which may therefore recur again and again.

Such laws reflect our tendency to respond to what the philosopher Kwame Anthony Appiah has termed "moral emergencies." We tend to feel much greater moral compulsion to act when people's needs are "up close and personal," than when they are more impersonal, distant, and abstract. The philosopher Peter Unger provides a nice illustration of these contrasting moral intuitions through two hypothetical scenarios. In the "Vintage Sedan" scenario, you are driving your much-loved vintage Mercedes when you see a man by the side of the road who has carelessly cut his leg on rusty barbed wire and is bleeding profusely. If you do not drive him to the nearby hospital, he will lose his leg. If you give him a lift, the blood will ruin your car's nice leather upholstery. In the "Envelope" scenario, you receive a letter from UNICEF requesting that you send one hundred dollars in a pre-addressed return envelope, otherwise thirty children in Africa will soon die.

Most people, Unger notes, feel it is wrong to leave the injured man bleeding by the side of the road in order to avoid the cost of cleaning the car's upholstery. Yet they do not feel it is morally monstrous to refuse to spend a smaller amount of money to provide life-saving assistance to the thirty children in Africa. The experimental moral psychologist Joshua Greene has conjectured that there may be an evolutionary explanation for these different reactions, noting that "our ancestors did not evolve in an environment in which total strangers on opposite sides of the world could save each other's lives" but they "did evolve in an environment in which individuals standing face-to-face could save each other's lives, sometimes only through considerable personal sacrifice."

Whatever the psychological explanation, the policy consequences of following these differing moral intuitions are striking. Take Hurricane Katrina, for example. The 2005 category 5 hurricane hit poor and minority communities in New Orleans especially hard. Those communities faced, and still face, systemic and deep-rooted hardships. Which is why they were living in the lowest-lying, lowest-value areas of the city, in some of the worst housing, lacking the means to leave New Orleans in the face of the oncoming hurricane. Dauber describes how the acute calamity of Hurricane Katrina

> conspire[d] to enable the same people to move from one state of moral blameworthiness to another. . . . reporters and politicians competed with each other to express outrage over the treatment of the same poor black residents of New Orleans who had been the targets of popular and sustained cuts in welfare and public housing programs. . . . What changed with Hurricane Katrina was not the people, but their ability to portray themselves as the victims of circumstances beyond their control.

This recategorization, however, was temporary. After the spotlight of public attention switched off, public policy quickly returned to business as usual. The experience, she notes, showed that an acute event can temporarily elevate a disadvantaged group to "successfully claim large-scale resources while leaving undisturbed their inability to receive help for their chronic condition."

She was speaking of the chronic conditions of inequality and injustice, but she might just as well have been speaking about chronic health conditions. Health, too, has its chronic and acute problems, and our history of policy responses illustrates a similar tendency to address the acute symptoms rather than their chronic origins.

Perhaps no example better illustrates the "disaster approach" to health-care policy than the programs we mentioned in the introduction, which are specifically designed to extend public health insurance coverage in the event of disasters—be they "natural," like COVID or Hurricane Sandy, or man-made, like 9/11 or the Flint water crisis. The blameless victims of the 9/11 attacks or the COVID-19 pandemic get additional access to health insurance—but only during that particular, acute crisis.

THE DESERVING AND THE UNDESERVING

Our history of policy responses to "moral emergencies" helps us understand why—in the absence of a coherent approach to universal health insurance—we have arrived at our existing patchwork of inefficient and inadequate health-care policies. If disaster strikes the unprepared, there is a strong moral impulse, at both the personal and the policy level, to "do something."

But that still leaves the question of what constitutes a "moral emergency." Why does a housing eviction or the threat of imminent starvation not prompt the same "emergency" policy response as a hurricane or a heart attack?

The answer lies in part in the long-standing emphasis in US social welfare policy to "attempt to classify people by merit," as the historian Michael Katz explained in his book *The Undeserving Poor*. American social policy incorporated the Victorians' emphasis on moral worth and blamelessness to a much greater extent than its progenitors across the Atlantic. As the sociologist Theda Skocpol has observed, "Institutional and cultural oppositions between the morally 'deserving' and the less deserving run like fault lines through the entire history of American social provision." These "fault lines" can be seen in nineteenth- and twentieth-century policies in areas as disparate as veterans' pensions, cash welfare for the indigent, natural disaster relief, and income support during economic downturns.

This same sensibility can be seen in the very origins of US hospitals, which, as we've discussed in the previous chapter, were first created in the late eighteenth and early nineteenth centuries primarily as a vehicle for charity. In a time when medical care could do very little, their purpose was to classify, not to cure. To identify the poor who were "deserving" of charity.

In the Victorian view, the "undeserving" poor were those who were responsible for their plight through their character flaws—idleness, improvidence, indolence, or intemperance. They should be condemned to the poorhouse—squalid, overcrowded institutions, where they would be isolated from relatives and neighbors and provided with a meager subsistence. The poorhouses were abhorrent by design, in order to inspire fear and inculcate a work ethic. And they were no place for the deserving poor, whose plight had arisen through no fault of their own. Someone suffering from poor health without family nearby to nurse him was a prime candidate for the "deserving" label. For no matter how hard he had worked, or how virtuous his character, an individual in the newly emerging cities could easily fall ill without anyone around to tend to him. He should not suffer the deliberate ignominy and inhospitality of the poorhouse.

Illness in the nineteenth century thus served the function of what the Nobel Prize–winning economist George Akerlof would later call a "tag." That is, an easily visible and largely immutable trait that signaled that the individual in question was more likely to be one of the "deserving poor"—genuinely needy through no fault of his own. But illness was only the initial tag. Patients who applied for admission to a nineteenth-century hospital were then subjected to more direct vetting of their moral worth by an admissions committee, composed not of physicians who could evaluate the applicant's medical condition, but of laymen. These "trustees" based their admissions decisions on criteria such as the applicant's church membership, record of service to particular families, and personal comportment. They often required a letter of recommendation about the applicant's character, ideally from a trustee or patron who had previously made contributions to the hospital. An excerpt from one such recommendation letter, written on behalf of a patient seeking admission to Pennsylvania Hospital in 1885 by a prominent Philadelphian, reads in part:

> I have known Mrs. Milne since four or five years: and she is well known to Mrs. Jackson, my sister Mrs. Henry, to Mrs. [Buckley], and to many other ladies. I believe we can all testify that she is deserving, industrious, well-behaved and respectable.

All told, the admissions process for nineteenth-century hospitals—which in some places even required a written application—bore more resemblance to that of twenty-first-century colleges than of twenty-first-century hospitals. So too did the pricing, with nineteenth-century hospitals offering both need-based and merit aid. Patients were charged more for their hospital admission if they were admitted because of a venereal disease, because that reflected poorly on their character.

The legacy of this Victorian morality persists to this day,* and the usefulness of illness as a tag for moral desert pervades modern health policy. "We accept without reservation our obligation to help . . . those unfortunates who, through no fault of their own, must depend on their fellow men," declared that famous proponent of limited government, Ronald Reagan, in his first inaugural address as governor of California. We've already seen how, as president, the Gipper directed his staff to make a patch to Medicaid so that little Katie Beckett—clearly suffering through "no fault of her own"—could get the medical care she needed.

Medicaid itself was created in 1965 not as health insurance for the poor but, as the political scientist Sandra Tanenbaum has noted, "for the 'deserving' poor . . . who were excluded from normal market relationships through no fault of their own." This was why Medicaid eligibility was tied to belonging to specifically designated groups—children, pregnant women, the disabled, or the elderly—who were seen as "deserving." Likewise, President Richard Nixon, presiding over the 1972 policy patch that expanded Medicare to provide health insurance coverage to the long-term disabled—the program described in chapter 1 that covered Mama's son Tommy once his illness left him

---

*Indeed, it is so deeply ingrained in the American psyche that we'll hazard a guess that any American-born reader knew instinctively what we meant by the phrases *deserving poor* and the *undeserving poor*. Whereas, Liran—who was born and raised in Israel—initially understood the meaning of the terms in reverse, assuming that the phrase *deserving poor* referred to those who "deserved" to be poor, while the "undeserving" were those who were poor through no fault of their own. This had never occurred to Amy, who has lived her entire life in the US.

sufficiently disabled—noted that the policy "reaffirms and reinforces America's traditional efforts to assist those of our citizens who, through no fault of their own, are unable to help themselves."

The view of illness as a tag for blamelessness, combined with our tendency to respond to moral emergencies, can help explain the empirical observation that our policies always have and always will try to provide care to those who are ill and lack the resources to care for themselves. They are rooted in a societal obligation that has existed throughout American history, as the creation of eighteenth- and nineteenth-century hospitals as charitable institutions illustrated.

As we will see next, the realization of the appropriate way to meet this obligation also dates back to our earliest days.

What Is to Be Done

Why universal health insurance is the only answer

There was a time when the US led rather than lagged the rest of the world in enacting policies to fulfill our health-care commitments. Did you know, dear reader, that the United States Congress enacted the world's first national compulsory health insurance law?

In 1798.

No, that's not a typo.

Alexander Hamilton was a key proponent of this early, compulsory health insurance. Unlike many other Hamiltonian endeavors—the Constitution, a national bank, the US Coast Guard—it has not lasted into the modern era. Nor does it get a mention in the eponymous hit Broadway musical.

Nonetheless, Hamilton's argument for compulsory health insurance anticipated the modern argument for universal health insurance coverage. It is an argument that, in the last several decades, has been embraced by prominent figures throughout the political spectrum, from a scholar at the conservative Heritage Foundation, to a moderate Republican governor, to a notorious (and notoriously liberal) Supreme Court justice.

HISTORY HAS ITS EYES ON US

Our story takes us back to the late eighteenth century, the early days of our new republic. It was then that the brand-new Congress enacted compulsory, tax-financed health insurance for commercial seamen.

In an era in which medical care was primarily provided by the family or neighbors, the peripatetic life of the commercial sailor left him singularly bereft of the standard form of support in times of illness. As we saw in chapter 4, charitable hospitals were created to fill this void. Indeed, it is no coincidence that the earliest hospitals were located in port or river towns—Philadelphia, New York, Boston, New Orleans, Louisville—where a seaman might fall ill, with his family too far away to care for him in his moment of need. But the scale and scope of the problem demanded more than private philanthropy. It necessitated—then and now—public policy.

The problem was that seamen—hailing from throughout the nation—became a concentrated burden on the local port communities. As a congressional committee's 1797 report noted, "Numbers of seamen . . . arrive at the different ports of the United States in such a disabled situation that they either become a great burden to the public hospitals, where any such are established, or are left to perish for want of proper attention." The burden was too great for local charity. And yet local charity felt compelled to try to come to the aid of such individuals in time of illness and need.

Alexander Hamilton had the solution. Compulsory health insurance for seamen. As the then Treasury secretary explained in a letter to Congress in April 1792,

> The interests of humanity are concerned in it, from its tendency to protect from want and misery, a very useful, and, for the most part, a very needy class of the Community.

In the face of this "tendency," compulsory health insurance would relieve local communities of the financial burden that they would otherwise bear. In other words, given that we are going to provide for seamen who fall ill in ports far from home, Hamilton reasoned that we should formalize and finance this arrangement. On July 16, 1798, Congress signed off.

Here's how it worked. Whenever a US ship arrived back from a foreign port, each shipowner had to deduct twenty cents per sailor per month at sea from the sailors' wages and hand this tax over to the customs agent. The customs agent in turn transmitted the tax revenue to the federal government "to provide for the temporary relief and maintenance of sick or disabled seamen, in the hospitals or other proper institutions." Shipowners who were caught avoiding the tax faced fines of one hundred dollars.

Requiring that sailors pay in advance to create a fund to finance their health care ensured that they wouldn't need to rely on local charity to shoulder the financial burden when they fell ill. For this reason, the resulting 1798 act explicitly noted that "the moneys collected in any one district, shall be expended within the same." In other words, the places where sailors would fall ill were also the places that should receive the tax revenue that would help cover the costs of ministering to the unfortunate seamen. The medical sociologist Robert Straus—whose 1947 PhD dissertation gives a fascinating description of the history and politics behind the legislation—summarized its purpose thus: "To assure seamen of the care they needed and which they would pay for."

FAST-FORWARD

The eighteenth-century congressionally mandated health insurance law bears a striking resemblance to the twenty-first-century—and, we dare say, more widely known—congressionally mandated health insurance law, colloquially known as Obamacare. Naturally, there are differences. The entire text of the 1798 Act for the Relief of Sick and Disabled Seamen occupies only one page. The 2010 Patient Protection and Affordable Care Act was almost one thousand pages, prompting snickering that even several years later no one had actually read the bill in its entirety. But the similarities are nonetheless remarkable. Both were politically controversial. Both coupled the insurance mandate with a fine for noncompliance, although the Obamacare fine was removed within a decade, while the eighteenth-century one lasted over seventy-five years.

Most important, both were rooted in the same basic rationale. Recognizing that we will ultimately feel compelled to help those who are sick and economically destitute, we should formalize and fund those commitments up front. The policy solution, in both cases, is what Hamilton came up with over two centuries ago. Economic theorists arrived at it more recently: make health insurance compulsory.

In modern times, this solution has been repeatedly invoked as an argument for universal coverage. We can see it at play, for example, when Switzerland introduced a mandate on individuals to purchase health insurance in 1996, creating mandatory universal coverage out of what had previously been a voluntary insurance system. The Swiss health minister who had overseen the reform explained its rationale:

> We will not let people suffer and die when they need health care. The Swiss believe that in return, individuals owe it to society to make provision ahead of time for their health care when they fall seriously ill. At that point, they may not have enough money to pay for it. So we consider the health insurance mandate to be a form of socially responsible civic conduct.

United States Supreme Court justice Ruth Bader Ginsburg made a similar point in her 2012 opinion supporting the constitutionality of the Obama administration's mandate for health insurance. There, the Notorious RBG noted:

> The cost of emergency care or treatment for a serious illness generally exceeds what an individual can afford to pay on her own. Unlike markets for most products, however, the inability to pay for care does not mean an uninsured individual will receive no care. Federal and state law, as well as professional obligations and embedded social norms, require hospitals and physicians to provide care when it is most needed, regardless of the patient's ability to pay.

Perhaps more surprisingly, the reality that society will provide care even to those who cannot pay is also accepted by many conservatives who, like their liberal peers, therefore embrace a policy of mandatory, universal health insurance coverage. The famously free-market economist F. A. Hayek seethed with contempt for the British National Health

Service for imposing a "system of state medicine" in which doctors were transformed from "members of a free profession primarily responsible to their patients, into paid servants of the state." Yet he nonetheless embraced the Hamiltonian rationale for compulsory health insurance. That's because, as Hayek observed:

> Once it becomes the recognized duty of the public to provide for the extreme needs of . . . sickness . . . irrespective of whether the individuals could and ought to have made provision themselves . . . it seems an obvious corollary to compel them to insure (or otherwise provide) against those common hazards of life . . . [otherwise] they would become a charge of the public.

Conservatives in the US have reached the same conclusion. Robert Moffit, a scholar at a prominent conservative Washington think tank, spoke out in support of the contentious, and ultimately unsuccessful, Clinton proposal for mandatory universal coverage in the early 1990s. As he argued:

> The entire moral and cultural tenor of our society . . . [is that] those who are uninsured and cannot pay for their care will be cared for, and those who are insured and working will pay for that care. So, we already have a mandate. But it is both inefficient and unfair.

Two decades after the failed Clinton mandate, in 2006, Massachusetts Republican governor Mitt Romney successfully introduced a mandate for health insurance coverage in his state. Several years later, it became the prototype for the Obamacare mandate. Romney's argument for the Massachusetts mandate was based on the same practical reality as Alexander Hamilton's and Switzerland's. The existing system of waiting till the uninsured got sick and then treating them in expensive settings didn't make financial sense. It would be more sensible to recognize that patients who lack insurance will ultimately get free care, and to respond by mandating that they purchase insurance up front. "No more free riders," declared Romney, who couched the mandate in Republican watchwords like "personal responsibility."

From the merchant marine to modern Massachusetts, from Alexander Hamilton to the Affordable Care Act, the necessity for mandatory insurance coverage has been the enduring moral obligation to provide essential health care to people who are ill and cannot afford that care. Society—and the taxpayer—will ultimately feel compelled to provide medical care for those without coverage who are extremely ill. Whether you agree that this should be the social contract, or despair along with Buchanan about our Good Samaritan tendencies, the policy implications are the same. As long as it is an unavoidable function of government to try to provide health care for those in need, then universal health insurance coverage is the right vehicle for fulfilling that obligation in a full and sensible manner.

This is also why—whatever other social policies we do or do not enact—the solution to the Samaritan's dilemma must be health-care specific. A striking illustration of this point arose in some of the discussions about a universal basic income—or UBI, as it is colloquially known—in which the government would provide everyone with enough cash to live on. Like compulsory health insurance, the argument for UBI can trace its origins in the US back to the eighteenth century. Also like with compulsory health insurance, the modern proponents of UBI run the political gamut, from the liberal senator Bernie Sanders to the controversial conservative scholar Charles Murray. Murray, who has argued for the elimination of all social welfare programs in the United States, sees UBI as a vehicle for taking the money that the government spends on these programs and "[giving] it back to the American people in cash grants." Murray's UBI proposal, however, has a noteworthy twist. The only restriction he would impose on his proposed $13,000 annual cash grant is a requirement that $3,000 of it must be used to purchase catastrophic health insurance.

———

It's telling when even a famously libertarian thinker like Murray exempts universal health coverage from his attempts to limit government activity. He's not alone in this health-care exceptionalism. As we'll see in the next chapter, there's also a rich philosophical tradition of treating health care as a "special social good" when it comes to public policy. But our—and Murray's—reason for making a policy distinction for health care is practical, not principled. When people inevitably end up ill and unable to afford their essential medical care, the Good Samaritans in us all—and in our public policies—will compel us to act. We will be unable to follow Buchanan's injunction to ignore the hapless traveler lying injured by the side of the road.

There are, of course, limits to how much we will feel compelled to do. At some point, our moral obligations end. Universal health insurance is a solution to the Samaritan's dilemma. It is not a solution to all dilemmas. We'll take this on next.

Adequacy, Not Equality

What universal coverage won't do

O f all the inequalities that exist," the Reverend Dr. Martin Luther King Jr. declared in 1966, "the injustice in health care is the most shocking and inhuman." Those inequalities persist to this day.

Richer Americans and White Americans live substantially longer than poorer Americans or Black Americans. A forty-year-old American woman, for example, can expect to live ten years less if she is one of the poorest 1 percent of Americans rather than one of the richest 1 percent. That gap in life expectancy expands to almost fifteen years for men, roughly the same as the gains in life expectancy that Americans achieved over the last fifty to one hundred years. Black children who live in the richest parts of the United States have higher mortality rates than young White children in the poorest parts of the country. Maternal mortality is 2.5 times higher for Black mothers than White mothers.

The health disparities that exist within the US are enormous, and enormously distressing. Uwe Reinhardt, the late and much-beloved health economist, issued an impassioned call for a more egalitarian health policy approach, famously posing the rhetorical question: "Should the child of a poor American family have the same chance of avoiding preventable illness or of being cured from a given illness as does the child of a rich American family?"

We'll take that bait. For those who, like Reinhardt, admirably aspire to reduce health inequality, we'll explain why health insurance policy is not the lever to lean on.

HEALTH VERSUS HEALTH CARE

"In the western United States there are two contiguous states that enjoy about the same levels of income and medical care and are alike in many other respects, but their levels of health differ enormously." So began economist Victor Fuchs's now-famous "Tale of Two States." Fuchs is widely considered to be the founding father of the economic study of health. In the early 1970s, he told his tale to pose and then unravel a puzzle.

In one state, the people were among the healthiest in the US. Their neighbors in the other state were among the least healthy, with annual death rates that were 40 to 50 percent higher. Yet the two states were similar on many of the dimensions believed to be important for health—including medical care, income, schooling, climate, urbanicity. You may get an inkling of where Fuchs was going with this comparison when we tell you that the two states were Utah and Nevada. And that the residents of Utah were the ones enjoying much better health.

Fuchs famously attributed the lower mortality rates of the clean-living, predominantly Mormon residents of Utah to their better health behaviors. Their Nevada neighbors enjoyed what he referred to as "more permissive" norms. Rates of smoking and drinking were much lower in Utah than in Nevada. And differences in mortality between the two states were particularly pronounced for diseases for which there was a direct link to such behaviors, such as lung cancer and cirrhosis of the liver.

Fuchs's simple tabulations of publicly reported death rates by age and gender for Utah versus Nevada appear antiquated by modern data science standards. But his central argument has stood the test of time. A large body of subsequent confirmatory work has hammered home a somewhat surprising point. Differences in access to medical care—let alone health insurance—are not the main drivers of health disparities.

Almost a half century after Fuchs's "Tale of Two States," a team of researchers conducted a similar analysis of health differences across the United States, but on a much larger scale. And by larger scale, we really mean larger. The team linked fifteen years of government tax records on the annual income of every single American—over 1.4 billion tax records in all—to information on whether and when each of those hundreds of millions of individual Americans had died. Using these data, they documented pronounced differences in life expectancy among people of the same age, race, income, and gender living in different parts of the US. And when they looked at where in the US residents were living longer, this Fuchs-on-steroids study confirmed the original finding. The higher-life-expectancy places didn't enjoy a greater quantity or quality of medical care, or higher rates of health insurance coverage. Rather, higher-life-expectancy places had populations that smoked less, exercised more, and were less likely to be obese. Half a century later, residents of Salt Lake City were still faring much better than those in Sin City.

The experiences of the elderly in the US provide further evidence in support of Fuchs's thesis about the relative unimportance of medical care and health insurance in driving differences in population health. All of the elderly in the US are covered by Medicare. Yet among elderly individuals of the same race, age, and gender, average life expectancy at age sixty-five ranges across different parts of the country from eighty-one to eighty-six years. There are also striking differences across these different parts of the US in the use of medical care among Medicare enrollees. A team of economists and physicians at Dartmouth has documented that medical spending for Medicare enrollees of the same race, age, and gender varies by almost a factor of two across different cities. To put that spending difference in perspective, Jon Skinner—an economist at Dartmouth and a key contributor to this work—likes to point out that, added up over their retirement, the difference in Medicare spending by a retiree in Miami compared with one in Minneapolis is enough to buy the Minneapolis retiree a decent used Ferrari. But here's the kicker: places where the elderly use more medical care don't seem to have much to show for it in terms of higher life expectancy or better health outcomes.

The surgeon and author Atul Gawande brought these decades of research to the attention of the general public with his widely read 2009 *New Yorker* article describing the large differences in medical practice—and medical spending—between the elderly in McAllen, Texas, and their demographically similar counterparts in El Paso. Gawande's McAllen–El Paso comparison quickly entered the lexicon of health policy, just like Fuchs's Nevada–Utah comparison had done decades earlier. But in Gawande's tale of two cities, health behaviors like smoking were pretty similar. So too was health. The only thing that was actually different was how medical care was practiced. Doctors in McAllen tended to go for more aggressive patient treatment than their counterparts in El Paso. More tests, more images, more hospital admissions, more surgeries. Patients with first-time gallstone pain and no other complications, for example, might be more likely to have their gallbladders surgically removed in McAllen, rather than treated with short-term pain medication and diet modification as in El Paso, even though the less aggressive treatment is a sensible—and often successful—initial approach. These different practice patterns translated into big differences in medical spending: health-care spending per elderly individual was twice as much in McAllen than in El Paso at the time Gawande wrote his article. But McAllen residents were not enjoying better health than their counterparts in El Paso. Once again, this suggests that something other than differences in health insurance or medical care is important for health.

Of course, it's possible that some of the differences in health and health care between these "seemingly similar" elderly Americans arise because they are not, in fact, as similar as they seem. Maybe people in Miami are in worse health than their Minneapolis doppelgängers, in ways that are hard to measure and control for.

It turns out that such health differences are indeed driving some of the geographic variation in medical care and mortality that has been observed. But not all of it, or even most of it. Amy and her collaborators realized this when they followed elderly individuals who move across the United States. They look at what happened as people moved, for example, from high-spending Miami to low-spending Minneapolis, or the other way around. When people move, they take with them—along with their photo albums and their taste in music—their health conditions, or lack thereof. Yet, the researchers found that within a year of the move, the elderly's medical treatments and mortality rates started to look substantially more like those of their new neighbors than their previous ones. The kicker remains: the places to move to if you want to increase your life expectancy aren't the same as the places to move to if you want more medical care.

It's not entirely clear what it is about different areas that cause the discrepancies in medical care and in life expectancy. Amy and her collaborators are still working on that one. But one thing it isn't is insurance coverage. Everyone in these studies has Medicare.

In case you're thinking that what's different across these areas is access to health insurance before Medicare coverage begins at age sixty-five, think again. Countries with universal health insurance also experience substantial health inequality. Indeed, evidence from Sweden and Norway—two Nordic countries with universal health insurance (as well as a generous cradle-to-grave social safety net)—indicates that differences in life expectancy between adults in the top 10 percent and bottom 10 percent of the national income distribution are similar to those in the US.

Fuchs was clearly onto something. Today, there is widespread agreement among researchers that variation in medical care or in health insurance is not a major driver of variation in health.

WHAT ARE WE SMOKING?

We realize that the received wisdom of the research community may seem absurd. How can differences in health insurance and access to medical care not be an important contributor to health disparities? Especially in light of the evidence we described in chapter 1 that providing the uninsured with health insurance increases their use of medical care and improves their health. In fact, these statements are not in conflict. Health insurance can improve health—we stand by that evidence. But it turns out that the magnitude of those improvements is too small to make much of a dent in the large income-health gradient.

Once you stop and think about it, as we finally did, the relatively unimportant role of health insurance in achieving health equality should not be that surprising. It can be explained by two phenomena we have already discussed.

One factor is the Fuchsian observation that medical care is not the only—or even the most important—determinant of health. Indeed, there is now increasing emphasis on what is called the social determinants of health, "the conditions in the environments where people are born, live, learn, work, play, worship, and age." As the physicians and public health researchers David Stuckler and Sanjay Basu nicely summarized this literature in their book, *The Body Economic*, "Good health doesn't start in hospitals and clinics; it starts in our homes and neighborhoods, in the food we eat, the air we breathe, and the safety of our streets. Indeed, the top predictor of your life expectancy is your zip code."

This explains why even countries like Sweden and Norway with universal health insurance still exhibit substantial health disparities by income. Indeed, the same researchers who documented the striking income-health gradient in Sweden also found that differences in health literacy—information and knowledge about the drivers of health—may be an important driver of those health inequalities. They compared individuals who had a doctor or nurse in their families to individuals who were otherwise similar in terms of income, education, age, gender, and the like, but who did not have a health expert in their family. They found that individuals who had family health experts lived longer. They also smoked less when pregnant, were less likely to be addicted to alcohol and drugs, engaged in more preventive health behaviors, and had fewer chronic medical conditions. In other words, as the economist Adriana Lleras-Muney aptly put it, "access to good doctors and hospitals will lengthen your life if you have a heart attack, but simply not having a heart attack (or delaying its onset) will have a far greater impact on longevity."

The other factor behind the relatively small role of health insurance in affecting health in the US is what we discussed in chapter 4: the nominally "uninsured" in fact receive a substantial amount of medical care. Indeed, there's a lot more commonality in the medical care received by the insured and the uninsured than those labels might suggest. People are generally not left to die in the streets.

This puzzle and resolution reminded Amy of an argument she used to have with her mother. Leaving the house on a winter morning as a child, Amy would frequently find herself admonished to put on a hat. The morning maternal mantra was "you lose 70 percent of your body heat through your head." This puzzled young Amy. After all, it seemed implausible that she would really be warmer wearing only a hat and taking off her winter jacket and her pants. Her mother must be mistaken. Although perhaps Amy didn't express it quite so politely back then. Only as an adult did Amy finally realize that what her mom meant was that given all the other clothes Amy was already wearing, most of the remaining heat loss was through her head. No one was arguing that a winter jacket and clothing of the arms and legs were not essential for warmth. Likewise, medical care is of course essential for good health. But given all of the medical care that is provided because of our social contract, most of the remaining differences in health are not driven by medical care or health insurance.*

---

*It turns out Amy's mother was not the only one to make these claims, and Amy wasn't the only one to (eventually) realize that the real point is that in cold weather almost all other body parts are already covered. See, for example, Susan Davis, "Do We Lose Heat through Our Heads?," WebMD, January 4, 2011, webmd.com/a-to-z-guides/features/do-we-really-lose-most-of-our-heat-through-our-heads. The adult Amy continues to go to the doctor, and to wear a winter jacket but no hat.

Because access to medical care or health insurance is not a major driver of health disparities, we don't have to engage in a principled discussion of whether or not health insurance policy should be designed with an aim toward reducing health inequality. The question is, as they say, academic. (A phrase we hate!)

But because we are academics after all, we're also game for considering a what-if. What if, in fact, health insurance and access to medical care were essential to reducing health disparities? Would our social contract compel us to address them? The philosophers tell us no.

A FLOOR, NOT A CEILING

The normative approach—inspired by the twentieth-century political and moral philosopher John Rawls—arrives at the same place we do. At the importance of universal health insurance for providing essential health care, but not for pushing for equality in health care. Rawls insisted that fair equality of opportunity—the ability for individuals to freely and fairly pursue their life plans—is a key principle of justice. Fair equality of opportunity in turn, he argued, requires universal health care, as well as universal education.

The philosopher and medical ethicist Norman Daniels—who was influenced by and in turn influenced Rawls—expounded further on this rationale for universal health care. Daniels emphasized that, for policy purposes, health care is "a special social good," because of health's "great strategic importance for opportunity."

What is the great strategic importance of health? It allows us to "maintain normal species functioning," Daniels explained, and "normal functioning in turn has a major impact on an individual's share of the normal opportunity range for his society." Philosophers are not alone in such views. The World Health Organization has declared that justice requires that everyone is able to "attain their *full potential* [emphasis added] for health and well-being." The Centers for Disease Control and Prevention declares likewise.

Nevertheless, in the end, Daniels's moral reasoning produces the same conclusion as our empirical reasoning. Universal health care must provide a basic minimum of health-care access for everyone, but it need not strive for equality in that access. This is because his normative argument for universal health care stems from the need to create "fair equality of opportunity." This requires that individuals have access to sufficient health care so that their health does not restrict their ability to "choose reasonable plans of life," to participate in society to the full extent of their potential abilities.

This is a standard of adequacy. Indeed, Daniels goes to great lengths to explain that his (and Rawls's) philosophical argument for universal health care is "compatible with, though it *does not imply*, a multi-tiered health-care system." Not all health care is essential for "normal species functioning."

Daniels recognizes that his willingness to accept a "multi-tiered health-care system" may not be a palatable one. He even admits, "My own egalitarian inclinations pull me in a different direction from the pro-tiering argument." Nonetheless, he concludes that he cannot find any principled objection to inequality in access to medical care that is beyond the essential.

We're happy to defer to the learned philosophers on the lack of principled objections to inequality in medical care. We can, however, articulate a practical objection to such inequality. It arises out of the concern that making additional health-care resources available to the rich may detract from the availability of essential ones for everyone else. Consider the media exposé of a secret "VIP program" in the public health-care system of the University of California, Los Angeles. The program allowed wealthy individuals to jump ahead of the queue for medical care by making generous donations to the UCLA system. The exposé complained that this "highly unethical" behavior came at the direct expense of less fortunate patients, who experienced longer wait times as a result. "If California's UC system wasn't so short on beds..." the article observed, "if the state's healthcare system wasn't already so overburdened, if UC hospital workers weren't ordered to prioritize VIP patients, if California's taxpayers weren't forced to subsidize wealthy people's healthcare, maybe this privileged access program would be okay."

In other words, the objection is not to the perks themselves, but to their conjectured consequence: reducing the amount of taxpayer-financed medical care available to less well-off patients. Universal health-care systems around the world have likewise grappled with how to make sure that the ability of wealthier individuals to buy additional medical care does not impair the quality of the basic care that is guaranteed for all. We'll return to this important issue in chapter 13, where we'll describe how some countries have managed to navigate this issue with reasonable success.

And navigate it we must. In modern times, the use of private resources to augment the basic health-care system is ubiquitous, condoned by the state virtually everywhere in the world. In the aughts, commentators liked to point out that the only places that outlawed private health insurance for services already provided by the public system were Cuba, North Korea, and six Canadian provinces. More recently, one of those Canadian provinces has reversed itself in the face of a successful legal challenge, while Sanders's "Medicare for all" would join the list of programs that prohibit private insurance, although it, too, would likely face legal challenges if enacted.

The experiences of other countries suggest that supplemental health insurance—and inequality in access to medical care—is inevitable. It may also be desirable. One size rarely fits all, and that's certainly the case for health care. Even among people with the same income, tastes for medical care can vary. As long as the government has fulfilled our social contract to provide access to necessary medical care, health inequality is not synonymous with inequity or injustice.

We can—and should—strive to achieve for all Americans the higher life expectancy enjoyed by richer Americans and by White Americans. The health of the best off in society gives us a benchmark of what is feasible to achieve for the worst off. But that does not suggest that—in pursuit of greater equality—we should *restrict* access to additional medical care for those with the resources to procure it. This has never been part of our social contract.

The nineteenth-century philanthropists who financed hospitals to provide charity health care created what the historian Charles Rosenberg has called a "two-tier approach to medical care," deliberately stratified by class. The paying customer got a private room, while charity cases were relegated to the wards. The goal was to ensure some sort of basic standard for individuals, whatever their financial circumstances may be, but not to ensure that everyone had the access to the *same* type of care.

A similar approach has pervaded US policy in other domains. The US was a leader in establishing universal, publicly funded, publicly provided education, but the focus has always been on providing an adequate minimum education—deemed essential for an informed and productive citizenry—rather than on providing educational equality. Moving to better school districts or attending privately funded schools has always been an option for those with enough resources. Indigent criminal defendants are guaranteed an attorney. But those with resources to pay for their own counsel are allowed to do so. The national government funds our "common defense," and state and local governments fund the police force. But we do not prevent people from purchasing additional security for their businesses and their homes, from personal security systems all the way to private, gated communities.

━━━━━

The function of universal health insurance should now be clear. On both practical and principled grounds, it should not be confused with a vehicle for addressing inequalities and inequities. Rather, as we've argued in earlier chapters, universal coverage is the only way to sensibly and coherently fulfill our implicit social contract to provide access to essential health care regardless of resources.

It's hard to argue against sense and coherence. But it's fair to ask: To what end? We've just argued that universal health insurance is not going to produce dramatic improvements in population health or reductions in population health inequality. So why replace the current, haphazard approach with universal coverage? What would be the benefit? And for whom?

The answer lies in the material we covered in part I, which described the inadequacy of our existing attempts to fulfill our social contract. For the millions of Americans who currently lack formal insurance, universal coverage would provide financial protection against medical expenses, less anxiety, and greater peace of mind. For the many more Americans who currently have formal health insurance, universal coverage would remove the omnipresent risk that their current coverage may disappear right when they need it most. Well-designed universal coverage would also remove the risk that their health insurance will prove woefully inadequate in taking care of their medical expenses when they fall ill. The dearth of that security and peace of mind under the existing "system" may help explain why surveys consistently indicate that the US population is unsatisfied with its country's (medically excellent) health system, and much more unsatisfied than respondents from other high-income countries.

The health-care sector is almost one fifth of the US economy. But it punches below its weight. It delivers far less than it could for that price tag. We should design a system that gets us considerably more bang for that (considerable) buck.

Now that we understand the function, we can turn to form.

PART III

THE BLUEPRINT

Writing the unwritten contract

Proponents of universal coverage speak eloquently of making health care "not a privilege for a few, but a right for all." That's not going to get us very far. That much is clear from the experience of the only group of Americans that has already secured a constitutional right to health care: the incarcerated.

This right exists thanks to the Eighth Amendment's prohibition against "cruel and unusual punishments," a Texas inmate, and a landmark Supreme Court decision. In the fall of 1973, J. W. Gamble was unloading bales of cotton from a truck as part of his prison labor assignment when a six-hundred-pound bale fell on him and crushed him. He received only a cursory medical exam. Although he complained of chest and back pains, he was punished with solitary confinement when he said he was unable to return to work. In a handwritten petition, Gamble sued the state corrections department. In 1976, in an 8–1 decision written by Justice Thurgood Marshall, the Supreme Court concluded in *Estelle v. Gamble* that "deliberate indifference to serious medical needs of prisoners" was unconstitutional.

The decision didn't actually help Gamble. His failure to receive proper medical care was deemed "inadvertent"—not the result of "deliberate indifference"—and thus not a violation of his constitutional rights. Gamble was not alone. The establishment of a "right to health care" did little to produce decent or accessible medical care for inmates. In practice, legal scholars have observed, the courts are "often hostile to prisoners' assertions of those rights." Their right to health care, moreover, does not entitle them to free, or even affordable, health care. Most states allow prisons to charge inmates for their medical care. Prisoners often try to pay for their care through prison jobs, which may pay only pennies per hour; minimum wage laws don't apply to prisoners. In West Virginia, for example, the hourly wage for an incarcerated worker can be literally a few pennies. As a result, the co-pay for a single visit to the doctor costs almost an entire month's wages.

We must get beyond this vacuous language of rights. No one would hire a builder to build a house without any specifications. We must likewise delineate the essential components of universal coverage. Equally important, we must grapple with what does not need to be in that coverage and can be left for people to purchase for themselves if they choose to.

Moral commitments are not limitless. Even FDR implicitly acknowledged this in his Second Bill of Rights. He spoke of rights such as "a decent home," "a good education," and "adequate medical care." The economist Arthur Okun, writing a few decades later, likewise espoused a right to health care while simultaneously cautioning that these rights are not unbounded. With the customary bluntness of an economist rather than a politician, he described "a heated debate with an audience of medical administrators." As Okun described it, "Taking what I viewed as an outlandish example, I suggested that any national health program should not grant me at public expense all the pairs of eyeglasses I might like. I learned to my surprise that they favored an unlimited right to eyeglasses."

In the remainder of this book, we discuss how to realize Roosevelt's (and Okun's) vision of our social contract: to ensure access to adequate health care for every American, without unlimited rights to eyeglasses. We turn, in other words, from the lofty language of societal obligations to the practical elements of design. From function to form. From ideology to eyeglasses.

———

At its core, the design is simple. It has only two main elements. First, there must be universal coverage for an essential set of services. We'll call this "basic coverage." Second, for those who want and can afford more, there must be the option to buy what we'll call "supplemental coverage."

This two-part form is dictated by the two-part function we described in part II: a social contract that requires a standard of adequacy, hence the basic set of medical services that are covered, but not equality—hence the option to buy additional coverage.

That is the entire blueprint. The rest is commentary.

That commentary is, of course, important. The devil is always in the details. In this final part of the book, we'll therefore describe the essential design elements. In doing so, we'll impart the silver lining to being a policy laggard. We have an abundance of both academic research and real-world prototypes to draw from for the key design choices.

We'll argue that basic coverage must be provided automatically, and financed by the taxpayer, rather than by charging people premiums for their health insurance. We'll also insist that any medical care included in basic coverage be available to patients for free, without asking them to pay anything out of their own pockets. That may seem intuitive, but it goes against decades of economics doctrine.

We'll emphasize that basic coverage should be very basic. Compared with what most people with insurance are currently accustomed to, basic coverage should have longer wait times, less patient choice over their doctor and their medical care, and much less comfortable hospital accommodations. That's because the purpose of basic coverage is to fulfill our social contract, not our heart's desires. Focusing on the purpose of basic coverage will help keep taxpayer costs down. So too will our insistence that, for the very first time, the US set—and enforce— a health-care budget for taxpayer-financed health care.

For the many Americans who would like to have a better-than-basic experience, we'll explain how to design a market for supplementary coverage that they can purchase out of their own pockets. We will be able to draw on a wealth of research, including some of our own as well as the experiences of other countries, to describe how to make sure that such a market can function well.

Equally important are the design elements we will deliberately not discuss. We won't weigh in on many of the hot-button health policy topics that receive a lot of attention and debate. Such as whether or not to have "single-payer" health care, as in Medicare for all—although as we'll now see, Medicare itself has a number of different payers. Or whether to have "socialized" or "privatized" medicine. Again, we'll soon see that both can be found within the US context. Each of these design elements has its virtues and limitations and can be accommodated—or not—within the scope of our proposal. None are indispensable for fulfilling our social contract. A firm focus on function clarifies which design elements are—and are not—up for debate.

The Foundation

Coverage must be automatic

The United States has already enacted universal coverage. It just hasn't achieved it.

Republican governor Mitt Romney led the way in 2006 with a requirement that everyone in Massachusetts have coverage. The Massachusetts law imposed fines on those who didn't comply, and offered financial help to those who couldn't afford to. The rest of the country followed suit in 2010 with the Obamacare mandate that everyone have insurance.

Calling it universal doesn't make it so. As we described in chapter 1, many people are not aware of their insurance options. Or of the requirement to have insurance. Or that their coverage has disappeared. Others try to enroll but don't succeed. Some may not even bother trying. They may be young enough or healthy enough that they just aren't interested in doing so.

It doesn't have to be this way. We can get to universal coverage. We can do it the hard way or the easy way. You can probably guess which one we'll recommend.

The hard way is to enact a mandate for universal coverage, as we've already done. And to strictly enforce that mandate, which we haven't. A few countries have gone this route. As we've already discussed in chapter 6, the Swiss created a mandate for universal coverage in 1996. It was the very same approach that Romney and Obama subsequently took. But unlike its US counterparts, the Swiss mandate comes with teeth, an escalating series of protocols to ensure that everyone ends up covered. First come warnings to those who are uninsured. These are followed by fines for being uninsured, fines that can be considerably higher than health insurance premiums would have been. After three months, if the warnings and the fines haven't done the trick, the government automatically enrolls the uninsured individual into a health plan, and then charges them premiums—both prospectively and retrospectively. Thanks to this ruthless enforcement, coverage in Switzerland is close to 100 percent.

The Dutch subsequently copied the Swiss playbook when they enacted their own insurance mandate in 2006. They added some additional touches, like garnishing the wages of those who don't enroll in insurance in order to recover the premiums they are supposed to pay. They've enjoyed similar success.

In the US, by contrast, the government has no authority to auto-enroll the uninsured, or to garnish wages to pay for their coverage. Indeed, as of 2019 there were not even any financial penalties for being uninsured. The US insurance "mandate" thus calls to mind the classic Robin Williams line about the impotence of the British police, who do not carry guns. The most intimidating threat an officer can make, Williams deadpanned, is to yell "Stop! Or I'll . . . say stop again!"

Even when the US briefly had a small financial penalty in place for noninsurance, from 2014 to 2018, enforcement was toothless. It relied on individuals voluntarily reporting their noncompliance—and therefore the fact that they owed the penalty—on their tax returns. There were also numerous exemptions from owing a penalty, including ones for financial hardship. By one estimate, over three quarters of those who were uninsured in 2016 were exempt from the penalty. The Dutch, by contrast, allow exemptions only for a small number of individuals who are conscientious objectors to insurance, typically for religious reasons. And even then, the government levies an additional income tax on these individuals, with the revenue earmarked to fund their medical care.

There's an easier way to get to universal coverage. One that doesn't require Dutch courage. It's the way that most other high-income countries have chosen to go. Provide the coverage automatically, without an enrollment step. As an entitlement, to use a politically charged term. Just do it, as Nike would say.

The US has already experienced success with this approach. BASIC COVERAGE TO BE AUTOMATIC read the *New York Times* headline on July 31, 1965, the day President Johnson signed Medicare into law. Almost all of the elderly were automatically enrolled, and mailed their health insurance card. Reporting on Medicare's first sixty days, then Social Security commissioner Robert Ball focused his concerns on the resistance of some Southern hospitals to comply with Medicare's requirement that they discontinue their long-standing racial segregation of patients. He made no mention at all about any issues of patient enrollment. Automatic enrollment worked with Swiss-watch-like efficiency.

In modern times, Medicare coverage for hospital and physician services is still automatic for the vast majority of the elderly. Those who are collecting Social Security are automatically enrolled in Medicare the month they turn sixty-five. Three months before their birthday, they are mailed a Medicare card and a welcome booklet. The result: virtually all of the elderly have health insurance.

Not so with Medicare coverage for prescription drugs, which was added in 2006. Most of the elderly have to actively sign up for that coverage. The process is neither automatic nor as smooth as the one developed in the 1960s. The result: even fifteen years later, many of the elderly still did not have drug coverage, even though the government would have footed most of their bill.

We can take two different paths to get to universal coverage. Make it difficult to be uninsured, as the Swiss do, or make it easy to be insured, as most other countries do, and as the US does with Medicare coverage for hospitals and doctors. Our experiences with both approaches make it clear: the easy route is, well, easier.

Requiring coverage did not get us to universal coverage. We must therefore provide it. Automatically. Only then will we achieve universal coverage. This is why basic coverage must be taxpayer financed. Charging premiums for basic coverage is at odds with providing that coverage automatically.

It's not just the basic coverage itself that should be provided for free. As we'll now argue, any medical care that it covers should also be completely free for patients.

9

Free and Clear

No patient fees

An exasperated President Truman once demanded a one-handed economic adviser. He was fed up, he said, with his economic advisers' constant hedging of "on the one hand . . . but on the other hand." His quip helped cement economists' reputation for equivocation. For the most part, we deserve this rap.

But there's one area of health policy where, for most of the last half century, Truman would have been able to find his one-handed economist. On the question of whether patients should have to pay part of the cost of their covered medical care, our profession's advice has been unequivocal. More than five decades of research—both theoretical and empirical—has produced an unambiguous recommendation. Patients must pay something for their care, otherwise they'll rush to the doctor every time they sneeze.

We've done some of the research on this topic ourselves, and preached the gospel to generations of students.

We take it back.

THE OTHER KENNEDY-NIXON DEBATE

Our story begins about fifty years ago, when Nixon and Kennedy publicly sparred over this very question. It was part of a lesser-known set of Nixon-Kennedy debates, involving a lesser-known Kennedy.

These debates took place in the early 1970s. Medicare and Medicaid had recently been enacted to cover the elderly and the indigent. They were hailed by many contemporary pundits as the first step toward universal health insurance coverage. And for a while it seemed that it would be so. Both parties had introduced bills in Congress for universal coverage.

In the Senate, Massachusetts Democrat Ted Kennedy had introduced a proposal for universal coverage in which patients would not have to pay anything out of their own pockets for covered medical care. This so-called "first-dollar coverage" was the approach that had already been embraced by the universal coverage systems in the UK and Canada. President Nixon's Republican administration had a different plan for universal coverage. Theirs required patients to contribute to some of the costs of their covered medical care, just like the elderly had to do under Medicare.

The Nixon administration saw cost sharing as an essential way to rein in excess use of medical care—needless tests and procedures—that drove up health-care spending without producing tangible benefits for the patient. Kennedy and his supporters countered that such cost sharing merely burdened the patient financially, while doing nothing to rein in spending.

This debate had been raging for decades. Physicians and insurers advocated for cost sharing in order to discourage "sniffle claims" and "hypochondriasis." Organized labor tended to oppose it. A similar debate had taken place in the design of Medicare a few years earlier, with the proponents of cost sharing winning out. At the time of these Nixon-Kennedy debates, the question of whether co-pays and deductibles would lower medical spending was also the source of active disagreement among economists. The two-handed economist was alive and well.

On the one hand, the economist Mark Pauly had recently outlined a theory that supported the Nixon camp. The economics were simple, he argued. When goods and services are less expensive, people will buy more of them. Demand curves slope down, as we say in Econ 101. And health insurance, by design, lowers the cost of medical care for patients. Ergo, Pauly theorized, it encourages them to use more medical care. More checkups, more tests, more medical procedures, more hospital admissions. "Like ants at a picnic" as Pauly put it. By the same token, raising the price of medical care for patients through cost-sharing would reduce their use of medical care, and thus reduce health-care spending. Some economists had produced studies claiming that the reductions in health-care use from co-pays and deductibles could be large and consequential.

On the other hand, the economist Rashi Fein considered this argument absurd. In 1971, Fein testified before Kennedy's committee that Nixon's proposed cost sharing would not change the use of medical care, it would merely concentrate the costs of that care on the sick. "I don't think we have any data that demonstrates that deductibles and coinsurance lead to lower utilization," he declared. Health-care spending was fixed, Fein argued. It was determined by disease, not dollars. By medical needs, not medical costs. The only question was who would pay for it. And the point of health insurance was to spread that cost across everyone so that those who fell ill didn't have to bear the full financial burden. Health insurance had nothing to do with health-care spending. "We are speaking of a transfer of funds," Fein testified, "not of new dollars. It is not—I repeat—it is not new money."

The debate boiled down to one question: Does the use of medical care follow the same iron law of demand as other consumer products? Pauly conjectured that it did, that patients choose whether to buy doctor visits the same way they choose whether or not to buy docksiders. Fein speculated that the two decisions had nothing in common. Medical care is different from other goods. It's not even a *good*. "No one *wants* to receive chemotherapy, have a colonoscopy, or move into a nursing home," one critic of the Pauly premise put it. We go to the doctor grudgingly, and only when we need to. And when we do go, we don't typically *choose* how much medical care to get. Physicians make treatment decisions for us, based on their diagnosis and their belief about the appropriate treatment. In such a setting, it's not clear that what patients "demand" plays any role at all in what medical care they receive. Let alone whether their "demand" increases as the price of that care falls.

Only one thing was sure: there was little rigorous evidence available to adjudicate this dispute. Both sides had to rely on rhetoric.

What followed is the stuff of legend, at least in the circles we travel in. To settle the debate, the federal government sponsored and paid for one of the most expensive social experiments conducted to date, the RAND health insurance experiment. Across the United States, researchers in the mid-1970s randomly assigned two thousand families to different types of health insurance plans, just as patients in a clinical trial are randomly assigned to different drugs. Some families were randomly assigned to the Kennedy-style free care. Others, in the spirit of Nixon, were put in plans that required them to pay for some or all of their medical care, at least initially. The research team tracked the families over five years to see what medical care they used, and what happened to their health. All told, the study cost over $300 million in 2019 dollars.

When the results came in, they left no room for doubt. Pauly was right.

Families assigned to the free-care plan subsequently went to the doctor more than those whose plan required them to pay something for their doctor visit. Families with the free-care plan also had more hospital admissions. It turns out that medical care is just like any other consumer product. People use less of it when the price is higher. No one wants to go to the hospital, but they want to go even less when they have to pay for it.

Decades of subsequent empirical work have repeatedly confirmed the findings of this landmark study. We've done some of this work ourselves. The accumulated evidence is overwhelming. When patients have to pay more for medical care, they use less of it. Fewer trips to the doctor, fewer prescription drugs, fewer visits to the emergency room, and fewer hospital admissions. The basic law of demand applies to all of health care, just as Pauly conjectured it would.

It is not possible for a reputable economist to claim today—as Fein could in 1971—that expanding health insurance coverage wouldn't increase health-care spending. It's no longer a subject of debate. A research paper titled "Health Insurance Increases Use of Medical Care" has become the academic equivalent of the headline DOG BITES MAN. It's not news.

The RAND experiment produced an additional influential finding. Co-pays and deductibles didn't seem to have much in the way of negative repercussions for health. Yes, people assigned to the Nixon-like plans with cost sharing went to the doctor and hospital less than those in Kennedy's free-care plans, but this had little or no measurable impact on their health. As a result, a major lesson from the experiment was that Kennedy's "first-dollar coverage" wasn't such a good idea. As Joe Newhouse, the principal investigator of the RAND experiment, summarized the policy implications of the massive experiment, "For most individuals the cost of [providing them with] free care seems substantial and health benefits minimal. As a result, there is a good case for initial cost sharing for the majority of the population." Nixon had been rehabilitated once again.

Not that it made a difference for the Nixon-Kennedy debate. As we all know, neither got his way on universal health insurance. And it wasn't because of anything the experiment did—or did not—find. Rather, by the time the experimental results began to come out, the bipartisan consensus for expanding health insurance had shattered, along with the Nixon presidency and the economy. A nation reeling from the budgetary nightmares of stagflation and of rapidly rising medical spending had changed its focus from expanding health insurance coverage to controlling health-care costs.

WHEN RESEARCH RULED THE DAY

Nonetheless, the lessons from the RAND experiment have reverberated throughout the country and the world. Its findings have shaped how insurers insure, how think tanks think, and how legislatures legislate the design of health insurance. This real-world influence is the kind of feel-good story that academic economists love to tell their children.

Its fingerprints are everywhere. Since the early 1980s, private insurers have been steadily increasing the amount that patients had to pay for their medical care, even for hospital care that had once been assumed to be unresponsive to price. The government subsequently created tax incentives to encourage the purchase of high-deductible private health insurance plans. Every major proposal for health insurance expansion in the US since the Kennedy-Nixon era—from the failed Clinton health-care reform in the 1990s to the enactment of the 2010 Affordable Care Act—has embraced cost sharing. Even health insurance for the poor was swept up in the doctrine. Originally, Medicaid had no patient cost sharing, but starting in the early 1980s, states were allowed to introduce some cost sharing, and many did. In all of these cases, the lessons from the RAND experiment have loomed large, and commentators have been quick to credit the RAND experiment for the changes.

Its influence has also extended abroad. By the time of the experiment, most other high-income countries already had universal coverage. They had made different choices when it came to whether—and how much—patients had to pay for that care. At one end of the spectrum were countries like Canada and the UK, where patients generally do not have to pay anything for covered services. At the other extreme, French patients almost always had to pay something out of their own pockets for covered care. Then came the RAND experiment and decades of additional confirmatory studies.

Our profession preached the gospel: Go the way of the French, not the French Canadians. Health insurance should cover medical expenses, providing much-needed economic security against catastrophic costs. But it shouldn't cover all of those costs.

The world listened. Over the last several decades, many countries have introduced or increased cost-sharing requirements for universally covered medical care. Japan began requiring elderly patients to pay for some of their medical care. France, Switzerland, and the Netherlands all increased the amount that patients have to pay. Germany introduced co-pays for doctor visits. The list goes on. A victory for science.

In working on this book, however, we realized that it's time to turn our back on the conventional wisdom. On a half century of economics research and the decades of policy reforms around the world that it has influenced. It turns out that, with consumer cost sharing, economists have developed a cure that is often worse than the disease.

Not because economists were wrong about the facts. We stand by our research, and that of legions of others. The science was right. Health insurance coverage increases health-care spending. But, as we'll now explain, the implications we drew from these findings were not.

COST SHARING AND ITS DISCONTENTS

If cost sharing is large enough to have a meaningful impact on medical spending, it interferes with the primary function of health insurance, which is to protect people against the risk of having to pay large medical expenses. We've already described some of the problems with substantial cost sharing, such as high-deductible health plans or out-of-pocket payments that increase without limit as medical expenses rise (see chapter 2). With this type of "insurance," patients still can be burdened by large medical bills that they cannot afford to pay. Insurance that leaves patients exposed to crushing medical debt is not serving its purpose. It makes no sense to give patients such substantial "skin in the game" that they risk being skinned alive.

This means that large or unlimited amounts of patient cost sharing must be off the table in any sensible design of universal basic coverage. That's presumably why most universal coverage systems around the world, even when they do require patient cost sharing, put very strict limits on the amount that patients have to pay. Their logic is that most people can chip in a small amount as a co-pay or deductible and still be protected against catastrophic expenses.

Smaller amounts of cost sharing expose patients to less risk, but also do less to reduce medical spending. And they still come with problems. There will always be people who can't manage a five-dollar co-pay for a prescription drug, or a twenty-dollar co-pay for a doctor visit. Which will put the government right back in the mess we're trying to get out of, albeit on a smaller scale. In an effort to make sure that everyone can access essential care, the government will once again be compelled to create the myriad types of exceptions and patchwork policies that our blueprint is designed to avoid.

The experiences of other countries over the past decades have made this clear. In fact, we were stunned to discover that as countries have added or increased modest cost-sharing requirements in their national health insurance plans, they have, time and again, simultaneously added programs that reduce or eliminate that cost sharing for large sections of the population! The net result has been to add complexity and uncertainty, as well as hassles for patients and administrative costs for the government, with little impact on the patients' share of total healthcare costs, or total national health-care spending.

Consider, for example, the UK experience. Universal health insurance coverage began in 1948 with the creation of the British National Health Service (NHS), birthed by the Welsh coal miner and Labour Party politician Aneurin "Nye" Bevan. The bedrock principle of the new system was that everything connected to health care would be free to all patients at the point of use. That initially included vision and dental care, as well as prescription drugs.

That didn't last long. Budgetary pressures soon got in the way. In 1951, patient charges for dentures and eyeglasses were added. Bevan resigned in protest. Co-pays for prescription drugs came next. The exemptions quickly followed. Today in Britain, drugs, dental care, and vision care all require cost sharing. All also have copious, specific exemptions to that cost sharing. So many exemptions, in fact, that they have proven to be the rule rather than the exception. In 2019, only about 10 percent of all prescriptions in England involved patient co-payments. The rest were dispensed for free.

Exemptions from cost sharing are available for people with particular diseases, below certain incomes, or below (or above) certain ages. For people with disabilities or work-related injuries. For full-time students, women who are pregnant or recently have given birth, and veterans of certain wars. There are different exemptions for people in Scotland and Wales and Northern Ireland compared with those in England. Eligibility rules for the exemptions differ across types of treatments so that a patient may be exempt for charges for dental treatment, but not vision, or for vision charges but not prescription drugs.

The UK is not unique or even unusual in this regard. Every country we looked at that had cost sharing had cost-sharing exemptions as well. A list of Israel's cost-sharing exemptions, for example, runs to over six pages long. Many of the exemption categories are similar to the those of UK—such as diseases, income, age, and veteran status—although the details vary. Some exemptions are likely uniquely Israeli, such as the one for Holocaust survivors.

If this sounds familiar, it's because it is. It is the same American patchwork approach to cobbling together health insurance for 90 percent of the population, played out for the case of cost sharing for a few specific treatments. And it has created the same types of problems.

We previously described the Katie Beckett waiver that President Reagan advocated for in the early 1980s, which provided coverage for certain disabled children, but failed to anticipate the medical progress that would enable them to live to adults and risk losing that coverage. In a similarly shortsighted move, in the late 1960s the UK decided to waive prescription drug co-pays for children with cystic fibrosis. At that time, such children typically did not survive to adulthood. Now they do, and when they do, they have to start paying for their medication.

Think back to the problems we described of people failing to enroll in free health insurance in the US, or not realizing when they had lost their coverage. This pattern has repeated itself with the cost-sharing exemptions in Britain. It's up to the patient to tick the right box to indicate that they are exempt, and to deal with the surprise bills that can arise when they don't realize their exemption has expired. One single mother took her child to what she thought was a free dental checkup only to learn after the fact that she owed money because her child had just turned eighteen. A part-time chef killed herself with an overdose of antidepressants after receiving unexpected charges for these medications; her exemption had lapsed because her depression was in abeyance.

The UK's experience illustrates how modest consumer cost sharing is part of the problem, not part of the solution. The end result has been little savings, but plenty of headaches. This became apparent in 2009, when the Labour government added an exemption for prescription drug charges for cancer patients, and pledged that it would soon also abolish charges for patients with chronic conditions. A subsequent report determined that, were they to do so, the costs of collecting the remaining small number of co-pays could outweigh the revenue collected from them.

US states that tried incorporating small patient fees into Medicaid have had similar experiences. It turned out to be a substantial administrative burden to identify who was required to pay those fees and who qualified for the many exemptions. Sometimes the administrative cost of collecting the fees exceeded the amount to be collected.

Many of the fees went unpaid. Some states gave up and discontinued their attempts to impose these fees at all.

In several European countries, the government has likewise thrown in the towel and abolished recently introduced attempts to impose cost sharing. In 2004, for example, Germany introduced a Praxisgebuhr, or practice fee. For the first time, Germans had to pay something to visit the doctor. It was only a small amount—ten euros for the first doctor visit in each quarter. The hope was that it would encourage Germans—who had among the highest rates of doctor visits per capita among rich countries—to think twice before going to the doctor for a minor health issue. It was just what Mark Pauly would have ordered.

Eight years later, Germany abolished these practice fees. The Germans had learned the hard way what the experience of the UK could have taught them. Between the negligible impact the fees had on the decision to visit a doctor, and the costs of collecting the fees and administering the exemptions, they saved much less money than expected. The juice wasn't worth the squeeze. The practice fees were also wildly unpopular in Germany—among both patients and physicians. Having to pay to go to the doctor was a totally new experience for Germans, which surely didn't make the medicine easier to swallow. But even in countries where such cost sharing has a long policy tradition, there's often an equally long policy tradition of undermining it.

The French experience is a case in point. Their national health insurance has always required high patient co-payments. Patients are responsible, for example, for 20 percent of hospital bills, 30 percent of doctor bills, and 40 percent of their lab costs, sometimes with no ceiling on how much patients have to pay. This is unusually bare-bones coverage, even by American standards.

As it increased cost sharing in recent decades in an effort to save money, the French government found itself simultaneously enacting policies to reduce the number of people who have to face this cost sharing. It has always covered patient charges for the very poor. But it enacted new policies for individuals whose income is low—but not low enough to qualify for government coverage; they now receive a voucher (called a cheque santé, or health check) that can be used to purchase supplemental insurance. The government also introduced tax subsidies and mandates for employers to offer supplementary coverage. The end result: almost everyone in France—95 percent of the population—now has supplemental insurance that covers their cost-sharing obligations.

A similar story has played out in the US with Medicare, which requires patients to pay for a substantial part of their care. The first $1,400 of hospital expenses each year, for example, as well as one fifth of all their doctors' bills, no matter how high. As we discussed in chapter 2, these kinds of costs can create substantial financial problems for the patients. Which may be why, after the introduction of Medicare, private policies to supplement Medicare coverage (so-called Medigap policies) quickly sprang up. Indeed, AARP (formerly the American Association of Retired Persons) originally got its start in the early 1970s by selling Medigap policies. These days, only about one in ten Medicare enrollees actually face all of the Medicare cost-sharing requirements. The rest have supplementary coverage for the cost-sharing requirements, some of it paid for by the government.

These experiences underscore the unavoidable tension between the social commitment to ensuring access to essential care and the economists' goal that patients should share in some of the costs of their care. At home and abroad, governments have time and again introduced cost-sharing requirements with one hand and then undid them with the other. Perhaps one-handed policy makers are needed, too, along with one-handed economists. Until that day, we'll skip the equivocation and cut out the cost sharing.

BUT WHAT ABOUT THE COSTS?

Will Kennedy-style "first-dollar coverage" lead to more national health-care spending than Nixonian cost sharing? Indisputably. But if that cost sharing comes in the form of small co-pays and deductibles, it won't be the silver bullet for reining in medical spending, even in the unlikely event that the US government is able to avoid creating exceptions to these co-pays (as in the UK), subsidizing coverage for those co-pays (as in France), or throwing in the towel (as in Germany).

Part of the reason relates to the nature of medical care, and the original debate between the proponents of Pauly and the friends of Fein. Fein and the other opponents of cost sharing were wrong in asserting that medical care was insensitive to price. But they were right that, in other ways, the demand for medical care is unlike that for most other goods and services that can be purchased. For one thing, the demand for medical care is inherently self-limiting. Almost everyone would prefer a bigger house if it were cheap enough. The same goes for fancier cars, or additional clothing. But no one (well, almost no one) wants to treat a disease they don't have—or to keep treating it after they are cured—even if they could do so for free.

Another unusual aspect of medical care is that, as the Nobel laureate economist Ken Arrow observed, there are important *nonmarket* forces that affect how much medical care a patient receives. Arrow is widely credited for launching the field of health economics. Yet, in a gentle rejoinder to Pauly's article, Arrow noted that although the economic forces Pauly identified surely exist, their quantitative importance was likely tempered by factors such as the "professional ethics of physicians not to prescribe frivolously expensive . . . treatment" as well as the "willingness of the individual to behave in accordance with some commonly accepted norms."

There's also a much more basic reason why cost sharing isn't much of a cost saver: Medical care is highly concentrated in a relatively small share of very sick patients. The top 5 percent of the population accounts for 50 percent of annual medical spending, the top 1 percent for almost one quarter. As a result, most medical spending is on patients who face little or no out-of-pocket costs for their (expensive) medical treatments.

The top 1 percent of patients have about $100,000 a year in medical bills. They are typically grappling with multiple overlapping chronic health problems. They're taking—or are supposed to be taking—many different kinds of medication. They're cycling in and out of the hospital. By the time a patient is on her second hospital visit in a year—or yet another course of chemotherapy—she's blown past her annual deductible, even if she had one of those $4,000 high-deductible plans. Indeed, most likely she's now paying nothing—or next to nothing—out of pocket for the high-cost medical care she is receiving, because insurance policies typically have an annual cap on the amount a person can pay out of pocket. Which is as it should be. It would undermine the purpose of insurance if patients had to keep paying for a portion of their care even as expenses climb into the stratosphere.

Any medical care that is included in basic coverage must be completely free to the patient. If not, the lesson is clear: we'll end up back in the same mess of trying—and not fully succeeding—to come to the aid of patients who cannot afford the required payments for that basic coverage. Asking people to pay for the care we have committed to provide puts form in conflict with function.

But basic coverage won't be all sweetness and light. We've described what basic coverage *must* do—it must be provided automatically, with no patient payments for covered services. We now must turn to the equally important, albeit less pleasant, subject of what basic coverage must *not* do.

A Shack, Not a Chateau

Basic coverage should be very basic

Over two thousand years ago, the first emperor of China arranged to be buried with a terra-cotta army—thousands of life-size terra-cotta soldiers and hundreds of terra-cotta horses and chariots for them to use. Whether or not they helped him in the afterlife as he intended, we'll never know. But they've been extremely effective as a tourist attraction, drawing millions of visitors every year to Xi'an to gape at the incredible mausoleum. It's a jaw-dropping experience.

Or so Liran has been told.

He wouldn't know. Liran spent his family's visit to Xi'an in the public hospital, with a very sick three-year-old daughter. Libby had a very high fever. Liran and his wife, Shirit—who is a physician—found themselves waiting with Libby in a room crowded with other patients, and with nowhere to sit down. They stood with these other families, many (like them) holding their sick child. They stood for a long time. They waited for their turn to see a doctor, who eventually looked at Libby, listened to her chest with a stethoscope, and sent her for a blood test. They waited in another long line for the blood test, and then waited some more for the results. Eventually the doctor came back with a prescription for an antibiotic. A few days later, Libby was completely fine.

In the end, after spending half a day in a crowded and bare-bones facility, Libby got the medical care she needed. From the perspective of her health, the treatment she got was as good as what she would have gotten if she'd been home in California. Shirit has since confirmed this. The care part—not so great.

And that is just fine. Basic coverage should provide minimalist (yet adequate) care, and no more. The rest is gravy. The social contract is about restoring essential function, not providing a high-end experience.

An analogy with airline travel may be useful. The main function of an airplane is to move its passengers from point A to point B. Almost everyone would prefer more legroom, unlimited checked bags, free food, and high-speed internet. And those who have the money and want to do so can upgrade to business class. They might also want to upgrade from their perfectly adequate pilot to one like Sully Sullenberger, who famously accomplished the so-called Miracle on the Hudson with a safe emergency landing of a commercial flight on that river.

But if our social contract were to make sure everyone could fly from A to B, a budget airline would suffice. Anyone who's traveled on one of the low-cost airlines that have transformed airline markets in Europe knows it is not a wonderful experience. But they do get you to your destination without crashing.

NO BILLS, NO FRILLS

There are two distinct words in health care: health and care. When it comes to basic coverage, it's important to separate them. Our social contract is about health—maintaining and restoring function to what the philosopher Norman Daniels called the normal human range. The care part of health care is all the nonmedical aspects of the experience— the amenities, as it were. Here, basic coverage can be quite, well, basic.

Many countries have taken exactly this approach to separating health from care. In Singapore, hospitals offer a range of hotel-like amenities. The VIP treatment, known as a Class A1 ward, gets the patient a single room, with a private attached bath and television; it also comes with air-conditioning, no small matter in Singapore's notoriously hot and humid climate. At the other end of the spectrum, the no-frills accommodation has eight beds in a room, a shared bathroom, and what is euphemistically referred to as "natural ventilation." Patients can pay out of pocket to upgrade to the VIP treatment. They can also pay less and upgrade only partway, to a five-bed room, for example.

Australia's system is similar. Its universal basic system covers no-frills doctors and clinics with patients paying nothing out of pocket. Those who want more need to pay for it, and the government encourages people to take out private insurance for this; about half the population has done so. The private insurance primarily improves upon nonmedical aspects of care. Consider, for example, the experience of childbirth. Basic public coverage can mean four new mothers and their crying newborns together in a room, with only thin and decidedly not soundproof curtains separating them. Private insurance gets the new mom a private suite in a hotel. Literally—the Grand Hyatt is one option. And while public hospitals serve the usual, unappealing institutional slop, the food in private hospitals is generally considered terrific. One new mom recalled having poached eggs on toast and smoked salmon for breakfast one morning. She also got her choice of doctor, who was with her from her first prenatal appointment through delivery. Physicians who practice in both systems in Australia—which includes about half of all specialists—describe a more relaxed and high-touch environment at the private hospital, where they can devote more time to getting to know their patients and establishing a relationship. But the consensus is that the medical care the public sector hospital delivers, while lacking in amenities, is adequate.

Private rooms, good food, and air-conditioning are certainly desirable. But they are quite separable from the medical function of health care. Liran's firsthand experience with an extreme version of no-frills but functional medical care in Xi'an made this clear. Far from offering such no-frills options, the US has gone in the opposite direction, with some states limiting hospitals to a maximum of one or two beds per room.

THE DOCTOR MAY SEE YOU NOW

Another area where basic coverage can be minimalist is wait times for nonemergency care. Of course, at some point wait times become sufficiently long that they make a mockery of the commitment to basic coverage. It does not fulfill our obligation to provide essential medical care to everyone if that essential medical care requires a three-year wait. But access doesn't have to be instantaneous either.

Any discussion of universal coverage invariably evokes the specter of extremely long wait times for nonemergency care. Stories abound. The twenty-seven-year-old Scotsman who is told that he will have to wait for up to three years to have his decayed tooth removed. The middle-aged Englishwoman suffering from depression who was unable to see a therapist for over six months. The forty-year-old Canadian with chronic pain whose family physician wanted her to see a neurologist but who faced an over four-year wait.

Although these stories are extreme by design, long wait times are indeed a central issue in many universal coverage countries. But not all. When surveyed, about three out of five people in Canada or Norway report that they would have to wait a month or more to see a specialist. But in Germany and Switzerland, only one in four people say they would have to wait that long, a rate similar to that reported in the US. Nor is the US itself a stranger to long wait times, particularly for primary care. About 30 percent of people in the US say they wouldn't be able to get a same-day answer to their medical concern from their doctor's office; this is only a slightly lower share than what Canadians report, and about double what the Germans and Swiss experience.

Within the US, wait times vary substantially based on what type of insurance—if any—a patient has. We know this from the results of numerous "secret shopper" studies, in which trained auditors posing as patients with a specific type of insurance call local physicians to try to schedule an appointment.* The studies consistently find that if a

---

*These "secret shopping" (or "audit") studies have a fascinating history. They arose originally in the 1940s and 1950s as a way of detecting racial discrimination in housing markets: a White "tester" couple would be sent to pose as would-be renters where a Black couple had just been told there was nothing available for them to rent. The use of individual audits for legal purposes was subsequently adapted for use in larger-scale research studies. These have examined discrimination in a wide range of markets—housing, hiring, loan applications, and sharing platforms such as Airbnb and Uber—and on a wide variety of dimensions, including race, ethnicity, age, criminal record, religious affiliation, sexual orientation, and military service. See Michael Gaddis, "An Introduction to Audit Studies in the Social Sciences," in *Audit Studies: Behind the Scenes with Theory, Method, and Nuance* (Cham, Switzerland: Springer International, 2018), 3–44.

patient says she has Medicaid, she is much less likely to be able to get a doctor's appointment than if she says she has private insurance, and will have to wait longer for that appointment if she does get one.

Medicaid wait times may not be ideal. But they nonetheless appear to be reasonable. We know this because the United States has explicitly delineated what kind of wait times and travel times are reasonable. It has done so for one of our oldest public health insurance programs: health insurance for veterans. The Department of Veterans Affairs (VA) provides veterans with medical care from government-employed health-care professionals at government-owned facilities, paid for by congressional funds. This publicly-run-and-operated system is strikingly similar to the much-derided system of "socialized medicine" in the UK. And like its counterpart in the UK, the VA has struggled with long wait times.

In 2014, a series of scandalous stories about excessively long wait times for VA care—along with allegations that veterans were dying as a result—prompted a public outcry. The outcry prompted congressional legislation requiring that veterans receive "timely and accessible care." The VA in turn delineated what that meant with military precision. Initially, the VA ruled that a patient must be able to get treatment within thirty days at a VA facility within forty miles. Subsequently, it tightened its standards, limiting wait times to twenty days for primary care and mental health care, and twenty-eight days for specialty care, with acceptable drive times now set at thirty minutes and sixty minutes, respectively. Typical wait times for Medicaid patients fit within these VA standards. Medicaid wait times tend to be about ten to fourteen days for a primary care appointment and about twenty days for a specialist appointment.

Put differently, a universal basic insurance system that had wait times comparable to what many Medicaid patients experience would be considered "reasonable" from the perspective of what has been deemed reasonable for American veterans. The VA standards in turn seem to fit within the general consensus of what other countries mean by "reasonable access" when they have set their own wait time standards.

To enforce the VA standards, Congress specified that any veteran whose access to VA care did not meet the wait-time or drive-time limits could get care outside of the VA, on the VA's dime. Likewise, a number of countries—including Norway, Denmark, and Portugal—have agreed to pay for patients to go to the private sector if wait times exceed what they have deemed to be the maximum allowable limit. Portugal even prophylactically gives out vouchers for services that are considered important and that it knows the public sector cannot easily provide; pregnant women, for example, are given vouchers to pay for private dental appointments. In 2010, in Denmark, about 3 percent of surgical patients received their operations at a private hospital paid for by the public program.*

---

*In countries where the private sector is not big enough to provide a sufficient safety valve—or where using it for this purpose is considered politically untenable—meeting self-proclaimed wait-time standards can be more difficult. In some cases, countries have resorted to a combination of financial sanctions and strong regulatory oversight of health-care providers. In England—which implemented these unpopular policies from 2001 to 2010—they became known as the "targets and terror" method. Finland implemented its own version of this approach. Both countries were able to bring down wait times substantially. For England, see Carol Propper, Matt Sutton, Carolyn Whitnall, and Frank Windmeijer, "Did 'Targets and Terror' Reduce Waiting Times in England for Hospital Care?," in "Health Care Economics and Policy," ed. Ching-to Albert Ma, B.E. Journal of Economic Analysis & Policy 8, no. 2 (December 2008): 1863, doi.org/10.2202/1935-1682.1863; Gwyn Bevan and Christopher Hood, "Have Targets Improved Performance in the English NHS?," BMJ 332, no. 7538 (February 16, 2006): 419–22, doi.org/10.1136/bmj.332.7538.419; Luigi Siciliani, Valerie Moran, and Michael Borowitz, "Measuring and Comparing Health Care Waiting Times in OECD Countries," Health Policy 118, no. 3 (December 2014): 292–303, doi.org/10.1016/j.healthpol.2014.08.011; and Catherine Foot, "What Will Replace Targets and Terror?," King's Fund, June 21, 2010, kingsfund.org.uk/blog/2010/06/what-will-replace-targets-and-terror.

(NOT) FREE TO CHOOSE

Defining and enforcing wait times is not the only similarity between the VA system in the US and the universal systems in other countries. In both, the insurer also plays an active role in determining what medical care a patient can get, like a bouncer deciding who can enter the nightclub. The idea is that the insurer can help reduce costs by eliminating unnecessary medical care that a patient and a physician—who don't bear the financial costs of treatment choices—might otherwise be tempted to try.

It will be important for basic coverage to also play this type of "gatekeeping" role if it is to remain basic. For most of the currently insured in the US, this won't mean much change. Most insurers in the US—both public and private—play a gatekeeping role. But there's one very important exception: Medicare.

Medicare is unusual in imposing essentially no constraints or guardrails on the medical care that patients can seek or physicians can deliver. It is decidedly hands off when patients and physicians try to receive or deliver that covered care. Patients with Medicare are free to see whichever doctor they want. Their doctors in turn are free to order whatever tests and procedures they deem warranted. Medicare is a passive bill payer. The originating statute explicitly prohibits Medicare from interfering with the practice of medicine or limiting patient access to physicians.

Consider a patient who has a runny nose and itchy eyes and wants to see an allergist, or a patient with stomach pain who wants to see a gastroenterologist. If she is covered by Medicare, she can simply make these appointments. By contrast, in most other insurance systems both in the US and abroad, she would first have to see her primary care provider, who would need to perform an exam to determine whether further care—such as diagnostic tests or a visit to a specialist—is warranted. The primary care physician in turn might be required to document the existence or persistence of certain symptoms or to get advance approval from a higher-up before pursuing further care. Such hoops are designed to prevent your cousin, who used WebMD to diagnose herself with brain cancer after a night of drinking and an early-morning headache, from getting a costly MRI right away.

To the proponents of gatekeeping, Medicare's approach is a big mistake. They argue that gatekeeping offers the elusive win-win, the ability to lower health-care spending while also ensuring higher-quality patient care. Their argument is that gatekeeping—or what they prefer to call "primary care case management"—sets up the primary care physician as the "general contractor" for all of the patient's medical care. The patient will then get a coordinated and sensible set of treatments, and avoid unnecessary care or risky—potentially contraindicated—treatments. As one physician, herself a specialist, wrote in support of this view:

> There are so many specialty organizations . . . each vigorously guards its turf. Imagine building a house by allowing each workman to do his own thing. The plumber would put a sink in every room. The electrician would install chandeliers on every ceiling. The carpenter would panel every room in luxurious wood.

It's a compelling metaphor and one that, needless to say, we're quite partial to. But that doesn't mean it's right. There's a danger that even an ostensibly sensible set of checks and balances can create a snarl of red tape that denies patients timely and important treatments. And there's certainly a perception that this is indeed what "gatekeeping" does, which was memorably encapsulated in the late-1990s movie *As Good as It Gets*. Midway through the movie, Helen Hunt—playing a New York City waitress and single mother—lashes out against her managed care insurer with a string of expletives. Moviegoing audiences across America responded with whoops and applause.

In practice, our read of the evidence is that gatekeeping and guardrails are likely neither as idyllic as the general contractor analogy is designed to suggest (and besides, who hasn't had problems with their general contractor as well?), nor as awful as Hunt's Academy Award–winning performance implies. Like most health-care institutions, gatekeeping involves trade-offs. It can be a useful constraint on the amount and nature of medical care received, but this can come at the cost of decreased patient satisfaction and well-being.

We see this in the evidence from a study of Medicaid patients in New York State who were randomly assigned to one of ten different Medicaid plans because they failed to choose a plan. All the plans covered the same benefits and imposed no consumer cost sharing. But the plans varied in how they "managed" care. This included their network of physicians and hospitals, as well as what restrictions they imposed on accessing specific medical services and technologies. Patients who were randomly assigned to plans with more gatekeeping had substantially lower medical spending. But they were also less satisfied with their plans. Aspects of their health also appeared to suffer. In particular, compared with patients randomly assigned to higher-spending plans, those assigned to lower-spending plans were more likely to be hospitalized for a condition that might have been avoidable with appropriate care. "Somewhat contrary to the popular myth in the broader health-care landscape," the authors concluded, "lower-spending plans are not achieving savings by keeping people healthy. They are restricting access to a broad set of services."

Just because gatekeeping isn't a panacea, however, doesn't mean we should avoid it. It must be an integral part of basic coverage. Just as it is in almost every insurance system *except* Medicare. It's the only option on the table to try to guard against excessive or unnecessary health care. In an imperfect world, gatekeeping—like a general contractor—is a necessary evil.

———

We've said that basic coverage must be automatic and free. But it can also be minimalist on nonessential dimensions. Wait times to see a doctor are longer than what most insured patients in the US are currently accustomed to. Patients and their physicians not at liberty to get any medical care they both want, as they currently are under Medicare. Uncomfortable waiting rooms, and hospital rooms with four or ten people in them. No air-conditioned private room where avocado toast is served, as the privately insured actually receive in several other countries.

But we aren't quite done describing basic coverage. We still need to define what medical care it must cover, and what can be excluded.

Trust the Process

Deciding what to cover

One early autumn evening in 1986, audiences across the United Kingdom turned on their television to watch a new game show. In *The Life and Death Game*, a studio audience had to decide which patients should get medical care paid for by the British government and which should not. Should they pay, for example, for life-saving kidney dialysis for a *single* patient like Carol, a young mother in her thirties? Or instead use that money to fund a hip replacement for *fifty* patients like Joan, a retired woman in her sixties whose osteoarthritis of the hip was causing debilitating pain?

The patients on the show and their health problems were real, although the decisions made by the studio audience were not. Still, the game show had a real purpose, which was revealed at the end. After the studio audience made several decisions between different patients' treatments, University of York health economist Alan Maynard appeared on the show to explain how he thought they—and the British government—should prioritize medical care across different types of treatments. It was all part of an effort by Maynard and his health economist colleagues to socialize the British to the idea of using the trusty economic tool of cost-effectiveness analysis to prioritize what health care would be covered through the British National Health System. Foreshadowing some of the reactions against this approach, one audience member described Maynard's approach as "codswallop."

Codswallop or not, this decision-making is unavoidable. As we'll describe in this chapter, certain types of care must be included in basic coverage in order to fulfill our social commitments. But there's also a large gray area of medical care that could be excluded from basic coverage. We'll discuss how to make these difficult decisions without resorting to a TV game show.

LET'S BE SENSIBLE

We'll start with the easier part—what basic coverage must include. It must systematically cover all essential medical care for the critically ill. For all conditions. Not just the "niche" programs we encountered in part I, which provide coverage once breast cancer is diagnosed, or once the end stage of kidney failure is reached.

Basic coverage must also include primary and preventive care for patients who are not yet critically ill. Primary care is cheap. Among insured individuals in the US, it accounts for only about 5 percent of total health-care spending. But our argument for including primary and preventive care in basic coverage is not based on potential cost savings. Rather, it reflects what it really means to fulfill our social contract. Sensibly. In spirit, not just in letter.

A strict reading of our revealed social contract indicates that we try to respond in times of medical emergency or crisis. But limiting basic coverage to those circumstances would be a mistake. That narrow definition of our social contract is hard to justify, even if it's easy to understand where it comes from.

As we discussed in chapter 5, individuals feel compelled to act when directly confronted with an immediate crisis, but we feel considerably less obligation to address chronic problems. Our social contract has mirrored these individual impulses. Our policies tend to be reactive, requiring action in an acute crisis, but allowing complacency when the specter of disaster hovers in the background.

We don't fault people for their moral intuitions. We suspect we may have similar impulses ourselves. But we can't advocate for encoding these psychological biases into public policy. Good policy doesn't merely react to knee-jerk impulses. It develops a sensible approach to fulfilling the commitments we have identified. Public policy should be less impulsive and more rational than individual people.

Lack of universal access to primary care is arguably the single biggest factor that distinguishes US health care from that of other high-income countries. Indeed, most countries' universal systems prioritize primary care, typically making its coverage more generous than coverage for more specialized care. As lower-income countries work to improve access to health care, they often focus first on primary care. Costa Rica, for example, achieved universal coverage of primary care by 2006, while coverage for specialist care and hospitalizations is still a work in progress. What the US has done, by contrast, is the health-care equivalent of committing to provide universal free high school, while leaving K–8 education inaccessible to large portions of the population.

Primary care should be the first point of contact for preventing illness, for diagnosing and treating new medical issues, and for managing ongoing chronic conditions. It makes no sense to commit to provide care once someone is experiencing a medical crisis, but not to provide the primary care that could prevent or manage a condition before it becomes a crisis. If you know you're going to rescue the sinking ship, you don't let a leaking ship leave port. You make sure it is seaworthy before it sets out, and equip it with life vests. Our moral intuitions may prompt us to react only in the event of disaster, but sensible policy demands more. Basic coverage should not kick into gear only once the crisis has arisen.

The big picture is clear. Basic coverage should include primary and preventive care, specialist, outpatient, emergency room, and hospital care. Now comes the harder part.

MORE THAN FIFTY SHADES OF GRAY

Once we try to go beyond that high-level description, there will inevitably be a multitude of gray areas. There are many aspects of medical care that can be excluded from basic coverage while still fulfilling our social contract: infertility treatment, dental care, vision care, physiotherapy, various forms of long-term care, and the list goes on and on.

We won't take a stand here on what in this gray area *should* be excluded from basic coverage. These are hard choices. But they are just that—choices. There's room for reasonable arguments for excluding all of them, some of them, or none of them. That's why most countries have a formal process for making these decisions, and why different processes reach different results. It's also why we'll insist that the US have a policy process for making these decisions.

Prioritizing which treatments to include in basic coverage isn't merely an issue for the transition to universal coverage. It is something that will have to be done on an ongoing basis. Standards for what is essential for achieving normal function will change over time as medical technology improves and income grows. When the US created Medicare in 1965, it didn't cover prescription drugs. Since then, there has been a revolution in drug development. New antihypertensives and statins, for example, have been key contributors to the dramatic reduction in cardiovascular mortality, the leading cause of death. Eventually, in 2006, Medicare was expanded to include prescription drug coverage.

Likewise, notions of what constitutes disease can change. Since 2000, countries such as England, Denmark, and Australia have expanded mental health benefits to include psychotherapy for mild to moderate mental health disorders. Medicare coverage in the US has similarly expanded to fully cover depression screening and to reduce cost sharing on outpatient mental health treatments to the same level as other health conditions.

An evolving definition of the standard of adequacy is not unique to health care. Thirty years ago, high-speed internet was considered a pipe dream. Now it's increasingly seen as a basic human necessity that governments are responsible for ensuring all citizens have access to. In the early twentieth century, US states grappled with whether "basic" education that the government would provide for everyone for free should expand beyond primary school to also include high school. Now, in the first few decades of the twenty-first century, we're asking whether the definition of "basic" education should again be expanded to also include two years of community college, preschool, or both.

This is why most countries have a formal, multistep process for considering whether to cover new treatments under universal health care. Some countries make these decisions on an "as-needed" basis, while others do it on a preset schedule—annually in the Netherlands, for example, or every five years in Switzerland. They typically use a centralized, two-step process. The first step is a formal assessment phase involving scientific experts. Its aim is to quantify the clinical impacts of the treatment. The ultimate decision, however, relies primarily on a second phase, in which other stakeholders—such as health-care professionals and government officials—weigh a range of criteria. These include not only the results of that first-phase technical assessment, but also other factors, including "societal values."

Health economist Alan Maynard was advocating for a particular process for coverage decisions when he appeared on that British game show in the mid-1980s. His would have considered only the technical assessment of the treatment's costs and medical benefits. Maynard argued that the National Health Service should prioritize coverage for the most cost-effective medical care. In other words, the procedures and treatments with the highest ratio of benefits to costs, the highest bang for the buck, as it were.

Maynard's views were not unusual. Certainly not among economists. And it turns out it's not only crazy academics who think this way. Prioritizing medical treatments based solely on cost-effectiveness has actually been tried, both at home and abroad. And it's proven impossible to fully adhere to.

BACK ON THE OREGON TRAIL

In 1987, Coby Howard, a seven-year-old boy in Oregon, died. Coby had Medicaid coverage. He also had acute lymphocytic leukemia and needed a bone marrow transplant. Medicaid would not pay for that transplant. Earlier that year, the state legislature had removed certain transplants from Medicaid coverage in order to cover prenatal care for around 1,200 pregnant women and basic care for about 1,800 children. Coby's story—and that of other Oregonians on Medicaid in desperate need of newly-not-covered transplants—made national news.

So too did Oregon's response. The state created a commission tasked with ranking all medical services by their cost-effectiveness. Their idea: eliminate coverage for high-cost treatments with limited or unclear benefits and use the savings to expand insurance coverage to more low-income Oregonians. "Rationalize" coverage, Maynard style.

The eleven-member commission—which included physicians, a social worker, and representatives of the public—immediately set to work. The commissioners worked assiduously, for long hours and without pay. Aided by hundreds of clinical specialists as well as their own original analyses, they ultimately produced a priority list based on detailed estimates of the benefits and costs of 1,600 different medical treatments for particular conditions—hip replacements, appendectomies, medical therapies for diaper rash, childhood immunizations. All were measured and ranked.

The first version of the commission's priority list—released in June 1990—provoked another outcry. Critics quickly pointed out that many of the rankings were counterintuitive. Tooth capping, for example, was estimated to be more cost effective than surgery for an emergency appendectomy or an ectopic pregnancy. The dental procedure therefore received a higher priority ranking than either of those life-saving surgeries.

The underlying estimates were not the issue. The committee had done its work well, and these all appeared sensible. For example, relative to no treatment, an appendectomy was deemed to improve quality of life by 97 percent (just shy of the maximum 100 percent that denotes the difference between being alive in perfect health rather than being dead), while dental caps improved quality of life by only 8 percent.*

---

*The technical term for this quality of life measure is *quality adjusted life year,* or QALY (rhymes with *jolly*). A year in perfect health is given a QALY score of one, a year of being dead scores zero. Much scientific effort and squabbling go into assigning scores to all the various ways a year can be spent in less-than-perfect health.

The problem was that reasonable estimates did not produce a reason-able ranking. Abdominal surgery is much more expensive than tooth capping. So even though the benefits of abdominal surgery are much higher than those of tooth capping, the *ratio* of benefits to costs is not. And prioritization was based on cost-effectiveness—benefits *relative* to costs—not absolute benefits.

The faithful and accurate application of cost-benefit analysis had produced unacceptable results. Even the commissioners agreed, acknowledging that their rankings often conflicted with their own in-tuition. They quickly abandoned the formulaic application of cost-effectiveness rankings in favor of a more "holistic" approach. They used their judgment—and that of members of the community who provided input through public forums—to create broad categories of health care that they ranked in order of importance. Effective care for acute fatal conditions (such as appendectomies) was ranked high, while minimally effective treatments for nonfatal conditions (such as tooth capping or medical therapy for diaper rash) were in a category near the bottom. Each of their original 1,600 medical treatments for spe-cific conditions was then placed within a category, where all were ranked according to their benefits—with no accounting for cost. In the final step of the process, the commissioners looked over the whole list line by line and made adjustments to the rankings by hand—"list-jockeying," in their own terminology—to about one quarter of the line items. At this final stage, the committee appears to have consid-ered the costs of the treatments. They never explicitly acknowledged this, but tellingly, many high-cost treatments were moved lower on the priority list.

In moral philosophy, this type of process is known as "reflective equilibrium." A theory is proposed, tested against specific, practical implications, and revised when those implications conflict with moral intuition. The process is repeated until there are no more conflicts, and stability ("equilibrium") has been achieved. We think of it as the same approach that Supreme Court justice Potter Stewart famously used to define hard-core pornography: you know it when you see it.

And it's the same approach the Brits have ended up with when they, too—prompted by the likes of Alan Maynard—tried unsuccessfully to make coverage decisions based on a pure application of the cost-effectiveness principle.

GOD SAVE THE KING, IF IT'S COST EFFECTIVE

The British National Health Service enjoys extraordinary public support. When London hosted the 2012 Olympics, its opening ceremony paid homage to the NHS with a segment featuring dancing nurses and sick children. The next year it was the NHS itself that took home the gold—coming first in a nationwide poll of what institutions made people proudest to be British—ahead of the army and the monarchy, as well as the recent Olympics. "The NHS is the closest thing the English people have to a religion," declared one UK politician (apparently forgetting Henry VIII's famous split with the Roman Catholic Church).

Despite their pride, the British have struggled with the grim realities of rising health-care costs and budgetary pressures. In response to these issues, Britain created the National Institute for Health and Care Excellence in the late 1990s. NICE—as it is colloquially, and perhaps optimistically, called—is a public institution charged with recommending which new medical treatments the National Health Service will, and will not, cover. NICE issues this guidance based on evidence of a treatment's cost-effectiveness—how much health benefit is obtained per dollar (or pound) of medical spending. NICE tends to recommend that the NHS cover treatments that cost less than about £20,000 to

£30,000 to produce a year of perfect health. One of its first decisions was to recommend that the NHS not cover the precautionary removal of healthy wisdom teeth. Needless to say, the British Dental Association objected.

If this path sounds similar to the Oregon Trail, it's because it is. But while the principle of cost-effectiveness has been more closely adhered to in the Isle of Portland than in Portland, Oregon, there have been bumps—and detours—along the UK motorway as well. NICE was controversial from the get-go. And just as in Oregon, some of these controversies have compelled the National Health Service to explicitly deviate from the principle of cost-effectiveness.

The exceptions are along predictable lines. Drugs approved for a small number of terminally ill patients, for example, are evaluated against a more lenient cost-effectiveness limit of about £50,000 rather than the normal £20,000 to £30,000. The cost-effectiveness limit is even more lenient for drugs that treat very rare diseases. In some cases, it has risen as high as £300,000 to produce a year of perfect health, ten times higher than the normal limit.

One of the more telling controversies and resulting exceptions concerns the coverage of cancer drugs. Toward the end of the aughts, a number of new, expensive cancer drugs were developed. The US Medicare program and other European countries' national health insurance programs covered many of these new drugs, like Avastin for colorectal cancer, which did not meet NICE's cost-effectiveness limit. The NHS therefore decided not to cover these drugs. This provoked a storm of public criticism, with headlines like GRAN LOSES CANCER DRUG APPEAL and NOT SO NICE—MUM LEFT TO FIGHT CANCER WITHOUT A PILL, along with dramatic stories of patients who had sought help from elderly parents or sold their homes to pay for treatment.

Facing public and political pressure, NICE raised the cost-effectiveness limit for some end-of-life drugs. But that wasn't high enough to satisfy critics. The Conservative Party used the issue of cancer drug coverage in its 2010 election campaign. When it came to power, it quickly created (and funded) a special Cancer Drugs Fund to which patients could apply for coverage of cancer treatments that NICE had refused to cover. Ultimately, a tenuous compromise was reached in which NICE has yielded to approving some additional cancer drugs, and the special cancer fund was closed in 2016.

Coverage decisions in most countries have ended up in a similar place as NICE. Most other high-income countries now also require economic evaluation of a new treatment, including analysis of budgetary impact and cost-effectiveness relative to existing alternatives. But their ultimate coverage decision involves additional criteria. Sweden made this approach explicit with its 1997 Health and Medical Services Act, which spelled out the principles that should guide what had to be covered by its publicly financed, universal health care. The answer: coverage must respond first to what it called "the principle of need," and only secondly to the principle of cost-effectiveness. That's why Sweden, like most countries, doesn't cover the highly cost-effective Viagra. Erectile dysfunction has been judged to be a "lifestyle" issue rather than a "disease." But Sweden does cover Rivastigmine—a very expensive drug designed to slow the progression of Alzheimer's—as well as extremely expensive lung transplants for patients with terminal lung disease. In both cases, the needs of the patients—the gaps between their current state and the normal range—are considered to be large enough to warrant the treatment, even though it scores poorly on cost-effectiveness.

The Swedes' "principle of need" goes by other names in other countries: "severity of condition" in Norway, "necessity" in the Netherlands. The World Health Organization calls it "priority to the worse off."

Whatever you call it, we've already encountered this tendency of public policy to encode our individual predilection to respond to "moral emergencies." We saw it, for example, in the outrage in Oregon when Medicaid stopped covering expensive but life-saving transplants. We also saw it in the creation of the US health insurance program that pays for expensive, life-saving dialysis for patients with kidney failure, even though such treatment ranks low on a cost-effectiveness scale.

Once again, it's not obvious to us that public policy should be guided by this psychological impulse. But it appears in practice to be the route most countries have taken.

———

Another route most countries have taken is to have and enforce a health-care budget. That's what creates the need to prioritize which treatments to cover in the first place. These difficult choices exist only when we can't cover everything that's on the wish list.

We're long overdue in this book for a discussion of the health-care budget. So too, it turns out, is the US government.

Budget Matters

Relax, we can afford it

Once upon a time, Congress tried to set and enforce a budget for Medicare spending. As part of the so-called Balanced Budget Act of 1997, Congress set a target for Medicare spending growth, and specified automatic cuts to physician spending if growth exceeded that target.

But it flinched. Over and over again. Every single time the politically unpopular cuts were about to go into effect, Congress voted to delay. It was the legislative equivalent of the movie *Groundhog Day*. All told, Congress passed seventeen deferrals in about the same number of years. Finally, in 2015, in a rare act of bipartisan agreement, Congress threw in the towel. It voted to eliminate the policy entirely.

We won't accept this. We will insist on a binding budget for basic coverage, just like all other high-income countries have. We won't set the specific dollar amount for this budget. That's because there's a lot of flexibility in what the budget for basic coverage can be. And that's a good thing. We will note, however, that basic coverage could plausibly be financed out of existing tax revenue, without having to raise taxes.

ON BUDGET

The idea that we need to set and enforce a budget for taxpayer-financed health-care spending is simultaneously banal and radical. Banal because of course any policy requires a budget. That seems incontrovertible. Radical because the US government has never had to live within a health-care budget. That, unfortunately, is also incontrovertible.

Every year, Congress decides how much the federal government can spend on infrastructure, on education, and on agriculture, but it sets no budget limit on federal health-care spending. When the media or politicians talk about the "Medicare budget," they are talking about how much the government has spent, or how much it is projected to spend. They are not describing a budget in the usual sense of the word, a limit on how much the government *can* spend.

Here's how Medicare spending is determined. Patients choose medical providers. Those providers choose treatments. The government imposes no guardrails or restrictions on those treatments (recall chapter 10). Providers then submit bills for those treatments. The government pays them (essentially), no questions asked. If hospitals or physicians submit more bills, or larger bills, the government simply spends more. From the patient and their doctor's perspective, why not run a few extra tests and scans to be on the safe side, or send the patient to a specialist when in doubt? If the sky's the limit, why not reach for the stars?

The federal government's expenses-be-damned attitude is unique to Medicare. The Department of Defense doesn't ask Boeing for some (barely specified) fighter planes and tell Boeing to just send the bill when it delivers the planes. States don't tell school districts to teach the students and just submit bills. School districts face budget limits and have to decide how to meet them. Some may pay teachers less. Some may be open for fewer hours. Some may cut back on arts or athletics. Some may decide to raise taxes to expand their budget.

These are the kinds of choices other countries have made when it comes to their health-care budgets. In essentially every other high-income country, the government sets an explicit and fixed budget for major categories of health-care spending. In the UK, for example, the House of Commons approves the annual budget for the NHS. In Norway, the Ministry of Health and Care Services sets the budget for four regional associations, which in turn deliver budgets to hospitals. In Canada, a fixed, overall budget is then devolved to increasingly decentralized units, with individual hospitals ultimately each given an annual budget to cover their costs. These budgets put a ceiling on taxpayer-financed health-care spending, and on the growth of that spending. It helps that the government agency responsible for the health-care budget often also has the final say in decisions about covering new treatments.

Often there is also a distinct budget—and process—for expanding national coverage as medical technology evolves. In Israel, for example, the "health basket committee" is given an annual budget that it can use to add coverage of new technologies. Recent decisions have added coverage for a sports-friendly prosthetic leg, and new treatments for depression and alcohol reduction. Some committee members have (perhaps not surprisingly) argued that their budget is too small—noting that it's "equivalent to purchasing two new tanks." But because there is a budget, that debate can be had.

Those debates are often quite vigorous. In Canada, political parties explicitly campaign on different platforms about the level of the

health-care budget. Some promise to rein in costs, while others advocate expanding the health-care budget and paying for it through higher
taxes or more government debt. In the UK, any increased funding for
the NHS involves heated debates about how much to raise the budget
and how to pay for it. The Conservative prime minister Theresa May,
for example, spoke openly about the need to increase taxes in order to
increase funding for the NHS.

Not so for Medicare. It's as if the government contracted with a
builder to construct a house but gave her no cap on expenses, and left
her a whole lot of leeway on what to build. Footprint, number of stories, choice of materials, whether to put in a pool—it's all up to her.
Nor does she need to check in before making decisions.

This lack of a budget has had extraordinary consequences. Fifty
years ago, the health-care sector in the US was about the same share of
the economy as it was in these other countries. Since then, US health-
care spending as a share of the economy has grown twice as fast as the
average in other high-income countries. The development and adoption of new medical technologies has been the main cause. New drugs,
new surgical procedures, and new treatment regimens are widely credited for much of the dramatic improvements in US health that have
occurred over the last half century. They're also widely blamed for the
equally dramatic rise in US health-care spending over the same period. Medical technologies are constantly evolving. There are always
promising (if expensive) new treatments to try. And without any limitations imposed on them, patients and physicians are apparently eager
to try them.

As we saw in the previous chapter, other countries take costs into
account (along with "societal values") in deciding what new treatments
to cover. Not so Medicare. By law, it is explicitly forbidden from con-

sidering costs in making coverage decisions. And private insurers—who can pass off rising health-care costs to their customers in the form of higher health insurance premiums—tend to cover the technologies that Medicare covers.

As a result, in US health care, "the gradient of technical feasibility becomes a moral imperative," the historian Charles Rosenberg has observed. "That which might be done, should be done."* Some economists have argued that this is as it should be—that as we grow richer, we may want to spend an increasing share of our resources on medical care. Whether or not they are right that health-care spending *should* become an increasingly large part of our economy, history has made clear that it *will* become so unless a binding health-care budget is set and enforced.

Indeed, where US policy has successfully deviated from Medicare's no-holds-barred approach, health-care spending has grown more slowly. One clear example is Medicaid, the public health insurance program for low-income Americans. Unlike Medicare, whose costs are paid for entirely by the federal government, states are responsible for funding a large portion of Medicaid's budget. And unlike the federal government, most states are required by law or by their constitution to balance their budgets. As a result, states have imposed binding budget constraints on their Medicaid programs. The result: over the last few decades, Medicaid spending per enrollee has been relatively constant (after adjusting for inflation), in striking contrast with the non-Medicaid portion of

---

*Writing at the height of the Cold War—during the era of Star Wars and Reagan—Rosenberg also drew an analogy between the US approach to government health-care spending and to defense spending. In both cases, he observed, "normal budgetary constraints and compromises have come to seem niggling and inappropriate." Charles Rosenberg, *The Care of Strangers: The Rise of America's Hospital System* (New York: Basic Books, 1987), 350.

health-care spending. The state of Maryland provides another instructive example. Since 2014 it has imposed a global budget on all hospital spending in the state, and experienced a substantial decline in spending compared with other states.

Refusing to set and enforce a budget for Medicare hasn't meant that we've avoided trade-offs. Taxpayer money spent on health care is money not spent on schools. Or Social Security. Or lower taxes. We just haven't grappled with these trade-offs explicitly. As the philosopher and medical ethicist Norman Daniels (whom we already encountered in chapter 7) observed, "Since health care is not the only important good, reasonable resource constraints will require judgements about which medical needs are more important to meet than others . . . meeting health care needs should not and need not be a bottomless pit." If even moral philosophers can bow to practical reality, surely the rest of us can—and must—as well. We must set—and enforce—a health-care budget.

THE TAXMAN

That health-care budget would come out of taxpayers' pockets. As we discussed in chapter 8, the only viable path to achieving universal coverage is to provide basic coverage automatically. We lack the resolve of countries like Switzerland or the Netherlands to actually enforce a mandate that people purchase this coverage. For coverage to be automatic, it must be financed by the government out of tax revenue.

As a result, there's a real possibility that taxes would rise in the US to finance a universal basic coverage that fulfills our social contract. But that's a choice. Taxes would not *need* to rise to finance basic coverage.

To see this, consider the level of government health-care spending in countries whose basic coverage—automatic coverage with (almost) no consumer payments—looks similar to what we propose. The UK is one example. Canada and Germany are others. In 2019, taxpayer spending for basic coverage in these countries was about 8 to 9 percent of their economy. Guess how much US taxpayers spent in that same year on health care? Answer: also about 9 percent of the economy.

It may come as a surprise that taxpayer-financed health-care spending in the US is already large enough to pay for universal basic coverage. After all, there's a popular narrative that health care in the US is "private," not "socialized medicine" as in other countries. But in fact, the government already pays for about half of all US health-care spending, and all of that is financed by taxpayers. Tax dollars are the single biggest source of health-care funding in the United States. Our taxes are already paying for the cost of universal basic coverage. We're just not getting it.

To be clear, total spending on health care in the US as a share of national income is much larger than it is in any other country—17 percent in the US in 2019, compared with 12 percent in the next highest-spending country that year, and to 9 percent on average across high-income countries. That higher US spending, however, primarily reflects higher *private* spending. Not higher public spending.

Of course, we might choose a more expansive—and expensive—basic system, which would mean higher taxes. The operative word is *might*. For it is exactly that: a choice. The example of other countries shows that we could choose to fulfill our social contract without raising taxes.

The blueprint for basic coverage leaves open a range of budget-relevant decisions, creating a range of options for the price tag for basic coverage that sensibly fulfills our health-care commitments. It is our choice what treatments in the "gray area" of basic coverage will include, how much doctors and hospitals will be reimbursed for basic care, and what gatekeeping there will be, among other choices. As any home builder knows, the big-ticket items are not the essential elements of any home—walls, roof, floor, windows, and door—but the discretionary ones: its size, features, and materials. Every house has a kitchen, but the choice of appliances and other amenities can easily mean a fivefold difference in costs. As with your home, so with your health care.

The level of *total* health-care spending—government plus private spending—is also a choice. Private spending will depend on whether and how much supplemental coverage people choose to buy in order to get coverage for services that aren't included in the basic coverage, or to get shorter wait times or nicer nonmedical amenities than the basic coverage provides. Those choices are not our concern. We don't worry about how much of people's income they are spending on vacations or electronics. As long as the government fulfills the social contract, who are we to judge if people want to spend their own money to buy additional health-care coverage?

We realize of course that this blasé attitude toward the total level of health-care spending is an anomaly. It's much more common to hear Chicken Little cries about the unsustainable, sky-high levels of US health-care spending. Generations of presidents, policy wonks, and professors have repeatedly declared that level of health-care spending "unsustainable."

"In recent years," one eminent economist observed, "almost every American family has become acutely aware of the soaring costs of medical care.... According to many observers, the US health care system is in 'crisis.'" That's Vic Fuchs, he of the "Tale of Two States" from chapter 7, talking about the "soaring costs of medical care."

In 1974.

This was when US health-care spending was only about 7 percent of the economy, rather than the 17 percent it was in 2019. If we listen to the pundits, the sky appears to have been falling for quite some time.

We disagree. We don't subscribe to the general hysteria about the level of US health-care spending. The real crisis is not the level of health-care spending, or even—as some economists have emphasized—the level of *taxpayer* spending on health care. Rather, the real crisis is our failure to fulfill our social contract.

That said, we also don't subscribe to the Pollyannaish claims that there are easy ways to cut US health care without any noticeable effects on patients.

WASTE DISPOSAL

From Nixon, to Clinton, to Obama, presidents have bundled proposals for universal coverage with proposals to reduce the level of health-care spending. The instinct is understandable. After all, coverage and costs are arguably the two great problems in the US health-care system.

But these problems are eminently separable. We can tackle the problem of coverage—and fulfill our social contract—without tackling the problem of health-care delivery. We do not have to hold our health-care commitments hostage to finding a way to get more health for the same total level of spending, or for those whose proclivities point in a different direction, getting the same health benefits at lower cost. Which is a relief, because we don't (yet) have the silver bullet for dramatically lowering health-care spending while fulfilling the dictate to "do no harm" to the patient. Nor, we hasten to add, does anyone else. Despite what you may have heard on TV.

Wait, really? You'd have to be living under a rock not to have heard that there's an enormous amount of waste in US health-care spending that drives up taxes and insurance premiums but provides no benefit to patients. That we spend more than any other country on health care but have only middling health outcomes to show for it.

We could write a whole book on why that high level of health-care spending defies facile solutions. Maybe someday we will. But it would make for a depressing read.

What the pundits and the media say is true. There's a lot of waste in US health care. But the old adage about advertising is also true: half of spending is wasted, we just don't know which half. We've done our share of research on this topic, looking into some of the much-heralded proposals for how to dramatically improve the efficiency of US health care. And, unfortunately, a consistent theme—of both our work and others'—is that most of the supposedly "easy" solutions to reducing health-care spending with no impact on patients actually aren't that easy. Or they aren't solutions at all.*

There are three frequently touted "cut-waste-quick" schemes: Lower the prices for medical care. Why should the US pay higher prices compared with other countries on everything from prescription drugs to surgical procedures? Slash administrative costs. Why pay for adminis-

---

*For example, one frequently touted (and correct) statistic is that about one quarter of all medical spending on the elderly occurs in the last year of life. But the research we've done has undermined the typical follow-on claim that we can save a lot of wasted spending by cutting back on expensive, heroic, and futile care for people in their last days of life. The reason, in a nutshell, is that at the time most of this so-called end-of-life spending occurs, neither the doctor nor the statistician can be confident that the patient is in fact very likely at the end of life. For more details, see Liran Einav, Amy Finkelstein, Sendhil Mullainathan, and Ziad Obermeyer, "Predictive Modeling of US Health Care Spending in Late Life," *Science* 360, no. 6396 (June 29, 2018): 1462–65; and Dan Zeltzer, Liran Einav, Amy Finkelstein, Tzvi Shir, Salomon M. Stemmer, and Ran D. Balicer, "Why Is End of Life Spending So High? Evidence from Cancer Patients," *Review of Economics and Statistics* (July 9, 2021), doi.org/10.1162/rest_a_01066.

trative costs—that catchall term for the nonclinical costs of running a health-care system—which are also substantially higher than in other countries? And behind door number three: Eliminate unnecessary care. This one's a no-brainer—the name says it all.

And yet here we are, saying there's no easy way to reduce that waste. Surely we can't be serious! But we are. (And don't call us Shirley.) The catch is that each of these three big buckets of cut-waste-quick schemes would also reduce patients' access to medical care.

Cutting prices is a sure way to save money. That's incontrovertible. But so too is the large body of evidence that when physicians are paid less, patients get less care. And when drug prices are lower, fewer new drugs are developed. That's not to say we should accept paying through the nose for medical care. But we need to be aware that there are consequences to patients of not doing so.

Or consider administrative costs. Proponents of "Medicare for all" and other single-payer programs like to point to the fact that administrative costs in Medicare are only 1 to 2 percent of total medical spending, compared with 10 to 20 percent for commercial health insurance spending. Those numbers are correct. But what goes unmentioned is that one of the ways Medicare achieves lower administrative costs is by doing, well, less administering, as we discussed in chapter 10. Some of that may be a good thing; less administering can mean less hassle for patients and physicians to get the medical care the patient needs. But some of that red tape may serve a useful purpose. By making patients and their doctors think twice before ordering expensive and potentially unwarranted medical care, it may help reduce waste in the health-care system.

Which brings us to eliminating unnecessary care—care that costs money without delivering much or any benefit for patients. Unfortunately, a large body of evidence indicates that the tools we currently have at our disposal tend to throw the baby out with the bathwater—cutting high-value and low-value care alike. One reason is that physicians and regulators have already eliminated many demonstrably harmful or useless treatments. Patients are no longer offered patent medicines, routine bloodlettings, or lobotomies. It's true that ordering a CT scan for a patient the first time she complains of a nondescript headache is generally not a wise move. Neither is getting married after a first date. But occasionally that unnecessary scan catches a life-threatening problem before it's too late, and, once in a while, a whirlwind marriage leads to happily ever after. Unlikely isn't the same as never, which can make it hard for a well-intentioned physician or a hopeless romantic to resist. This is likely why, as we discussed in chapter 10, the evidence on "gatekeeping" suggests that it is a mixed bag, reducing spending but also lowering patient satisfaction.

It's also likely why medical care in most other high-income countries around the world is frequently described as rife with waste. One study estimated that, across high-income countries, about a fifth of health-care spending makes "no or minimal contribution to good health outcomes." Poorly coordinated care for patients with chronic diseases. Emergency room visits that could have been prevented with effective and accessible primary care. Preventable medical mistakes and infections that endanger patient health and increase hospital spending. Unnecessary tests and imaging. Overdiagnosis and overtreatment of diseases. And the list goes on. It's not just the US.

The absence of a holy grail for eliminating the substantial waste in health care—both at home and abroad—doesn't mean that we have to passively accept the unacceptable status quo. While we wait for the miracle cure, researchers have already identified a number of specific, identifiable small pockets of waste, and actionable steps that can be taken to surgically excise them. This type of incremental, evidence-based approach to reducing waste in US health care is similar in spirit to the approach that economist Esther Duflo has advocated for working toward alleviating global poverty, another pressing problem that defies facile solutions. Duflo used the term "plumbing"—going in and checking the taps, plugging the leaks—to describe the practical, small-step-by-small-step approach to reducing poverty that won her and her collaborators the 2019 Nobel Prize in economics.

We have no doubt that the US health-care sector could likewise benefit from the decidedly important but unglamorous work of "health-care plumbing." Indeed, we've discovered—and advocated for—one specific example of such plumbing: getting rid of an arcane, and idiosyncratically American, health-care institution called a "long-term-care hospital." These are hospitals whose patients tend to stay for a very long time, and are therefore paid more by Medicare than typical hospitals. They began as a regulatory carve out for a few dozen specialty hospitals in the early 1980s, but quickly turned into a profitable regulatory loophole large enough to drive hundreds of hospitals through. We've estimated that these hundreds of hospitals provide no measurable benefits to patients but cost the taxpayer an additional $5 billion per year. A prime candidate for some health-care plumbing.

This is not the only leak that can be plugged. A collection of health economists have compiled evidence on more than a dozen specific policy reforms that could each, individually, cut a small amount of spending without harm to patients. But we're also realistic. Even a dozen such repairs would make scarcely a dent in the $4 trillion of annual health-care spending.

—————

Our incremental approach to improving health-care delivery may seem jarring when contrasted with our approach to health insurance coverage. There, we're advocating for tearing down the existing "system" and building an entirely new system, de novo. Yet for health-care delivery, we're urging the kind of small, targeted solutions that have failed to address the fundamental problems with health coverage (recall chapter 3).

The explanation is simple. We don't yet know how to build a brand-new, solid delivery system that generates more benefits at lower cost. So it makes sense to try to at least plug the leaks that we can.

In a strange way, this bad news on the health-care spending front is also good news for universal coverage. The main drivers of health-care spending are not about how much insurance coverage people have, but about how much is paid for that care, and what guardrails are put on the choices patients and providers make. We don't in fact have to tackle the two issues at the same time. Universal coverage can—and should—be separated from health-care delivery reform.

At the same time, the realization that the major ways to rein in medical spending have consequences for the patient experience means that for the vast majority of the currently insured—that is, most Americans—basic coverage would be a step down. Not in what is covered. As we've emphasized, that wouldn't noticeably change. But covered care would likely come with longer waits for doctor appointments, more patients in a hospital room, worse hospital food and temperature control, and more hoops to jump through to see a specialist or to get the treatment of the patient's (or their doctor's) choice.

It wouldn't be all downside for the currently insured. Basic coverage would provide the certainty of continued coverage that the insured currently lack (see chapter 1). It would also eliminate the risk of crushing medical bills that many of the insured face (see chapter 2). Still, let's not kid ourselves: if you're one of the 60 million people on Medicare, or the 150 million people fortunate enough to have health insurance through an employer, basic coverage would in many respects be a lot more, well, basic.

Which is why some will want to upgrade their coverage beyond the basic. And that's why a sensible design for allowing people to buy supplemental coverage is also a key element of our proposal. We'll turn to that now.

Beyond Basic

Designing supplemental insurance

I n the late-1990s movie *As Good as It Gets*, Jack Nicholson plays a successful Manhattan writer with an obsessive-compulsive disorder who falls for a coffee shop waitress played by Helen Hunt. When the uncontrolled asthma of Hunt's son threatens to disrupt Nicholson's carefully ordered daily routine, Nicholson arranges for a physician house call.

Accompanied by his nurse, the doctor examines the boy in his bedroom, draws blood to run some tests, informs an incredulous Hunt that her son's lab results will be back later that day, and then sits down at the kitchen table to dispense medical advice. In the coup de grâce, he leaves his home number for Hunt to call if she has any further questions. This solicitous and effective medical treatment prompts Hunt to curse out the "f*ing HMO bastard piece of shit" insurance she has been working with to date, an Oscar-winning performance that we've already alluded to in chapter 10.

Hollywood's depiction of "dream coverage" clearly takes a few artistic liberties. "Did you know there are doctors who come to your house?" the little boy asks his mother with joy. "Not in the late twentieth century!" the health economist watching the movie wants to shout.

But the scene nevertheless encapsulates the ideal of high-end health care. Easy and rapid access to any doctor a patient might want, and to any test or treatment the physician (or patient) might dream up. All occurring in a setting that is convenient and comfortable for the patient. One imagines that if Hunt's son ever has to go to the hospital, he would be installed in a private, light-filled room, with plush carpeting, high-speed internet, and fresh-squeezed orange juice.

These types of upgrades—in kind if not in degree—are exactly the purpose of supplemental coverage, both as envisioned in our blueprint and as experienced in many high-income countries (recall chapter 10). The experiences of these countries—not to mention decades of economics research—have a lot to teach us about how to design this supplemental coverage. One clear lesson: people should be allowed to purchase an upgrade *on top of* existing basic coverage, rather than *instead of* that basic coverage.

HOW TO PAY FOR AN UPGRADE

Consider the contrasting cases of Singapore and the United Kingdom. In both countries, people can buy upgrades to the basic coverage. In both countries, these upgrades allow for greater choice of physician, better amenities—such as private hospital rooms with better food and ventilation—and faster access to care. But there's a crucial difference between these ostensibly similar arrangements. It relates to what people have to pay for that upgrade.

In Singapore, the upgrade is sold by the same insurers that provide the basic coverage; the additional amount the person has to pay for the upgrade reflects the additional cost of the additional benefits she will receive (plus perhaps a bit of a profit margin for the insurer). In the UK, however, one can't simply "upgrade" from the basic coverage. Instead, someone who wants more than what basic coverage provides must buy an entirely separate policy that pays for the entire cost of care—both the care that would have been provided by the universal system as well as the desired additions. For example, although the NHS will pay for cataract surgery with a standard lens implant, patients who prefer a special lens cannot simply have the NHS-funded operation and pay extra for the "upgrade" on the lens. They must pay for both the operation and the implants through private treatment. This is the same approach that the US uses when it comes to paying for private primary or secondary school. Parents who opt in to private schooling have to pay the whole cost of schooling, not just the incremental cost of the private school above and beyond what taxpayers would have spent to educate their child in the public school.

To see why the UK approach is problematic ("inefficient" in econspeak), let's explore a concrete example. Consider a patient with multiple sclerosis (MS), a disabling disease that affects the central nervous system. Most patients have a form of the disease known as relapsing remitting MS, in which patients experience an onset of symptoms (relapse) followed by a recovery (remission). It's the disease that President Jed Bartlet initially hid from the American public on the show *The West Wing*. There are a number of effective drugs available that reduce the frequency and severity of relapses. These were initially only available in injectable form. The patient had to go to a hospital several times a year to get an injection, or to self-inject at much higher frequency (sometimes daily). More recently, oral versions of these drugs have been approved. Some patients prefer the oral form because they find traveling to a hospital clinic onerous and the self-injections difficult to administer.

But the NHS doesn't cover the new oral drug. In 2021, NICE (which we encountered previously in chapter 11) judged that it was not cost-effective; the benefits from the oral medication were not worth the extra expense. As a result, an English patient with relapsing remitting MS faced a choice between receiving the injectable drug (Avonex) for free, or paying the full cost of about £1,400 per month for the new oral drug (Zeposia). She did not have the option—as she would in a Singapore-style system—of applying the amount that the NHS would have otherwise paid for injectable Avonex (about £650 per month) toward the cost of oral Zeposia. In Singapore, in other words, a patient would have to pay only the £750 difference in cost between the covered and uncovered drug, rather than the full £1,400 cost.

Some patients may be willing to pay the additional £750 cost for the oral alternative to the injectable drug, but not the full £1,400 cost of the oral drug. These patients will be worse off under the UK system than the Singapore system, even though government spending would be the same for these patients under both systems.*

The UK is not alone in making these kinds of take-it-or-leave-it health-care offers. Medicaid coverage for low-income individuals in the US operates similarly. By law, individuals cannot pay to "upgrade"

---

*In the Singapore system, the government will pay £650 toward the drug, and patients then either get the injectable drug for free or pay an additional £750 for the oral version. Those who choose to spend £750 to "top up" are doing so because they prefer that to getting the injectable drug for free. By contrast, under the UK approach, because anyone who wants the more expensive oral drug must pay its full cost (of £1,400), these same patients stick with the injectable drug. Government spending on these patients is the same, but they are worse off. They do not get their preferred type of treatment for their disease.

Medicaid; they cannot, for example, offer to pay a physician something extra to enhance the infamously low Medicaid fees. Individuals must either take Medicaid coverage "as is," or pay the full cost for a more generous private insurance policy. The result is that, perversely, some low-income individuals have reduced their insurance coverage when they become eligible for Medicaid.

We know this because of the evidence of what transpired when eligibility for Medicaid and other free, public health insurance programs gradually expanded, starting in the 1980s. A number of specific demographic groups gained eligibility, including kids of older ages and somewhat higher incomes, as well as many previously ineligible low-income adults. Two things happened as a result. First, as intended, many previously uninsured individuals enrolled in Medicaid and gained insurance coverage. These were people who hadn't been able to afford the private insurance. That was the purpose of expanding eligibility.

But, second, something unintended happened as well: a notable number of newly eligible individuals reduced the amount of insurance coverage they had, switching from private insurance to Medicaid. When their only option was to buy private insurance or to be uninsured, they chose to buy the private coverage. But now they had the option of getting a more limited, public health insurance policy for free. For many, it was no longer worth it to pay the full price for private health insurance. They thus dropped their private coverage and enrolled in free public coverage instead. In other words, they downgraded. And that's a problem. For the same reason it's a problem in the UK when people who would prefer to pay the additional cost for an oral MS drug go for the free injectable drug instead.

There's a better way to go. One in which the basic coverage continues to pay what it normally would, and individuals who buy supplementary coverage have to pay for only the *additional* costs incurred by that coverage. It's the Singapore way. It's also the approach taken by a number of other countries as well, including the Netherlands, Germany, and Israel. And, as we'll now see, it's the approach the US has used—with considerable success—in its other major public health insurance program: Medicare.

WHEN THE PRICE IS ALMOST RIGHT

Here are two of the better-kept health policy secrets rolled into one: Medicare has already been privatized, and the much-debated "public option"—the idea of a government-run health insurance agency that competes with private health insurers—already exists. In 2019, over one third of Medicare enrollees were in private Medicare, otherwise known as Medicare Advantage. Private Medicare must provide all the benefits in the public Medicare plan, and can also offer additional benefits.

The Medicare eligible make their choice of whether or not to enroll in private Medicare under a Singapore-like system. If they enroll in private Medicare, they have to pay only for the additional coverage, over and above the basic option. Here's how this works in practice: the private insurer assumes responsibility for all of the basic Medicare benefits, and the government pays the private insurer what it would have cost the taxpayer to cover the enrollee with the public Medicare plan. In other words, the Medicare eligible effectively get a voucher— to use a politically charged term. This "voucher" can pay for their public Medicare in its entirety, or it can be used toward paying for a private Medicare plan.

This private Medicare option has been around since the early 1980s, but enrollment was relatively modest until reforms in the aughts that encouraged its growth. Along with that rise in enrollment came a rise in research on private Medicare. The result is that we now have almost two decades of real-world experience as well as academic research (including some of our own) on how this Singapore-style system functions. Over sixty million Americans—almost one fifth of the country—are currently experiencing the approach we are advocating for supplemental coverage. And what all that experience and research teaches us is that the system works pretty well. That's not to say it is perfect. It has some very real problems. But it also has some fairly decent solutions.

One of the problems with this kind of "upgrade" system is that the government may end up paying private firms more than it intended to—and more than it would have paid itself—to provide basic coverage. This can happen if the people who enroll in the private plans are healthier—and therefore have lower medical expenses—than those who remain with only basic coverage. As a result, the government can end up overpaying private insurers to provide basic coverage. This can happen even if the government's payment to private insurers is lower than the average cost of an enrollee in basic coverage. That's because those who leave the basic coverage for the private coverage are not average. They are in fact below average in their medical costs, and would have cost the government substantially less than typical enrollees if they'd continued to be covered by the public option.

The experiences with private Medicare teach us about these dangers, and also about their remedies. Private insurers do manage to enroll customers who cost less to cover than the typical Medicare enrollee. Customers who are less likely to make frequent trips to the doctor or end up in the hospital than the typical Medicare enrollee. How do insurers manage to attract these more profitable customers? It isn't through mere happenstance, that's for sure. It is the result of their deliberate efforts. We could write a whole separate book on this. In fact, we already have.* We'll just treat you to some of the highlights here.

There are both obvious and less obvious strategies that insurers use to attract cheaper customers, and private Medicare insurers successfully use both types. An obvious strategy is to offer coverage only to customers who look like they will be low cost to cover. A person who is obese and suffering from diabetes and hypertension will be more expensive to cover than an avid jogger with no preexisting medical conditions. Insurers can look at a customer's current medical records before offering to enroll them. A less obvious—but common—strategy is to design the private insurance to appeal to the healthier customers and not to the sicker ones. Throw in a perk of a free gym membership, for example. It turns out that's an effective way to attract the healthy and spry enrollees—who at least can tell themselves they will really use that membership—rather than those with multiple health problems.

This problem is not unique to health care. The government faces the same issue, for example, when it comes to paying charter schools— an alternative form of public schools—for enrolling students who would otherwise be in traditional public schools. Some students—for example those with additional needs—are more expensive to educate. So charter schools often work to avoid enrolling such students.

You might think that the solution is simple: the government should just lower the amount it pays private insurers to provide basic Medicare. This seems only fair, because the private insurers' enrollees are

---

*Liran Einav, Amy Finkelstein, and Ray Fisman, *Risky Business: Why Insurance Markets Fail and What to Do about It* (New Haven, CT: Yale University Press, 2023).

healthier, and therefore less expensive to cover, than a typical public Medicare enrollee. Unfortunately, that won't cut it. If the government lowered the payment to private insurers, private insurers would simply be even more selective in whom they cover, in order to enroll only those people whose medical expenses are likely to be below the new, lower payment rate. The payment rate could be lowered again, but by this point you can probably guess what would happen. Round and round we'd go, until the problem of private Medicare customers being cheaper than what private insurers are paid to cover them is "solved" by driving everyone out of the private market.

Fortunately, there are other tools the government can deploy to try to keep private firms from serving only the cheapest-to-serve customers. And as private Medicare became an increasingly large and important part of the overall Medicare program over the last two decades, the government stepped up its game and deployed some of these tools.

For example, the government started customizing the payment to a private insurer based on the enrollee's medical history. It used to be that the government paid the insurer the same amount for enrollees of the same age and gender who lived in the same place. An insurer would get the same payment for enrolling two eighty-year-old Miami women, even if one was obese, had diabetes and high blood pressure, and spent her days channel surfing, while the other had no preexisting medical problems, was trim and fit, and diligently attended a weekly aqua aerobics class. Now, however, the insurer is paid less to enroll the healthier customer.

Payments that are tailored to the customer's health can go a long way toward reducing the selection problem, but they are unlikely to ever get rid of it entirely. That's because the insurer can design its plan to appeal to people who are healthier in ways that neither they nor the government can observe. For example, imagine two elderly individuals—Peter and Paul—of the same age, in the same town, with the same medical conditions. Peter may in fact be quite active—constantly going out for power walks and moving happily without any pain. He also knows his parents lived to a ripe old age. Paul may be more sedentary, and experiencing more aches and pains in the old joints when he tries to move about. He's also starting to worry about whether there's a lump in his abdomen, especially because both his parents died relatively young from cancer. Neither the government nor the insurer has an easy way to observe this directly—on paper, the two men look the same: the same weight and height, the same mild hypertension. But Paul is more likely than Peter to be put off from enrolling if the plan requires referrals to see specialists and also restricts which doctors he can see. He's worried he may want to go see someone soon about his joint pain and that aching lump. And if the private insurer throws in a gym membership discount as part of its insurance plan, Peter is going to be more likely to be enticed by that to enroll than Paul. Peter is also going to be cheaper to cover than Paul, not *because* Peter goes to the gym, but simply because he is active enough that he can delude himself into thinking he would.

Therefore, another tool the government uses is to limit people's opportunities to switch between public and private Medicare. People used to be able to switch between private and public Medicare every month if they wanted. Now, they can do so only during a fixed open enrollment period each fall and then are locked into their choice for the entire calendar year. What this means is that a healthy customer who chooses private Medicare for its gym membership can no longer switch out when they get an unexpected diagnosis or start to experience joint pain, and suddenly care a lot less about fitness and a lot more about their choice of doctor. (Ever wondered why your employer lets you change your health insurance plan only once a year in the fall? It's for the same reason—they don't want you to be able to wait till you get sick to switch to a more comprehensive health insurance plan.)

It's not perfect. Private Medicare enrollees are still somewhat healthier than public Medicare enrollees who "look the same" based on demographics and health conditions. Liran and his collaborators have estimated that even with all these adjustments, private Medicare enrollees are still about 1.5 percent healthier—as measured by their expected medical expenses—than public Medicare enrollees. As a result, private insurers are able to make a nice profit—which is presumably why they continue to exist.

But we're not striving for perfection. In the end, the government's payment system for the private Medicare market works pretty well. Which may be why it has mostly flown under the radar, despite its substantial size. Outside of health policy circles, most people don't realize that two fifths of Medicare enrollees have exercised their option to leave the public system.

DRIVEN TO TIERS

A much bigger danger with supplemental insurance is the possibility that its existence will erode the basic coverage to the point where it is no longer fulfilling our social contract. This danger lurks regardless of whether the pricing of that supplemental insurance follows the approach we advocate for (à la Singapore or Medicare) or the one we caution against (à la the UK or Medicaid).

And it is why about half of Canadian provinces outlaw supplemental coverage that pays for "better" versions of what the basic coverage already pays for—paying to "jump the queue" for hip surgery, for example, or to have the surgery performed by your first-choice surgeon.

This is one of the key purposes of supplementary coverage in many countries, including the UK, Germany, Israel, Singapore, and Australia, to name a few. The other key purpose is to pay for care that is not included in basic coverage, such as dental care, or private or semiprivate hospital rooms. Canadians have no issue with this type of upgrade. In fact, almost all the provincial governments actively encourage that kind of supplemental insurance through tax subsidies, and about two thirds of Canadians have this coverage.

There's an important difference between supplementary coverage that has no interaction with the basic universal system—such as coverage for a private hospital room—and so-called duplicative coverage that pays for a more attractive version of what the basic system would pay for—such as a shorter wait time for hip surgery. After the universally covered hip surgery, a patient can be wheeled into a private room in Canada without having any impact on the cost of the hip surgery itself, or on the surgeons who provide it. But this may not be true if the private alternative offers a shorter wait time—or first choice of physician—for that hip surgery.

Concerned Canadians can point to many Latin American countries as cautionary tales of what allowing "duplicative" supplementary coverage can mean. Many of these countries have publicly funded universal health-care systems that are chronically underfunded and widely considered inadequate. As a result, the better off buy into an entirely separate private system, a situation that some have likened to "medical apartheid." When Liran's mother broke her femur during a family vacation in southern Argentina, the paramedics on the scene made it clear to Liran that he shouldn't try a repeat of his successful Xi'an approach of going to the local public hospital when a family member needed medical treatment (see chapter 10). In Argentina, the local public hospital would not provide adequate medical care; he should go to a private clinic.

All of this raises an important chicken-or-egg question. Do those who choose to avoid the public system do so *because* it offers substandard medical care? Or has this avoidance itself been a prime *cause* of the poor quality of basic coverage? Either is plausible. Allowing people to "buy out" of the universal basic system can adversely affect it.

Some of the potentially adverse impacts on the basic system are economic in nature. The supplementary system may pay physicians and other medical providers more in order to attract some of the best doctors and reduce wait times. And that can mean fewer doctors—or fewer of the best doctors—in the basic system. Of course, medical care is not in fixed supply. Existing doctors and other medical professionals may choose to work longer hours if the price is high enough, but there are limits to the number of hours in the day, even for a surgeon. More people may enter the medical profession if it is more lucrative, but such responses are not instantaneous.

Other sources of danger to the basic system are political. If more and more of the wealthier patients opt for private coverage, leaving the universal system to the poorest, this can erode political support for the requisite public funding of the basic system. Private schools create a similar set of concerns for the adequacy of public schools.

Together, these economic and political forces can leave the basic system struggling to care for some of the most difficult and complex patients, without some of the best physicians and other medical providers, and with dwindling financial resources. Such concerns loomed large in a landmark 2005 Canadian court case over whether Quebec could outlaw private insurance for care that was also provided by the public, universal system. The case, *Chaoulli v. Quebec*, centered on a man in his sixties, George Zeliotis, who had had to wait almost a year for hip surgery through the public system. In 1997, Zeliotis teamed up with a Quebec physician named Jacques Chaoulli to challenge the restriction on private insurance in court. They argued that Zeliotis's yearlong delay for hip surgery had caused great suffering, and therefore Quebec's legal prohibition on the purchase of private insurance for hip surgery was in violation of Zeliotis's right to be "free from physical, mental or psychological harm." Ironically, it took eight years for Zeliotis to get his case adjudicated.

The Quebec government argued in its defense that its prohibition on supplemental insurance was necessary to "preserve the integrity of the public system." Allowing for a parallel private system, it argued, would divert both doctors and resources away from the public system and ultimately harm the quality of public care. The result would be a dreaded two-tier system, in which those who could not afford private care would experience longer wait times and lower-quality care than they did before the introduction of a private alternative.

The Supreme Court of Canada ruled against Quebec. It found that if the wait time for a procedure was "too long," the prohibition on the purchase of private insurance violated the Quebec Charter on Human Rights and Freedoms.* It did not specify how long was "too long," but the following year the Quebec government enacted a bill allowing for

---

*The court ruled 4–3 that the prohibition violated the Quebec Charter of Human Rights and Freedoms, but split (a 3–3 ruling with one abstention) on the question of whether it violated the Canadian Charter of Rights and Freedoms. As a result, the ruling did not have legal implications for the other provinces. Indeed, both Ontario and Alberta subsequently upheld the prohibition. Sierra Dean, "Canada's Landmark Chaoulli Decision: A Vital Blueprint for Change in the Canadian Health Care System," *Law and Business Review of the Americas* 13, no. 2 (2007): 417; Christopher P. Manfredi and Antonia Maioni, "The Last Line of Defence for Citizens: Litigating Private Health Insurance in *Chaoulli v. Québec*," in "Symposium on Chaoulli," ed. Bruce Ryder, special issue, *Osgoode Hall Law Journal* 44, no. 2 (Summer 2006): 249; and Amélie Quesnel-Vallée, Richard A. McKay, and Noushon Farmanara, "*Chaoulli v Quebec*: Cause or Symptom of Quebec Health System Privatization?," in *Is Two-Tier Health Care the Future?*, ed. Colleen M. Flood and Bryan Thomas ([Ottawa, ON]: University of Ottawa Press, 2020), 93–122.

the purchase of private insurance for three specific procedures—hip, knee, and cataract surgeries. In subsequent years it expanded the list of procedures that could be covered by private insurance.

Quebec lost its case, but its fears proved unfounded. A decade after the landmark case, there was no indication this ruling had eroded the quality of the public system. Indeed, duplicative private insurance remained extremely rare, as did the use of private care for publicly covered services.

The supplementary system need not remain small for the universal basic system to remain unharmed. In Australia, about half of the people purchase supplementary insurance. In Singapore, two thirds of the population does so. Yet, in both cases, coverage under the basic system remains excellent, and many people with supplementary insurance continue to use the basic system, especially for nonelective procedures. In Singapore, for example, although the majority of the population has private insurance, about 70 to 80 percent of hospital stays are still delivered through the public system.

Far from being concerned about potential negative impacts of private insurance on the basic system, the Australian government has explicitly encouraged private health insurance purchases as a way to reduce strain on the public system. It offers tax subsidies to low-income groups to purchase private insurance, and imposes tax penalties for individuals above a certain income level if they do not. Likewise, government policy in the US has actively encouraged the growth of the private Medicare system. One reason to encourage supplementary insurance is that it may pay higher prices to doctors and hospitals than the basic insurance does. Indeed, a common argument—sometimes voiced as a complaint—is that private insurance in the US helps "pay for" the care of publicly insured and uninsured patients. We are still waiting for the research that may support that hypothesis, but it—and the actions of the US and Australian governments—certainly raises the possibility that a supplementary system can strengthen and support the basic one.

That's not to say that the concerns of the Quebec government were unfounded. Recent experiences in Israel provide a cautionary tale for how allowing duplicative supplementary coverage can undermine the adequacy of the basic coverage. Since 1995, Israel has had universal basic coverage, and has also allowed people to purchase supplementary insurance. That supplementary insurance can cover services the basic system does not, such as dental and vision, as well as "duplicative" services, such as more choice for your surgeon or shorter wait times for surgery. By the early 2010s, it had become clear that the standard of care provided by the basic system had been eroded beyond what was acceptable. For example, more than a quarter of patients with basic coverage experienced wait times of over a month for a primary care appointment. Wait times were even longer for specialist care and elective surgeries.

A government committee was formed to investigate and address concerns about the inadequacy of basic coverage. It concluded that the growth of supplementary coverage—which over 80 percent of the population had—was an important cause, eroding the finances of the basic system as well as public support for that financing. It was just what the Quebec government had feared.

We don't pretend to know the exact ingredients of the "secret sauce" that has allowed Australia, Singapore, and Quebec to stave off the problems that supplemental coverage in Israel created for the basic coverage. But fortunately, we don't have to. For the Israeli experience also underscored that when these problems materialize, there are some rather straightforward government solutions.

One is to increase funding for the basic system. Indeed, the government committee in Israel concluded that a big source of the problem was that the budget for the basic system had not kept up with the growth in health-care costs. This was part of what was driving people into the supplemental system. To remedy this, the Ministry of Health and Ministry of Finance agreed to a onetime increase in funding to restore the level of support, as well as a commitment to more appropriate indexing of funding going forward. The extra resources were put toward the basic public system: increasing the resources for community health-care clinics, emergency rooms, and hospitals; reducing wait times; and expanding training programs for doctors and nurses. Not surprisingly, maintaining adequate funding for the basic system is essential to ensure that the basic coverage remains adequate.

The government committee also proposed new financial and professional incentives for physicians to work full time in the public system, rather than splitting their time between the public and the private system. The UK had already enacted something similar, requiring physicians who want to work for the public system to work at least forty hours a week in that system before they do any private consulting.

———

In other words, basic coverage must be adequately funded and physicians sufficiently incentivized to provide care. But this is true regardless of whether supplementary coverage is allowed. As long as we continue monitoring the fulfillment of our social contract with respect to basic coverage, and respond when cracks appear, having a free and active market for supplemental coverage can nicely complement—and perhaps even benefit—the basic system. It's not rocket science. It's basic economics.

Taking stock

This book is our attempt to develop and articulate a considered response to the $4 trillion question: how can we fix the US health-care system? We're pleased that we now have an answer. We'll no longer have to duck and equivocate when we get that inevitable question from Amy's father-in-law, or from our token noneconomist friends.

Our answer can't be summarized by the kind of slogans that the typical cocktail party interlocutor seems to want—sound bites like "single-payer health care" or "free markets." We're not unduly concerned; we don't get invited to many such parties anyway.

It's not that we can't summarize our proposal succinctly. We can. Automatic, basic universal coverage for everyone, along with the option to buy additional, supplemental coverage. But this simple summary isn't enough. You can't embrace—or critique—our blueprint without first engaging in its remit. It constantly amazes and dismays us that most discussions about health insurance reform don't begin with articulating—and perhaps arguing over—the *reason* for policy in the first place. No wonder there's so much confusion and contention.

We've concluded that the key reason for health insurance reform is our personal and policy tendency to come to the aid of those who are critically ill and unable to afford their essential medical care. We described some of the psychological and philosophical origins of this impulse, but we also emphasized that you do not need to agree that this is how people should behave, or what policy should do. What is important is that this is how people *do* behave, and what US health-care policy *has* been trying—but failing—to do for over seventy years.

The haphazard policy patches we described in the first part of the book reflect attempts to fulfill our empirical social contract to provide medical care for those who need it and cannot afford it. Occasionally, these attempts have produced major reforms—health insurance coverage for groups deemed particularly "deserving," such as the elderly and the poor. More frequently, they have produced narrowly targeted policies aimed at "fixing" a particular coverage gap for a particular group whose problems have become politically salient at a particular moment. Whether broad-based or narrowly targeted, the patches always leave gaps at the seams. They aren't enough. They never can be.

Our health policy history to date has resembled a game of Whac-a-Mole. The moment we smash the mole down into one hole, he pokes his furry head out of another. The only way to finally fulfill our health-care commitments is to stop playing this game. Stop trying to patch and renovate the ramshackle, chaotically constructed health insurance policy house. Tear it down and build, from scratch, a brand-new edifice that finally gets it right.

Clarity of purpose elucidates the essential design elements of the brand-new home. Basic coverage must be provided automatically and without any premium payments, otherwise we won't achieve universal coverage. Basic medical care must be provided to patients for free, otherwise we'll end up back in the position of struggling to provide workarounds for people who cannot afford the out-of-pocket costs. Beyond that, however, basic coverage can be quite basic. Our social contract requires providing essential medical care to those who need it, but it is silent on the nature of nonessential medical care and nonmedical amenities.

For the thirty million Americans without formal insurance, basic coverage would be an improvement. It would provide reliable coverage of major medical needs without any costs to the patient—or attempts to collect costs from them. For the seventy million low-income Americans with Medicaid, basic coverage would be similar to the coverage they already have.

For the remaining two thirds of Americans, basic coverage would likely be worse on many—although not all—dimensions. We suspect that many of them would purchase supplementary insurance. This includes the one hundred fifty million Americans who have private health insurance and the sixty-five million elderly and disabled Americans with Medicare. For them, basic coverage would mean longer wait times, for example—along the lines of what those covered by Medicaid or the Veterans Affairs experience—and less well-apportioned waiting areas and hospital rooms. But on some dimensions basic coverage would be an improvement. No risk of losing coverage, and no need to mind those gaps in Medicare and private insurance coverage that we discussed in part I.

Automatic, universal basic coverage solves the problem we have been struggling with for decades: how to finally fulfill our health-care commitments in a sensible and efficient way. It does not, however, solve all problems with US health care. In particular, as we discussed in chapter 12, it does not tackle the problem of substantial waste in the health-care system, the large amounts of health-care spending that may produce little benefit. This is an important—and challenging— problem. It still needs to be solved. We continue to investigate the solutions in our academic research. But it is separate—and separable— from the problem that universal coverage is designed to solve.

We have also deliberately left unspecified many of the health policy debates that loom large in the public zeitgeist. Will basic coverage be provided through a single payer, or through multiple payers? Will basic coverage be provided by the public sector? Or will it be offered by private firms? Or perhaps by both in the so-called public option?

That's because we can fulfill our health-care commitments through a variety of answers to those questions. The experience of other countries makes this clear. Countries like the UK and Canada have a single-payer, public health insurance system,* akin to Medicare coverage for hospital and physician care in the US. Countries like Switzerland, Israel, and the Netherlands, however, provide universal basic coverage through multiple, private insurers, akin to Medicare coverage for prescription drugs in the US. Another thing that is clear: the "right" approach on these issues is far less clear than what the popular pundits— on either side—would have you believe. But that, as Kipling would say, is another story.

The experience of other countries provides another reassuring observation. Although we developed our proposal from first principles— by focusing on the problem that needs to be solved and what is essential

---

*More accurately, in the Canadian case there is a single public payer for each of its provinces and territories.

to that solution—we found that our blueprint does not require new institutions or mechanisms. No crazy new contraptions dreamed up on our blackboards and untested in the "real world."

The specifics of our proposal, however, can't be found lock, stock, and barrel in any existing country's system. They constitute a mix and match of particular aspects that, in our opinion, particular countries have managed to get right. Our insistence that patients be automatically covered and not pay anything for their covered care looks like the universal coverage programs in the UK and Canada, and very much unlike the programs in most other countries. But our advice on how to structure payments for the supplemental system is very different from the approach taken in the UK or Canada, to the extent that they allow such supplemental coverage at all. Rather, it is closer to the approach found in countries like Singapore, Israel, and Switzerland. These countries, however, also require substantial patient cost sharing in the basic coverage, something that we reject.

Closer to home, our proposal cannot accurately be described as "Medicare for all" nor as "Medicaid for all." But it does have elements of both. It would preserve the "upgrade" approach of the current Medicare program (see chapter 13), but basic coverage would involve restrictions on patient and physician choices, which the current Medicare program does not have (see chapter 10). These restrictions could make basic coverage closer to "Medicaid for all," but, unlike the current Medicaid program, people would be able to purchase upgrades without having to repurchase basic coverage.

Of course, a lot of daylight remains between a blueprint composed of existing elements and a newly constructed home. Chief among them is the elephant in the room (or more accurately the elephant and the donkey): the pesky politics of passing health-care reform.

"How can this ever happen politically?" is surely, by now, echoing from the peanut gallery. Indeed, most conversations about universal health insurance, including at those cocktail parties we aren't invited to, start by asking what we think we can do politically. It's presumably by now abundantly clear that we don't think that's the right place to start the conversation.

But we do think it's the right place to end, now that we've articulated what we *should* do.

Can it be built?

There's an old joke about health-care reform in the US. A leading advocate for universal coverage dies and goes to heaven. He is granted an audience with the Supreme Deity, who informs him that in return for a life well lived, he can ask God any question, and it will be answered.

The advocate asks, "God, will there ever be universal health insurance coverage in the United States?" God replies, "Yes. But not in my lifetime."

This cynicism about the chances for universal coverage has long existed, right alongside optimism that universal coverage is imminent. In 1916, the president of the American Medical Association—who was also the US surgeon general—prophesized that the spread of health insurance would be "the next great step in social legislation." In the early 1970s, "the feeling among experts was that we would have national health insurance by 1973." And in the early 1990s, the editor of the American Medical Association's flagship journal declared that "an aura of inevitability is upon us. It is no longer acceptable morally, ethically, or economically for so many of our people to be medically uninsured or seriously underinsured."

The famous saying has it that "revolution is impossible until it's inevitable." It has been variously—if apocryphally—attributed to Leon Trotsky, Rosa Luxemburg, and a few others who knew a thing or two about revolutions. Judging from the pundits, universal health care in the US has done revolution one better: it is simultaneously impossible and inevitable.

We've been on the receiving end of both views. In the fall of 2008, when Amy was trying to raise funds to study the impact of covering the uninsured through the Oregon health insurance lottery (see chapter 1), more than one prospective funder worried that understanding the consequences of lack of insurance would soon be irrelevant, because President Obama was about to enact universal coverage.* In early 2020, multiple prospective publishers for our book ruminated that by the time our book came out, President Biden would have likely already enacted universal coverage. Yet at the same time, multiple colleagues warned us of the reputational risk of tackling the "politically impossible" topic of universal coverage. We got it coming and going.

We have no particular expertise in predicting what will be politically possible—or impossible, or inevitable—and when. Even for the experts, politics is much less certain than death and taxes, and often as

*It was both comforting and disconcerting for Amy to learn from Joe Newhouse, who led the landmark RAND health insurance experiment we described in chapter 9, that he'd gotten similar comments from funders reviewing his RAND experiment proposals in the early 1970s.

hard to predict as the weather. And we're certainly no experts when it comes to politics.

That said, our reading of the historical record—both at home and abroad—leaves us sanguine about the possibilities for universal health care in the US. "No country has acquired national health insurance without a fierce and bitter political fight," the political scientist Jacob Hacker has observed. We won't go so far as to say that makes it inevitable that the US will get there, too, but we're confident it's not impossible either.

There is of course a popular narrative in which the US never had a chance at achieving universal coverage. We lacked a labor movement strong enough to push for it. We faced too strong an opposition from the powerful American Medical Association. The culture of rugged American individualism would never allow it. Incremental reforms such as coverage for the elderly and the poor effectively closed the door on more ambitious coverage goals. The list of explanations goes on and on.

But there's also another narrative out there. One that's less dramatic, and gets less attention, but is no less plausible. One in which several "near misses" suggest that—but for a quirk of fate—universal health insurance would have been adopted in the US at key junctures when other countries managed to do so. One in which enactment of universal coverage in other countries was also fiercely controversial, and had to overcome considerable obstacles, not dissimilar to the ones faced in the US. One in which everything is impossible, until it happens.

This narrative starts over a century ago, when a group of progressive reformers began to push for compulsory health insurance in the US, right after Britain succeeded in enacting compulsory health insurance for manual workers in 1911. This was decades before our neighbor to the north began to make a similar concerted effort. And the US re-formers almost succeeded. Their cause was taken up by national campaigns, including former president Teddy Roosevelt's 1912 bid to get back into the Oval Office, and by several state legislatures. New York got the closest in 1919, when a bill for compulsory health insurance was approved by the state senate, but failed to pass in the state assembly.

More near misses came a few decades later under President Truman, who tried both in 1945 and again in 1949 to enact national health insurance. His failed attempts occurred around the same time as a similarly unsuccessful effort in Canada to achieve national health insurance, and bracketed the successful enactment of universal coverage in Britain in 1948.

With the National Health Service now firmly entrenched as a beloved British institution, it's easy to forget its tumultuous—and by no means assured—origin. The British Medical Association (BMA) worked furiously to prevent the NHS from coming into existence. And when it lost that fight and the new system was only a few months away from taking effect, its physician members voted 10–1 against participating in the new program. One physician member declared— to cheers from his fellow doctors—that the plan would mean the "enslavement of the medical profession" and described the BMA's opposition as part of a "life and death struggle for our freedom and independence." Ultimately, when it came down to the wire, both sides blinked, just as was to happen two decades later with Medicare in the US. In the UK case, the government offered last-minute financial concessions that allowed doctors to practice privately rather than as salaried public servants, and the BMA didn't carry through with the threatened boycott.

Nor was it merely the government against the physicians. The two political parties also waged a fierce battle over whether to create universal coverage. Winston Churchill—the Tory leader and himself no stranger to difficult politics—later described it as "party antagonism as bitter as anything I have seen in my long life of political conflict." The Tories voted against the formation of the NHS on twenty-one separate occasions before the National Health Service Act was finally passed. The enactment was so contentious that on the evening before the NHS launch, Nye Bevan, the Labor health minister who had spearheaded its creation, publicly proclaimed his "deep burning hatred for the Tory party that inflicted those bitter experiences on me. So far as I am concerned, they are lower than vermin."

The idea that the creation of universal coverage in Britain in 1948 was the natural and predestined outgrowth of the postwar consensus is a gross misreading of history. As one leading scholar of the postwar British social policy wryly commented, "Whatever words may be used to describe th[e] train of events, 'consensus' is not one of them."

Universal coverage in Canada experienced a similar set of origin struggles. When Saskatchewan became the first province to introduce universal medical coverage in July 1962, its physicians—nearly a third of whom had left Britain to escape the NHS—went on strike. The strike lasted twenty-three days, with most physicians withholding all nonemergency services, and other doctors from the US and UK flying in to provide essential health care. That standoff also ended with concessions on both sides.

A few years later, when the Canadian federal government followed suit with universal medical coverage, it was opposed not only by the Canadian Medical Association and the Canadian Dental Association, but also by the private insurance industry, which was then providing health insurance to about half the population, the Canadian Chamber of Commerce, the pharmaceutical industry, and the Canadian

Manufacturers' Association, among others. Even after the federal government passed national health insurance in 1966, it was only fully implemented by all provinces in 1971, with the delay reflecting the fierce struggles involved in getting full provincial cooperation.

As the last of these Canadian provinces were implementing universal coverage in the early 1970s, the US experienced its nearest miss. We already encountered some of this history in chapter 9 when we described the competing Democrat and Republican proposals for universal coverage, and the debate between (Ted) Kennedy and Nixon over whether to include patient cost sharing. What wasn't up for debate at the time was universal coverage, which both parties supported.

Nixon made a concerted effort at universal coverage first in 1971 and then again in 1974. Some pundits believe that he was predisposed to favor universal coverage because of his own family's struggles with health problems; Nixon had two brothers who died from tuberculosis in childhood. Others take a more cynical view, arguing that his efforts were nothing more than a calculated political move, first to help with his 1972 reelection campaign and then to try to save a presidency engulfed in the Watergate scandal. Whatever his motives, Nixon's actions ushered in a short-lived period of bipartisan efforts to establish universal coverage. By the spring of 1974, Democrats in the Senate and in the House had cosponsored a proposal that had the tacit approval of the Nixon administration and that was successfully voted out of committee by the House Ways and Means Committee. Enactment of universal coverage felt inevitable.

There are various theories of what went wrong. One is that as the Nixon presidency lurched toward its ignominious end, liberals withdrew their support for the compromise proposal that had been voted out of committee, believing they would now be able to achieve something more ambitious. Another theory is rooted in scandal rather than strategy: progress toward passage was derailed when a key political supporter was publicly disgraced by an incident involving an illicit affair, inebriation, and a car crash.* Whatever the cause for delay, the opportunity was lost. By the next year, Nixon's price controls on the health-care sector had expired, and the nation was gripped by rising health-care costs as well as general stagflation. The enthusiasm for universal coverage had dimmed.

It is this reading of history—with near failures abroad and near misses at home—that convinced us that it was well worth our time and yours to lay out a solid blueprint for how to design a universal system. There are many paths for success. Now that we know what success looks like, we can start to pick our path. Like "surfers waiting for the right wave," in the famous words of political scientist John Kingdon, we can be ready when political fortunes next align to put universal coverage back on the political agenda, as it has been so many times over the last century, at both the national and state levels.

"Chance only favors the prepared mind," said Louis Pasteur, the great French microbiologist and chemist whose germ theory of disease ushered in the way for modern medicine at the end of the nineteenth century and created the modern need for health insurance as we now know it. It strikes us as fitting that Pasteur provides not only the genesis of the problem that this book tries to address but also the philosophy for its approach. We want to be ready when political fortunes align.

---

*For connoisseurs of the seamier side of American politics, we note that the politician involved was not Ted Kennedy. His eerily similar scandal occurred in 1969 on Martha's Vineyard. This one occurred in 1974, in Washington, DC, and involved the powerful Democratic chair of the House Ways and Means Committee, congressman Wilbur Mills.

In 1953, a British teenager working as a cowboy on a tropical cattle ranch in Guyana was bucked from a wild horse, trampled on, and crushed like "a human pancake." Stan Brock was over 350 miles—and a twenty-six-day trek—from the nearest doctor. Late in life, he could still vividly recall the "pain and fear that compounded [his] physical aches: the uncertainty of what would happen to [him] without access to medical care."

Decades later—after a career that included a brief stint as a movie star—Brock's near-death experience prompted him to found Remote Area Medical (RAM). Its aim was to bring temporary clinics to medically desolate areas of the world. Early forays included missions to Haiti, India, Kenya, and Guyana.

By this time, Brock had settled in eastern Tennessee. When his neighbors learned what he was up to, they urged him to focus closer to home, where millions of Americans were also suffering from lack of access to basic health care. Brock soon switched RAM's focus to providing pop-up medical clinics to underserved rural and urban areas within the United States. He has since passed away, but the organization he created lives on, providing free health-care services through pop-up clinics around the country. One of the largest of them has been held annually for over two decades in Wise, Virginia. Every year, over a three-day weekend in July, it serves several thousand patients who travel from more than fifteen states to receive free medical, vision, and dental care provided by volunteer clinicians.

Brock's youthful injury, his difficulty accessing needed medical care, and the profound impact that experience had on his life's work and the lives of millions of others bears a striking similarity to the story of another British émigré. In 1910, at the wee age of six, young

Tommy Douglas suffered a freak fall in Scotland that badly injured his knee.

Shortly thereafter, his family emigrated to Canada, and there they sought further medical care for Tommy's injury. The doctors treating him did not have the expertise to save his leg, and recommended amputation. The Douglas family could not afford other options that might not involve loss of limb. But by sheer luck, an orthopedic surgeon offered to operate on Tommy for free, in return for being able to use him in a surgical demonstration for his students. The operations were a success and Tommy's leg was saved.

Like Stan Brock, Tommy Douglas was moved by his experience to help others escape a similar fate. Struck by the role that luck had played in his care, he grew up determined that "no boy should have to depend either for his leg or his life upon the ability of his parents to raise enough money to bring a first-class surgeon to his bedside."

In 1947, as premier of the western Canadian province of Saskatchewan, Douglas pioneered the first, publicly funded universal hospital insurance in North America. In 1962, he doubled down with insurance for physicians as well, although not without some considerable pushback from those physicians, as we have just seen. In both cases, other provinces quickly followed his example, as did federal legislation making first hospital and then physician insurance universal throughout Canada, over a decade before Stan Brock founded his charitable organization.

Stan Brock and Tommy Douglas. Similar origins. Similar experiences. Similar impulses. Very different reactions. US charity care on the one hand, and Canadian national, universal health insurance on the other.

The contrasting endings of these similar tales can serve as a Rorschach test for people's intuitions about US health-care policy. Many may see it as an allegory for the impossibility of achieving universal health coverage in the US, and the inevitable need for charity care as a result. Others, perhaps fortified by our description of the near misses to achieving universal coverage in the US, may choose to see this story as yet one more example of a near miss in our attempts to achieve universal health insurance. If only Tommy had landed in Sacramento instead of in Saskatchewan.

We see something else entirely. We see yet more examples of the enduring and universal moral commitment to try to provide essential medical care for those in need. A commitment that the US, like every rich country, has always been on board with, but—unlike any other—has so far failed to fulfill. A commitment that is the function of universal health insurance, and that dictates its form. A form that we have now tried to provide. From the ground up. We've got you covered.

ACKNOWLEDGMENTS

Success has many fathers but failure is an orphan, as the old saying goes. It remains to be seen if anyone will acknowledge paternity for our book. But we do have many people to thank—without implicating—for their help and encouragement along the way.

Mark Cullen, Jeannie Suk Gersen, Emily Oster, and Emanuel Rosen read and provided helpful comments on our initial attempts to write a book proposal. We are particularly indebted to Emily for introducing us to our extraordinary agent, Margo Fleming. Margo provided invaluable advice throughout the process; the (good parts of the) finished product owe much to her suggestions and guidance. Above and beyond her substantive help, we are incredibly grateful for her ready availability, constant good humor, and impressive patience with our idiosyncrasies.

Our terrific editor, Merry Sun, was everything we had hoped and imagined an editor would be. She had the rare ability to provide clear and specific direction, while at the same time leaving us in control of the final product. We are very grateful for the time she took to read and comment on many drafts of the manuscript (and always within her promised time frame!). Her suggestions were always insightful and constructive. Early on, they helped us sharpen (and in some cases adjust) our argument. At later stages, her expositional suggestions and direct edits greatly improved the flow of the book.

A number of friends, family, and colleagues took the time to read and comment on the manuscript. We are extremely grateful to Gill Bejerano, Mark Cullen, Roni Einav, Rushika Fernandopulle, Alan Finkelstein, Joan Finkelstein, Jacob Glazer, Howard Glennerster, Jon Gruber, Bonnie Honig, Ben Jones, Jeff Liebman, Neale Mahoney, Greg Mankiw, Joe Newhouse, Ben Olken, Mark Olken, Pat Olken, Emanuel Rosen, Charles Rosenberg, Susan Sered, Mark Shepard, Jon Skinner, Jeannie Suk Gersen, and Kelvin Bryan Tan. Additional thanks go to Sarah Taubman for brainstorming with us the topic before we even knew it would become a book, and to Mani Honigstein for helping us procure the ITV video of *The Life and Death Game*.

A large number of research assistants provided invaluable help, educating us on new topic areas as well as tracking down hard-to-find facts. For their excellent work, as well as their much-appreciated good-natured attitude to our incessant follow-up questions and requests, we thank Fiona Chen, Brad Clark, Paul Friedrich, Kelsey Moran, Miray Omurtak, April Xu, and especially Lisa Turley Smith.

Liran thanks his wife, Shirit, and kids—Shiley, Yahli, and Libby—for always getting him covered. Amy thanks her husband, Ben, for always being on the side of truth, even when it's not in his strategic interest. And she thanks her children—Sam and Sarah—for modeling the kind of unconditional enthusiasm for her book that they would like her to provide for their own endeavors.

NOTES AND REFERENCES

PROLOGUE

viii **high health-care spending:** Dan Zeltzer, Liran Einav, Amy Finkelstein, Tzvi Shir, Salomon M. Stemmer, and Ran D. Balicer, "Why Is End-of-Life Spending So High? Evidence from Cancer Patients," *Review of Economics and Statistics* (July 9, 2021), doi.org/10.1162/rest_a_01066; and Liran Einav, Amy Finkelstein, Sendhil Mullainathan, and Ziad Obermeyer, "Predictive Modeling of U.S. Health Care Spending in Late Life," *Science* 360, no. 6396 (June 29, 2018): 1462–65.

viii **age at which women:** Liran Einav, Amy Finkelstein, Tamar Oostrom, Abigail Ostriker, and Heidi Williams, "Screening and Selection: The Case of Mammograms," *American Economic Review* 110, no. 12 (December 2020): 3836–70.

viii **market for pet health:** Liran Einav, Amy Finkelstein, and Atul Gupta, "Is American Pet Health Care (also) Uniquely Inefficient?," *American Economic Review* 107, no. 5 (May 2017): 491–95.

viii **demand for dental:** Liran Einav, Amy Finkelstein, Iuliana Pascu, and Mark R. Cullen, "How General Are Risk Preferences? Choices under Uncertainty in Different Domains," *American Economic Review* 102, no. 6 (October 2012): 2606–38.

INTRODUCTION: BREAKING GROUND

xiii **One familiar move:** There are two types of waivers that can be granted to expand disaster-specific coverage—a 1115 demonstration and a 1135 waiver. The type of waiver needed depends on the type of disaster, although both expand eligibility for health coverage and relax some of the application requirements. During the public health emergency from COVID-19, a 1135 waiver was implemented. For more information on these waivers, see: Centers for Medicare & Medicaid Services, "About Section 1115 Demonstrations," accessed May 5, 2022, medicaid.gov /medicaid/section-1115-demonstrations/about-section-1115-demonstrations /index.html; and Centers for Medicare & Medicaid Services, "1135 Waiver - at a Glance," CMS.gov, accessed May 5, 2022, cms.gov/Medicare/Provider-Enrollment -and-Certification/SurveyCertEmergPrep/Downloads/1135-Waivers-At-A -Glance.pdf.

xiii **New York had done:** New York used a Section 1115 demonstration to implement its Disaster Relief Medicaid program. For more information, see Katherine E. Finkelstein, "Disaster Gives the Uninsured Wider Access to Medicaid," *New York Times*, November 23, 2001, nytimes.com/2001/11/23/nyregion/disaster-gives-the -uninsured-wider-access-to-medicaid.html; Cornell University, School of Industrial and Labor Relations, Disaster Relief Medicaid Evaluation Project, December 2005, health.ny.gov/health_care/medicaid/related/docs/drm_report.pdf; and Michael Perry, New York's Disaster Relief Medicaid: Insights and Implications for Covering Low-Income People (Menlo Park, CA: Kaiser Commission on Medicaid and the Uninsured, Henry J. Kaiser Family Foundation, August 2002), files.kff.org /attachment/new-yorks-disaster-relief-medicaid-insights-and-implications-for -covering-low-income-people.

xiv **Louisiana after Hurricane Katrina:** Stephen Zuckerman and Jack Hadley, "Louisiana's Proposed Section 1115 Medicaid Demonstration Project: Estimating the Numbers of Uninsured and Projected Medicaid Costs" (issue paper, Kaiser Commission on Medicaid and the Uninsured, Henry J. Kaiser Family Foundation, Washington, DC, July 2007), kff.org/wp-content/uploads/2013/01/7669.pdf; and Centers for Medicare & Medicaid Services, "Medicaid Responds When Natural Emergencies Strike," Medicaid.gov, accessed May 5, 2022, medicaid.gov/about-us /program-history/medicaid-50th-anniversary/entry/47667.

xiv **Michigan during the Flint:** KFF, "Michigan's Medicaid Section 1115 Waiver to Address Effects of Lead Exposure in Flint," KFF, March 7, 2016, kff.org/medicaid /fact-sheet/michigans-medicaid-section-1115-waiver-to-address-effects-of-lead -exposure-in-flint.

xiv **Many low-income uninsured:** Munira Z. Gunja and Sara R. Collins, "Who Are the Remaining Uninsured, and Why Do They Lack Coverage?," Commonwealth Fund, August 28, 2019, doi.org/10.26099/h0xy-az24; and Louise Radnofsky, "Millions Eligible for Medicaid Go Without It," *Wall Street Journal*, January 31, 2016, wsj.com /articles/millions-eligible-for-medicaid-go-without-it-1454277166.

xiv **The federal government had made:** For more information on COBRA, the federal program that gives some workers who have lost their health benefits the right to pay to continue their previous coverage for a limited time, see US Department of Labor 2021 and Employee Benefits Security Administration 2011 and 2018. For information on how COBRA's requirements and deadlines were changed during COVID-19, see Rule 2020-09399. US Department of Labor, "Continuation of Health Coverage (COBRA)," accessed June 17, 2021, dol.gov/general/topic/health-plans /cobra; Employee Benefits Security Administration, "Fact Sheet: Celebrating 25 Years of COBRA," US Department of Labor, April 7, 2011, https://permanent .fdlp.gov/gpo10185/fsCOBRAanniversary.html; Employee Benefits Security Administration, An Employer's Guide to Group Health Continuation Coverage under COBRA (United States Department of Labor, October 2021), dol.gov/sites /dolgov/files/EBSA/about-ebsa/our-activities/resource-center/publications /an-employers-guide-to-group-health-continuation-coverage-under-cobra.pdf; and Rule 2020-09399, 85 Fed. Reg. 26351 (May 4, 2020).

xiv **The cost of that:** Gary Claxton, Matthew Rae, Anthony Damico, Gregory Young, Nisha Kurani, and Heidi Whitmore, "Health Benefits in 2021: Employer Programs Evolving in Response to the COVID-19 Pandemic," *Health Affairs* 40, no. 12 (December 2021): 1961–71.

xiv **Confronted with a brand-new:** For more information on the programs that would cover the costs of care specific to COVID-19, see Health Resources & Services Administration, "COVID-19 Claims Reimbursement to Health Care Providers and Facilities for Testing, Treatment, and Vaccine Administration for the Uninsured," HRSA, April 21, 2020, hrsa.gov/CovidUninsuredClaim; Karyn Schwartz and Jennifer Tolbert, "Limitations of the Program for Uninsured COVID-19 Patients Raise Concerns," KFF, October 8, 2020, kff.org/policy-watch/limitations-of-the -program-for-uninsured-covid-19-patients-raise-concerns; Families First Coronavirus Response Act, Pub. L. No. 116-127 (2020), congress.gov/bill/116th -congress/house-bill/6201; and American Rescue Plan Act of 2021, Pub. L. No. 117 –2 (2021), congress.gov/bill/117th-congress/house-bill/1319.

xiv **medical expenses of patients:** Michael Wysolmerski, Katie Garfield, Amy Rosenberg, and Robert Greenwald, "The Medicaid Tuberculosis Option: An Opportunity for Policy Reform" (issue brief, Center for Health Law and Policy Innovation, Harvard Law School, Jamaica Plain, MA, June 2015), chlpi.org /wp-content/uploads/2014/01/Issue-Brief-June-2015-The-Medicaid-Tuberculosis -Option.pdf.

xiv **breast and cervical cancer:** Andy Schneider, Risa Elias, and Rachel Garfield, "Chapter 1: Medicaid Eligibility" in *The Medicaid Resource Book* (Washington, DC: Kaiser Commission on Medicaid and the Uninsured, July 2002), kff.org/wp-content /uploads/2013/05/mrbeligibility.pdf.

xiv **Lou Gehrig's disease, end-stage:** Louise Norris, "Medicare Eligibility for ALS and ESRD Patients," Medicareresources.org, July 2, 2021, medicareresources.org /medicare-eligibility-and-enrollment/medicare-eligibility-for-als-and-esrd-patients; Social Security Administration, "President Signs S. 578, the 'ALS Disability Insurance Access Act of 2019,'" *Social Security Legislative Bulletin* no. 116-26, December 28, 2020, ssa.gov/legislation/legis_bulletin_122220.html; Centers for Medicare & Medicaid Services, "End-Stage Renal Disease (ESRD)," CMS.gov,

December 1, 2021, cms.gov/Medicare/Coordination-of-Benefits-and-Recovery /Coordination-of-Benefits-and-Recovery-Overview/End-Stage-Renal-Disease -ESRD/ESRD; and Richard A. Rettig, "Special Treatment—the Story of Medicare's ESRD Entitlement," *New England Journal of Medicine* 364, no. 7 (February 17, 2011): 596–98, doi.org/10.1056/NEJMp1014193.

xiv **HIV/AIDS:** Tom Engels, "HRSA Celebrates 30 Years of the Ryan White CARE Act," HIV.gov, August 18, 2020, hiv.gov/blog/hrsa-celebrates-30-years-ryan-white-care.act.

xiv **sickle cell anemia:** Victoria L. Elliott, *Maternal and Child Health Services Block Grant: Background and Funding* (Washington, DC: Congressional Research Service, August 28, 2017), fas.org/sgp/crs/misc/R44929.pdf; Health Resources & Services Administration, "Factsheet: Maternal and Child Health," HRSA, May 11, 2017, hrsa .gov/our-stories/maternal-child/factsheet.html; dfitzgerald, "Q & A: Medicaid Coverage for Sickle Cell Disease," National Health Law Program, July 23, 2013, healthlaw.org/resource/q-a-medicaid-coverage-for-sickle-cell-disease; and Kellie Moss, Lindsey Dawson, Michelle Long, Jennifer Kates, MaryBeth Musumeci, Juliette Cubanski, and Karen Pollitz, "The Families First Coronavirus Response Act: Summary of Key Provisions," KFF, March 23, 2020, kff.org/coronavirus-covid-19 /issue-brief/the-families-first-coronavirus-response-act-summary-of-key-provisions.

xv **John Druschitz experienced:** Sarah Kliff, "A $22,368 Bill That Dodged and Weaved to Find a Gap in America's Health System," *New York Times*, March 10, 2021, nytimes.com/2021/03/10/upshot/covid-bill-health-gap.html.

xvii **They invariably focus:** Katherine Keisler-Starkey and Lisa N. Bunch, *Health Insurance Coverage in the United States: 2019*, Current Population Reports, no. P60-271 (Washington, DC: US Government Publishing Office, September 2020), 26.

xvii **Indeed, along with one:** Neil Bennett, Jonathan Eggleston, Laryssa Mykyta, and Bryan Sullivan, "19% of U.S. Households Could Not Afford to Pay for Medical Care Right Away," United States Census Bureau, April 7, 2021, census.gov/library/stories /2021/04/who-had-medical-debt-in-united-states.html.

xviii **In the eighteenth century:** Adam Levinson, "Act for the Relief of Sick and Disabled Seamen," *Statutes and Stories* (blog), April 29, 2018, statutesandstories.com/blog _html/act-for-the-relief-of-sick-and-disabled-seamen; and Robert Straus, in *Medical Care for Seamen: The Origin of Public Medical Service in the United States*, vol. 1 (New Haven, CT: Yale University Press, 1950).

xx **Or, as the iconic:** *Borderline Medicine*, directed by Roger Weisberg (New York: PBS, December 17, 1990), Broadcast, pt. 55:35.

xxii **He argued that the role:** Milton Friedman, *Capitalism and Freedom*, 40th anniversary ed. (Chicago: University of Chicago Press, 2002), 14.

PART I: IT'S A TEARDOWN

1 **During the Democratic primary:** Margot Sanger-Katz and Tim Enthoven, "Is America's Health Care System a Fixer-Upper or a Teardown?," *New York Times*, September 19, 2019, nytimes.com/2019/09/19/upshot/health-care-home-metaphor.html.

CHAPTER 1: POOR DESIGN

3 **We are the only major:** Jon Greenberg, "Bernie Sanders: U.S. 'Only Major Country' That Doesn't Guarantee Right to Health Care," PolitiFact, June 29, 2015, politifact .com/factchecks/2015/jun/29/bernie-sanders/bernie-sanders-us-only-major -country-doesnt-guaran.

3 **The eminent economist:** Irving Fisher, "The Need for Health Insurance," *American Labor Legislation Review* 7, no. 1 (March 1917): 9–23.

3 **But if the thirty million:** Katherine Keisler-Starkey and Lisa N. Bunch, *Health Insurance Coverage in the United States: 2019*, Current Population Reports, no. P60-271 (Washington, DC: US Government Publishing Office, September 2020), 26.

4 **Consider this: In any:** Yunwei Gai and Kent Jones, "Insurance Patterns and Instability from 2006 to 2016," *BMC Health Services Research* 20 (April 21, 2020): 334.

4 **that we dug:** Liran Einav and Amy Finkelstein, "The Risk of Losing Health Insurance in the United States Is Large, and Remained So After The Affordable Care Act," *Proceedings of the National Academy of Sciences* 120, no. 18 (April 2023).

4 **Let's start with the precarious:** KFF, "Health Insurance Coverage of the Total Population," KFF, accessed January 13, 2023, kff.org/other/state-indicator/total -population.

5 **There's no natural reason:** Aaron E. Carroll, "The Real Reason the U.S. Has Employer-Sponsored Health Insurance," *New York Times*, September 5, 2017, nytimes.com/2017/09/05/upshot/the-real-reason-the-us-has-employer-sponsored -health-insurance.html.

5 **The "duty-free" nature:** Jonathan Gruber, "Taxes and Health Insurance," in *Tax Policy and the Economy*, ed. James M. Poterba, vol. 16 (Cambridge, MA: MIT Press, 2002), 37–66; and Melissa A. Thomasson, "The Importance of Group Coverage: How Tax Policy Shaped U.S. Health Insurance," *American Economic Review* 93, no. 4 (September 2003): 1373–84.

5 **It's also responsible:** Kip Hagopian and Dana Goldman, "The Health-Insurance Solution," *National Affairs 13* (Fall 2012): 95–111.

5 **that's about two fifths:** Erika Chen, "K-12 School Spending up 4.7% in 2019 from Previous Year," United States Census Bureau, May 18, 2021, census.gov/library /stories/2021/05/united-states-spending-on-public-schools-in-2019-highest-since -2008.html.

5 **The unintended reliance:** Jonathan Gruber, "The Tax Exclusion for Employer-Sponsored Health Insurance," *National Tax Journal* 64, no. 2.2 (June 2011): 511–30; and Mark V. Pauly, "Taxation, Health Insurance, and Market Failure in the Medical Economy," *Journal of Economic Literature* 24, no. 2 (June 1986): 629–75.

5 **For another, workers can:** Jonathan Gruber and Brigitte C. Madrian, "Health Insurance, Labor Supply, and Job Mobility: A Critical Review of the Literature," in *Health Policy and the Uninsured*, ed. Catherine McLaughlin (Washington, DC: Urban Institute Press, 2004), 97–178.

6 **this absurd state of affairs:** Employee Benefits Security Administration, *An Employer's Guide to Group Health Continuation Coverage under COBRA* (United States Department of Labor, October 2021), dol.gov/sites/dolgov/files/EBSA/about-ebsa/our-activities/resource-center/publications/an-employers-guide-to-group-health-continuation-coverage-under-cobra.pdf; and Employee Benefits Security Administration, "Fact Sheet: Celebrating 25 Years of COBRA," US Department of Labor, April 7, 2011, https://permanent.fdlp.gov/gpo10185/fsCOBRAanniversary.html.

6 **the patch had a catch:** For example, only some employees who lose their jobs are eligible for COBRA coverage, and to get that coverage they have to apply for it within sixty days (at least when there's no pandemic raging—Congress "fixed" the issue of a limited application window . . . for the duration of the pandemic). For more, see benefits.gov, "Facts to Help Determine Your COBRA Eligibility," Benefits.gov, September 30, 2020, benefits.gov/news/article/407; and Jason Sandoval, "Premium Assistance for COBRA Benefits," notice 2021-31 (Internal Revenue Service, March 2021), irs.gov/pub/irs-drop/n-21-31.pdf.

6 **The real problem is:** Gary Claxton, Matthew Rae, Michelle Long, Anthony Damico, and Heidi Whitmore, "Section 6: Worker and Employer Contributions for Premiums," in *Employer Health Benefits: 2018 Annual Survey* (San Francisco: Henry J. Kaiser Family Foundation, 2018), kff.org/report-section/2018-employer-health-benefits-survey-section-6-worker-and-employer-contributions-for-premiums.

6 **Now that she's:** Amy Finkelstein, Casey McQuillan, Owen Zidar, and Eric Zwick, "The Health Wedge and Labor Market Inequality," *Brookings Papers on Economic Activity*, Spring (2023).

6 **"Sticker shock" is:** Kerry Hannon, "Where to Get Health Insurance If You Lose Your Job," MarketWatch, April 21, 2020, marketwatch.com/story/where-to-get-health-insurance-if-you-lose-your-job-2020-04-21.

6 **One New Jersey woman:** Michael Sainato, "The Americans Dying Because They Can't Afford Medical Care," *The Guardian*, January 7, 2020, theguardian.com/us-news/2020/jan/07/americans-healthcare-medical-costs.

7 **It should therefore not:** Karen Pollitz, Matthew Rae, Cynthia Cox, Rabah Kamal, Rachel Fehr, and Greg Young, "Key Issues Related to COBRA Subsidies," KFF, May 28, 2020, kff.org/private-insurance/issue-brief/key-issues-related-to-cobra-subsidies.

7 **"[COBRA] is well named":** Jenny Deam, "Layoffs Expose Another Hole in the Health-Care Safety Net," *Houston Chronicle*, April 24, 2016, houstonchronicle.com/business/medical/article/Layoffs-expose-another-hole-in-the-health-care-7305850.php.

7 **While the privately insured:** Public insurance coverage for diseases such as end-stage renal disease (ESRD), breast cancer, and cervical cancer all end once the patient no longer has the disease. See Centers for Medicare & Medicaid Services, "End-Stage Renal Disease (ESRD)," CMS.gov, December 1, 2021, cms.gov/Medicare/Coordination-of-Benefits-and-Recovery/Coordination-of-Benefits-and

-Recovery-Overview/End-Stage-Renal-Disease-ESRD/ESRD; and Breast and Cervical Cancer Prevention and Treatment Act of 2000, Pub. L. No. 106-354, H.R. 4386 (2000), congress.gov/bill/106th-congress/house-bill/4386/text.

7 **Some of these gaps:** Laurie Kaye Abraham, *Mama Might Be Better Off Dead: The Failure of Health Care in Urban America* (Chicago: University of Chicago Press, 1993).

8 **Tommy had worked:** Abraham, *Mama Might Be Better Off Dead*, 28–29.

8 **Now officially disabled:** Abraham, 53; Centers for Medicare & Medicaid Services, "CMS Fast Facts," CMS.gov, April 15, 2020, web.archive.org/web/20210625091832 /https://www.cms.gov/fastfacts.

8 **Covers them, that is:** Social Security Administration, *Annual Statistical Report on the Social Security Disability Insurance Program, 2019*, no. 13-11826 (Washington, DC: Social Security Administration, October 2020), ssa.gov/policy/docs/statcomps /di_asr/2019/di_asr19.pdf.

8 **Robert had known:** Abraham, *Mama Might Be Better Off Dead*, 9–10; and KFF, "Medicare Beneficiaries with End-Stage-Renal-Disease (ESRD)," KFF, accessed February 2, 2021, kff.org/medicare/state-indicator/enrollees-with-esrd.

8 **By the time Robert:** Abraham, viii, 9–15.

9 **In a macabre sense:** A law enacted in December 2020—almost a half century after the original coverage—would allow coverage to continue after a successful transplant. That law is scheduled to go into effect in 2023. For more information, see National Kidney Foundation, "Expanded Medicare Coverage of Immunosuppressive Drugs for Kidney Transplant Recipients," National Kidney Foundation, February 5, 2021, kidney.org/atoz/content/faq-expanded-medicare-coverage-immunosuppressive -drugs-kidney-transplant-recipients; Centers for Medicare & Medicaid Services, "Kidney Transplant Coverage," Medicare.gov, accessed February 9, 2022, medicare. gov/coverage/kidney-transplants; and Lee Fifield, "CMS Proposes to Extend Medicare Coverage of Immunosuppressive Drugs for Kidney Transplant Recipients," AAPC Knowledge Center, May 3, 2022, aapc.com/blog/84942-cms-proposes-to -extend-medicare-coverage-of-immunosuppressive-drugs -for-kidney-transplant-recipients.

9 **This would have left him:** Elisa J. Gordon, Thomas R. Prohaska, and Ashwini R. Sehgal, "The Financial Impact of Immunosuppressant Expenses on New Kidney Transplant Recipients," *Clinical Transplantation* 22, no. 6 (November/ December 2008): 738–48.

9 **But uncertainty also pervades:** Centers for Medicare & Medicaid Services, "Medicaid Facts and Figures," CMS.gov, January 30, 2020, cms.gov/newsroom /fact-sheets/medicaid-facts-and-figures#_ftn1.

9 **Other eligibility pathways:** Usha Ranji, Ivette Gomez, and Alina Salganicoff, "Expanding Postpartum Medicaid Coverage," KFF, accessed July 29, 2020, web .archive.org/web/20191024044815/https://www.kff.org/womens-health-policy /issue-brief/expanding-postpartum-medicaid-coverage; and Emily M. Johnston, Stacey McMorrow, Clara Alvarez Caraveo, and Lisa Dubay, "Post-ACA, More

Than One-Third of Women with Prenatal Medicaid Remained Uninsured before or after Pregnancy," *Health Affairs* 40, no. 4 (April 2021): 571–78, doi.org/10.1377 /hlthaff.2020.01678.

9 **"The clock is ticking":** Susan Starr Sered and Rushika Fernandopulle, in *Uninsured in America: Life & Death in the Land of Opportunity,* updated ed. (Berkeley: University of California Press, 2006), 49–52.

9 **Some women repeatedly:** Sered and Fernandopulle, *Uninsured in America,* xviii.

10 **Income limits on eligibility:** While eligibility requirements vary by state, the cutoffs at ages one and six are when states may choose to make the eligibility requirement more stringent. See Brooks et al. 2020 and CMS 2014 for more information. For the most current information on each state's standards, see KFF 2022. Tricia Brooks, Lauren Roygardner, Samantha Artiga, Olivia Pham, and Rachel Dolan, "Medicaid and CHIP Eligibility, Enrollment, and Cost Sharing Policies as of January 2020: Findings from a 50-State Survey," KFF, March 26, 2020, kff.org/report-section /medicaid-and-chip-eligibility-enrollment-and-cost-sharing-policies-as-of-january -2020-findings-from-a-50-state-survey-tables; Centers for Medicare & Medicaid Services, "State Medicaid and CHIP Income Eligibility Standards" (Centers for Medicare & Medicaid Services, accessed January 18, 2023), medicaid.gov/medicaid /national-medicaid-chip-program-information/medicaid-childrens-health -insurance-program-basic-health-program-eligibility-levels/index.html; and KFF, "Medicaid and CHIP Income Eligibility Limits for Children as a Percent of the Federal Poverty Level," KFF, accessed January 18, 2023, kff.org/health-reform /state-indicator/medicaid-and-chip-income-eligibility-limits-for-children-as-a -percent-of-the-federal-poverty-level.

10 **And kids have a way:** Brooks et al., "Medicaid and CHIP Eligibility, Enrollment, and Cost Sharing Policies"; and Centers for Medicare & Medicaid Services, "Medicaid and CHIP FAQs: Coverage of Former Foster Care Children" (Department of Health & Human Services, December 2013), medicaid.gov/state-resource-center /downloads/medicaid-and-chip-faqs-coverage-of-former-foster-care-children.pdf.

10 **A pediatric cardiologist:** Arthur Garson, "Heart of the Uninsured," *Health Affairs* 26, no. 1 (January/February 2007): 230, doi.org/10.1377/hlthaff.26.1.227.

10 **All told, this Medicaid:** "Annual Medicaid & CHIP Expenditures," Medicaid.gov, Centers for Medicare & Medicaid Services, December 2021, web.archive.org/web /20211228185741/https://www.medicaid.gov/state-overviews/scorecard/annual -medicaid-chip-expenditures/index.html.

10 **If you—like us:** Office of the Under Secretary of Defense (Comptroller), *Defense Budget Overview: United States Department of Defense Fiscal Year 2019 Budget Request* (Department of Defense, February 2018), dod.defense.gov/Portals/1 /Documents/pubs/FY2019-Budget-Request-Overview-Book.pdf.

10 **Once you add:** These numbers include both traditional Medicare and Medicare Advantage. For spending information, see Centers for Medicare & Medicaid Services, "CMS Office of the Actuary Releases 2019 National Health Expenditures," press release, December 16, 2020, cms.gov/newsroom/press-releases/cms-office-actuary

-releases-2019-national-health-expenditures; and Wafa Tarazi, W. Pete Welch, Nguyen Nguyen, Arielle Bosworth, Steven Sheingold, Nancy De Lew, and Benjamin D. Sommers, "Medicare Beneficiary Enrollment Trends and Demographic Characteristics" (ASPE Office of Health Policy, March 2, 2022), aspe.hhs.gov/sites /default/files/documents/f81aafbba0b331c71c6e8bc66512e25d/medicare -beneficiary-enrollment-ib.pdf.

11 **No wonder a Treasury:** US Department of the Treasury, "Remarks of Under Secretary of the Treasury Peter R. Fisher to the Columbus Council on World Affairs Columbus, Ohio Beyond Borrowing: Meeting the Government's Financial Challenges in the 21st Century," press release, November 14, 2002, home.treasury .gov/news/press-releases/po3622.

11 **The result: many more:** Cynthia Cox and Daniel McDermott, "Millions of Uninsured Americans Are Eligible for Free ACA Health Insurance," KFF, November 24, 2020, kff.org/policy-watch/millions-of-uninsured-americans-are -eligible-for-free-aca-health-insurance.

11 **Here's a depressing:** Suzanne M. Kirchhoff, *Health Insurance Exchanges: Health Insurance "Navigators" and In-Person Assistance* (Washington, DC: Congressional Research Service, August 13, 2014), sgp.fas.org/crs/misc/R43243.pdf.

12 **Liberals were outraged:** Karen Pollitz, Jennifer Tolbert, and Kendal Orgera, "Navigator Funding Restored in Federal Marketplace States for 2022," KFF, September 29, 2021, kff.org/private-insurance/issue-brief/navigator-funding -restored-in-federal-marketplace-states-for-2022.

12 **Making people eligible:** Cox and McDermott, "Millions of Uninsured Americans Are Eligible."

12 **Many people simply:** Jennifer M. Haley and Erik Wengle, "Many Uninsured Adults Have Not Tried to Enroll in Medicaid or Marketplace Coverage" (Urban Institute, January 2021), urban.org/sites/default/files/publication/103558/many-uninsured -adults-have-not-tried-to-enroll-in-medicaid-or-marketplace-coverage.pdf; and Munira Z. Gunja and Sara R. Collins, "Who Are the Remaining Uninsured, and Why Do They Lack Coverage?," *Commonwealth Fund*, August 28, 2019, doi.org/10.26099 /h0xy-az24.

12 **these opaque formulas:** Qualifying for Medicaid varies by state and is calculated differently in each state. For an in-depth look on what states across the country require to be eligible for Medicaid, see Brooks et al., "Medicaid and CHIP Eligibility, Enrollment, and Cost Sharing."

12 **Multiple studies have shown:** See, for example, Richard Domurat, Isaac Menashe, and Wesley Yin, "The Role of Behavioral Frictions in Health Insurance Marketplace Enrollment and Risk: Evidence from a Field Experiment," *American Economic Review* 111, no. 5 (May 2021): 1549–74; Bill J. Wright, Ginny Garcia-Alexander, Margarette A. Weller, and Katherine Baicker, "Low-Cost Behavioral Nudges Increase Medicaid Take-Up among Eligible Residents of Oregon," *Health Affairs* 36, no. 5 (May 2017): 838–45; Jacob Goldin, Ithai Z. Lurie, and Janet McCubbin, "Health Insurance and Mortality: Experimental Evidence from Taxpayer Outreach," *Quarterly Journal*

of Economics 136, no. 1 (February 2021): 1–49; and Rebecca Myerson, Nicholas Tilipman, Andrew Feher, Honglin Li, Wesley Yin, and Isaac Menashe, "Personalized Telephone Outreach Increased Health Insurance Take-Up for Hard To Reach Populations, but Challenges Remain," *Health Affairs* 41, no. 1 (January 2022): 129–37.

13 **One father, Anthony:** Anthony P. Putney, "Across State Lines, a Family Navigates Medical Complexity and Medicaid Hurdles," *Health Affairs* 34, no. 7 (July 2015): 1241–44.

13 **In Massachusetts, for example:** Mark Shepard and Myles Wagner, "Reducing Ordeals through Automatic Enrollment: Evidence from a Subsidized Health Insurance Exchange" (working paper, December 5, 2021), scholar.harvard.edu /mshepard/publications/economics-automatic-health-insurance-enrollment.

13 **Staying enrolled is yet:** Brett Kelman and Mike Reicher, "At Least 220,000 Tennessee Kids Faced Loss of Health Insurance Due to Lacking Paperwork," *The Tennessean*, July 14, 2019, tennessean.com/story/news/investigations/2019/07/14 /tenncare-coverkids-medicaid-children-application-insurance-denied/1387769001.

14 **Ironically, the government:** Elizabeth Byrne, "Texas Removes Thousands of Children from Medicaid Each Month Due to Red Tape, Records Show," KERA News, April 22, 2019, keranews.org/politics/2019-04-22/texas-removes-thousands-of -children-from-medicaid-each-month-due-to-red-tape-records-show.

14 **Like the mother in Tennessee:** Kelman and Reicher, "At Least 220,000 Tennessee Kids Faced Loss of Health Insurance."

14 **Or the mother in Idaho:** Lexi Churchill, "The Trump Administration Cracked Down on Medicaid. Kids Lost Insurance," ProPublica, October 31, 2019, propublica.org /article/the-trump-administration-cracked-down-on-medicaid-kids-lost-insurance ?token=s6l9puJoKD2r75Z2Qhb3WrSSeO-JpYz3.

14 **In response, a number:** For some examples of these organizations, see "Enrollment Assistance Program," Covered California, accessed May 3, 2022, hbex.coveredca .com/enrollment-assistance-program; "Helping Californians Get the Health Care They Need," Health Consumer Alliance (HCA), accessed May 3, 2022, healthconsumer.org; "UHPP Basics," *Utah Health Policy Project*, accessed May 3, 2022, healthpolicyproject.org/uhpp-basics; "TennCare Enrollment and Appeal Help," Tennessee Justice Center, accessed May 3, 2022, https://www.tnjustice.org /tenncare-enrollment-appeal-help; and "About HLA," Health Law Advocates, accessed May 3, 2022, healthlawadvocates.org/about/what-we-do.

15 **The low-income mother:** Sered and Fernandopulle, *Uninsured in America,* xviii–ix.

15 **The domestic violence survivor:** Sered and Fernandopulle, 65–68.

15 **The blue-collar worker:** Sered and Fernandopulle, 104–6.

15 **The twentysomething uninsured:** Robert Vargas, *Uninsured in Chicago: How the Social Safety Net Leaves Latinos Behind* (New York: NYU Press, 2022), 1–2, 27.

15 **The data also provide:** For an overview of some of this evidence, see Amy Finkelstein, Neale Mahoney, and Matthew J. Notowidigdo, "What Does (Formal)

Health Insurance Do, and for Whom?," *Annual Review of Economics* 10, no. 1 (August 2018): 261–86.

15 **Some of that evidence:** *Oregon Blue Book: Almanac & Fact Book,* s.v. "Motto, State," accessed February 11, 2022, sos.oregon.gov/blue-book/Pages/facts/almanac /h-m.aspx.

15 **In 2008, Oregon:** William Yardley, "Drawing Lots for Health Care," *York Times,* March 13, 2008, nytimes.com/2008/03/13/us/13bend.html.

15 **Oregon heavily advertised:** Amy Finkelstein, Sarah Taubman, Bill Wright, Mira Bernstein, Jonathan Gruber, Joseph P. Newhouse, Heidi Allen et al., "The Oregon Health Insurance Experiment: Evidence from the First Year," *Quarterly Journal of Economics* 127, no. 3 (August 2012): 1057–1106.

16 **Oregon chose its:** Julia James, "The Oregon Health Insurance Experiment" (health policy brief, *Health Affairs* and Robert Wood Johnson Foundation, July 16, 2015), healthaffairs.org/do/10.1377/hpb20150716.236899/full /healthpolicybrief_141.pdf.

16 **Comedy host Stephen:** Stephen Colbert, "The Word—Pick Sicks," video, 4:06, in *The Colbert Report,* aired April 1, 2008, on Comedy Central, cc.com/video-clips /inwuqm/the-colbert-report-the-word-pick-sicks.

16 **The answer: those who won:** For an overview of the study, see J-PAL Policy Briefcase 2022. For information on clinical outcomes, see Baicker et al. 2013. For information on emergency department usage, see Taubman et al. 2014. For an overview of the first year of the study, see Finkelstein et al. 2012; J-PAL Policy Briefcase, "Understanding Medicaid Expansion: The Effects of Insuring Low-Income Adults," J-PAL Policy Briefcase (Cambridge, MA: Abdul Latif Jameel Poverty Action Lab, 2022), povertyactionlab.org/publication/understanding-medicaid-expansion-effects -insuring-low-income-adults; Katherine Baicker, Sarah L. Taubman, Heidi L. Allen, Mira Bernstein, Jonathan H. Gruber, Joseph P. Newhouse, Eric C. Schneider et al., "The Oregon Experiment—Effects of Medicaid on Clinical Outcomes," *New England Journal of Medicine* 368, no. 18 (May 2, 2013): 1713–22; Sarah L. Taubman, Heidi L. Allen, Bill J. Wright, Katherine Baicker, and Amy N. Finkelstein, "Medicaid Increases Emergency-Department Use: Evidence from Oregon's Health Insurance Experiment," *Science* 343, no. 6168 (January 17, 2014): 263–68; and Finkelstein et al., "The Oregon Health Insurance Experiment."

17 **A subsequent, much:** Goldin, Lurie, and McCubbin, "Health Insurance and Mortality."

17 **Or as one Oregon:** Heidi Allen, Bill Wright, and Katherine Baicker, "Personal Narratives from Oregon's Medicaid Expansion," in *Medicaid: Politics, Policy, and Key Issues,* ed. Daniel Lanford (New York: Nova Science Publishers, 2020), 16.

18 **The astute reader:** US Department of Health & Human Services, Digital Communications Division, "Who Is Eligible for Medicare?," HHS.gov, September 11, 2014, hhs.gov/answers/medicare-and-medicaid/who-is-elibible-for-medicare /index.html.

18 **That may help explain:** Steffie Woolhandler and David U. Himmelstein, "Medicare for All and Its Rivals: New Offshoots of Old Health Policy Roots," *Annals of Internal Medicine* 170, no. 11 (June 4, 2019): 793–95; and Abigail Abrams, "The Surprising Origins of 'Medicare for All,'" *Time*, May 30, 2019, time.com/5586744/medicare -for-all-history.

CHAPTER 2: SHODDY CONSTRUCTION

22 **Consider Medicare. PBS:** Philip Moeller, "Medicare Coverage for Aging Parents' Care Is Not Nearly Enough," *PBS NewsHour*, July 22, 2015, pbs.org/newshour /economy/medicare-coverage-aging-parents-care-nearly-enough.

22 **Cora Jackson's experiences:** Laurie Kaye Abraham, *Mama Might Be Better Off Dead: The Failure of Health Care in Urban America* (Chicago: University of Chicago Press, 1993), 74, 235.

22 **By law, Medicare:** Sidney Zahabizadeh, "How to Find Medicare Law," American Bar Association, October 1, 2016, americanbar.org/groups/law_aging/publications /bifocal/vol_38/issue_1_october2016/how-to-find-medicare-law.

22 **For example, one elderly man:** Philip Moeller, *Get What's Yours for Medicare: Maximize Your Coverage, Minimize Your Costs* (New York: Simon & Schuster, 2016), 76.

23 **For Cora, the "medically necessary":** Abraham, *Mama Might Be Better Off Dead*, 4.

23 **Not surprisingly, she therefore:** Abraham, 67–68.

23 **During the year described:** Abraham, 1–8, 236.

23 **Medicare patients are required:** US Centers for Medicare & Medicaid Services, "Medicare Costs at a Glance," Medicare.gov, December 17, 2019, web.archive.org /web/20191217040036/https://www.medicare.gov/your-medicare-costs /medicare-costs-at-a-glance.

23 **They must also pay:** Centers for Medicare & Medicaid Services, "2019 Medicare Parts A & B Premiums and Deductibles," CMS.gov, October 12, 2018, cms.gov /newsroom/fact-sheets/2019-medicare-parts-b-premiums-and-deductibles.

23 **their first three units:** Centers for Medicare & Medicaid Services, "Blood Transfusion Coverage," Medicare.gov, accessed March 21, 2022, medicare.gov /coverage/blood; and Choosing Wisely, "Blood Transfusions for Anemia in the Hospital" (Consumer Reports, 2018), choosingwisely.org/wp-content/uploads /2018/02/Blood-Transfusions-For-Anemia-In-The-Hospital-ASH.pdf.

23 **All told, such gaps:** Juliette Cubanski, Wyatt Koma, Anthony Damico, and Tricia Neuman, "How Much Do Medicare Beneficiaries Spend Out of Pocket on Health Care?," KFF, November 4, 2019, kff.org/medicare/issue-brief/how -much-do-medicare-beneficiaries-spend-out-of-pocket-on-health-care.

23 **These gaps are no:** Some examples of the discussions surrounding the decision to have Medicare patients pay for some of their care can be found in the following reports and bills: Advisory Council on Social Security, "Report of the Advisory

Council on Social Security: The Status of the Social Security Program and Recommendations for Its Improvement," *Social Security Bulletin* 28, no. 3 (March 1965): 3–41, ssa.gov/policy/docs/ssb/v28n3/v28n3p3.pdf; A Bill to Provide for Payment for Hospital Services, Skilled Nursing Home Services, and Home Health Services Furnished to Aged Beneficiaries under the Old-Age, Survivors, and Disability Insurance Program, and for Other Purposes, H.R. 4222, 87th Cong. (1961); and A Bill to Amend the Social Security Act and the Internal Revenue Code so as to Provide Insurance against the Costs of Hospital, Nursing Home, and Surgical Service for Persons Eligible for Old-Age and Survivors Insurance Benefits, and for Other Purposes, H.R. 4700, 86th Cong. (July 13, 1959).

23 **The result: Medicare covers:** For more on what Medicare does and does not cover, see Chandra and Garthwaite 2019. On comparing Medicare to other insurance plans, see McArdle et al. 2012; Amitabh Chandra and Craig Garthwaite, "Economic Principles for Medicare Reform," *The Annals of the American Academy of Political and Social Science* 686, no. 1 (November 2019): 63–92; and Frank McArdle, Ian Stark, Zachary Levinson, and Tricia Neuman, "How Does the Benefit Value of Medicare Compare to the Benefit Value of Typical Large Employer Plans? A 2012 Update," KFF, April 5, 2012, kff.org/health-reform/issue-brief/how-does-the-benefit-value -of-medicare.

24 **As a result of Medicare's:** Wyatt Koma, Juliette Cubanski, and Tricia Neuman, "A Snapshot of Sources of Coverage among Medicare Beneficiaries in 2018," KFF, March 23, 2021, kff.org/medicare/issue-brief/a-snapshot-of-sources-of-coverage -among-medicare-beneficiaries-in-2018.

24 **The grass is not much:** To see how health insurance deductibles have risen since 2003, see Claxton et al. 2021 and Rae et al. 2019. For some information on rising deductibles even before 2003, see Moon et al. 1996 and Max 2003; Gary Claxton, Matthew Rae, Gregory Young, Nisha Kurani, Heidi Whitmore, Jason Kerns, Jackie Cifuentes et al., *Employer Health Benefits: 2021 Annual Survey* (San Francisco: KFF [Kaiser Family Foundation], November 2021), files.kff.org/attachment /Report-Employer-Health-Benefits-2021-Annual-Survey.pdf; Matthew Rae, Rebecca Copeland, and Cynthia Cox, "Tracking the Rise in Premium Contributions and Cost-Sharing for Families with Large Employer Coverage," *Peterson-KFF Health System Tracker*, August 14, 2019, healthsystemtracker.org/brief/tracking-the -rise-in-premium-contributions-and-cost-sharing-for-families-with-large-employer -coverage; Marilyn Moon, Len M. Nichols, and Susan Wall, "Medical Savings Accounts: A Policy Analysis" (Urban Institute, March 1996), http://webarchive .urban.org/publications/406498.html; and Sarah Max, "Health Insurance Premiums up (Again)," *CNN Money*, September 22, 2003, money.cnn.com/2003/09/09/pf /insurance/employerhealthplans/.

24 **By 2019, almost:** Gary Claxton, Matthew Rae, Gregory Young, Daniel McDermott, Heidi Whitmore, Jason Kerns, Jackie Cifuentes et al., *Employer Health Benefits: 2020 Annual Survey* (San Francisco: KFF, 2020), files.kff.org/attachment/Report -Employer-Health-Benefits-2020-Annual-Survey.pdf.

25 **These large deductibles:** Blake Dodge, "Doctors Are Fed Up with Being Turned into Debt Collectors," *Bloomberg*, November 15, 2018, bloomberg.com/news/articles /2018-11-15/doctors-are-fed-up-with-being-turned-into-debt-collectors.

25 **A 2018 NPR story:** The story about this couple can be found in Aleccia 2018. While the numbers we give reflect their specific high-deductible health plan, Claxton et al. 2019 shows that a $3,000 deductible requirement before coinsurance kicks in is not uncommon; JoNel Aleccia, "Insured, but Indebted: Couple Works 5 Jobs to Pay Off Medical Bills," *NPR*, December 26, 2018, Your Health, npr.org/sections/health -shots/2018/12/26/678749817/insured-but-indebted-couple-works-5-jobs-to-pay -off-medical-bills; and Gary Claxton, Matthew Rae, Anthony Damico, Gregory Young, Daniel McDermott, and Heidi Whitmore, "Section 8: High-Deductible Health Plans with Savings Option," in *2019 Employer Health Benefits Survey* (San Francisco: Kaiser Family Foundation, September 25, 2019), kff.org/report-section /ehbs-2019-section-8-high-deductible-health-plans-with-savings-option.

25 **Another big source:** Zack Cooper, Fiona Scott Morton, and Nathan Shekita, "Surprise! Out-of-Network Billing for Emergency Care in the United States," *Journal of Political Economy* 128, no. 9 (August 13, 2020), 3626–77; and Zack Cooper and Fiona Scott Morton, "Out-of-Network Emergency-Physician Bills—an Unwelcome Surprise," *New England Journal of Medicine* 375, no. 20 (November 17, 2016): 1915–18.

25 **That can be a particular:** Eric C. Sun, Michelle M. Mello, Jasmin Moshfegh, and Laurence C. Baker, "Assessment of Out-of-Network Billing for Privately Insured Patients Receiving Care in In-Network Hospitals," *JAMA Internal Medicine* 179, no. 11 (November 2019): 1543–50.

25 **A number of states:** Jack Hoadley, Kevin Lucia, and Beth Fuchs, "Surprise Billing Protections: Help Finally Arrives for Millions of Americans," Commonwealth Fund, December 17, 2020, doi.org/10.26099/p80d-tp74; and Maanasa Kona, "State Balance-Billing Protections," Commonwealth Fund, February 5, 2021, commonwealthfund.org/node/27021.

26 **But these laws:** For example, a story from after the law was passed describes an $80,000 surprise bill that the parents of newborn twins received because the hospital and insurance couldn't agree on whether the NICU care was "an emergency." The couple had to eventually pay a professional company to resolve the dispute: Jay Hancock, "An $80,000 Surprise Bill Points to a Loophole in a New Law to Protect Patients," *NPR*, February 23, 2022, npr.org/sections/health-shots/2022/02/23 /1082405759/an-80-000-surprise-bill-points-to-a-loophole-in-a-new-law-to -protect-patients.

26 **The federal law, for example:** Ground ambulances are not covered; however, air ambulances are. For more on what the federal law—called the No Surprises Act—does and does not cover, see Centers for Medicare & Medicaid Services, "No Surprises: Understand Your Rights against Surprise Medical Bills" (Centers for Medicare & Medicaid Services, accessed November 19, 2021), cms .gov/files/document/nosurpriseactfactsheet-final508.pdf; and Margot Sanger-Katz,

"A New Ban on Surprise Medical Bills Starts Today," *New York Times*, December 30, 2021, nytimes.com/2021/12/30/upshot/medical-bill-ban-biden.html.

26 **Every year, about one quarter:** Liz Hamel, Mira Norton, Karen Pollitz, Larry Levitt, Gary Claxton, and Mollyann Brodie, "Section 1: Who Has Medical Bill Problems and What Are the Contributing Factors?," in *The Burden of Medical Debt: Results from the Kaiser Family Foundation/New York Times Medical Bills Survey*, KFF, January 5, 2016, kff.org/report-section/the-burden-of-medical-debt-section-1 -who-has-medical-bill-problems-and-what-are-the-contributing-factors.

26 **Even among the elderly:** Neil Bennett, Jonathan Eggleston, Laryssa Mykyta, and Briana Sullivan, "19% of U.S. Households Could Not Afford to Pay for Medical Care Right Away," United States Census Bureau, April 7, 2021, census.gov/library /stories/2021/04/who-had-medical-debt-in-united-states.html.

26 **Medical debt is also:** Raymond Kluender, Neale Mahoney, Francis Wong, and Wesley Yin, "Medical Debt in the US, 2009–2020," *JAMA* 326, no. 3 (July 20, 2021): 250–56.

26 **And here's the really shocking:** The share of debt held by insured and uninsured households is based on the author's calculations from the 2018 Survey of Income and Program Participation, an annual survey conducted by the US Census Bureau, as well as: Kluender et al., "Medical Debt in the US."

26 **Although Walter White's:** Arpit Gupta, Edward R. Morrison, Catherine Fedorenko, and Scott Ramsey, "Leverage, Default, and Mortality: Evidence from Cancer Diagnoses" (SSRN Scholarly Paper, SSRN, Rochester, NY, September 12, 2017), doi.org/10.2139/ssrn.2583975.

26 **Hospitals frequently resort:** Zack Cooper, James Han, and Neale Mahoney, "Hospital Lawsuits over Unpaid Bills Increased by 37 Percent in Wisconsin from 2001 to 2018," *Health Affairs* 40, no. 12 (December 2021): healthaffairs.org /doi/10.1377/hlthaff.2021.01130.

27 **An insured mother:** Laura Beil, "As Patients Struggle with Bills, Hospital Sues Thousands," *New York Times*, September 3, 2019, nytimes.com/2019/09/03 /health/carlsbad-hospital-lawsuits-medical-debt.html.

27 **Many of the hospitals:** Trevor Brown, "Oklahoma Hospitals Sue Thousands Each Year over Unpaid Medical Bills," *Journal Record*, August 9, 2019, journalrecord .com/2019/08/09/oklahoma-hospitals-sue-thousands-each-year-over-unpaid -medical-bills.

27 **If the suit is "successful":** Erin C. Fuse Brown, "IRS Rules Will Not Stop Unfair Hospital Billing and Collection Practices," *AMA Journal of Ethics* 17, no. 8 (August 2015): 763–69.

27 **But the hospital often wins:** Healthcare Finance Staff, "A Public Hospital Serves the Poor with Lawsuits," *Healthcare Finance*, December 30, 2014, healthcarefinancenews .com/news/public-hospital-serves-poor-lawsuits.

27 **In 2014, concerns:** "Our Mission," RIP Medical Debt, accessed December 27, 2019, web.archive.org/web/20191227153409/https://ripmedicaldebt.org/about.

27 **Buying up and forgiving:** "About Our Organization," RIP Medical Debt, accessed March 23, 2022, ripmedicaldebt.org/about.

27 **Indeed, hospitals often sense:** Jake Halpern, "Paper Boys: Inside the Dark, Lucrative World of Consumer Debt Collection," *New York Times Magazine*, August 14, 2014, nytimes.com/interactive/2014/08/15/magazine/bad-paper-debt-collector.html.

28 **The government has made:** Bureau of Consumer Financial Protection, Debt Collection Practices (Regulation F), Final Rule, 85 Fed. Reg. 76734 (November 30, 2020), federalregister.gov/documents/2020/11/30/2020-24463/debt-collection-practices-regulation-f.

28 **Estimates suggest that about 90:** Lucas Nathe and Ryan Sandler, "Paid and Low-Balance Medical Collections on Consumer Credit Reports" (Consumer Financial Protection Bureau, July 2022), files.consumerfinance.gov/f/documents/cfpb_paid-and-low-balance-medical-collections-on-consumer-credit-reports_2022-07.pdf; and Robert B. Avery, Paul S. Calem, Glenn B. Canner, and Raphael W. Bostic, "An Overview of Consumer Data and Credit Reporting," *Federal Reserve Bulletin* 80, no. 2 (February 2003): 47–73.

28 **But not before:** For evidence of the impact of medical debt on patients' credit rating, see Brevoort et al. 2020. There is less direct evidence on the potential costs of medical debt on stress and guilt, but these do appear in a range of interviews with industry professionals (e.g., debt and creditor attorneys and judges) discussed in Mann and Porter 2010. Kenneth Brevoort, Daniel Grodzicki, and Martin B. Hackmann, "The Credit Consequences of Unpaid Medical Bills," *Journal of Public Economics* 187 (July 2020): 104203; Ronald J. Mann and Katherine Porter, "Saving Up for Bankruptcy," *Georgetown Law Journal* 98, no. 2 (January 2010): 315–18.

28 **The key difference:** For some of the evidence on how health and mortality improve with higher income and education, see Adriana Lleras-Muney, "Education and Income Gradients in Longevity: The Role of Policy" (Working Paper 29694, National Bureau of Economic Research, Cambridge, MA, January 2022), doi.org/10.3386/w29694.

29 **Cora Jackson was caught:** Abraham, *Mama Might Be Better Off Dead*, 48–53.

30 **Fortunately, the wise men:** For more on the process of Medicare and Medicaid becoming law, see Wilbur J. Cohen, "Reflections on the Enactment of Medicare and Medicaid," *Health Care Financing Review* 1985, supp. (December 1985): 3–11.

30 **From the start, therefore:** For a very brief history on Medicaid eligibility, see the Medicaid and CHIP Payment and Access Commission "Eligibility" article. For current information on Medicaid eligibility pathways, see CMS's website. To be eligible for the "medically needy" pathway, you must also already fall into an assistance category—which at a minimum includes pregnant women and children, but also often includes seniors, people with disabilities, and low-income parents. If you belong to one of these categories, your monthly income after medical expenses and assets must fall below certain thresholds, which vary widely by state. For example, in Louisiana, you can be left with no more than $100 each month after medical expenses are paid; in Illinois, you can be left with over $1,000. For more

information on this eligibility pathway, including how states' medically needy requirements differ, see Musumeci et al. 2019. "Eligiblity," Medicaid and CHIP Payment and Access Commission, accessed November 16, 2022, macpac.gov /medicaid-101/eligibility; "Medicaid Eligibility," Medicaid.gov, Centers for Medicare & Medicaid Services, accessed March 22, 2022, medicaid.gov/medicaid/eligibility /index.html; and MaryBeth Musumeci, Priya Chidambaram, and Molly O'Malley Watts, "Medicaid Financial Eligibility for Seniors and People with Disabilities: Findings from a 50-State Survey" (Kaiser Family Foundation, San Francisco, June 14, 2019), kff.org/medicaid/issue-brief/medicaid-financial-eligibility-for-seniors-and -people-with-disabilities-findings-from-a-50-state-survey.

30 **Each state could then decide:** Musumeci, Chidambaram, and Watts, "Medicaid Financial Eligibility for Seniors and People with Disabilities."

30 **The key problem is that:** Michael Bihari, "Your Income Level May Put You in a Medicaid-Eligible Category," *Verywell Health*, March 7, 2020, verywellhealth.com /medically-needy-1738567.

31 **Cora Jackson had to requalify:** Abraham, *Mama Might Be Better Off Dead*, 50–52.

31 **As Jackie commented:** Abraham, 51.

31 **Many states still require:** Medically Needy—Income Eligibility, 42 C.F.R. 435.831 § (1994), ecfr.gov/current/title-42/chapter-IV/subchapter-C/part-435/subpart-I /subject-group-ECFR6418eede7d9fe81/section-435.831; and Musumeci, Chidambaram, and Watts, "Medicaid Financial Eligibility for Seniors and People with Disabilities."

CHAPTER 3: REBUILD, DON'T RENOVATE

33 **In July 1965:** History.com Editors, "President Johnson Signs Medicare into Law," History, November 24, 2009, history.com/this-day-in-history/johnson-signs -medicare-into-law; and John D. Morris, "President Signs Medicare Bill; Praises Truman," *New York Times*, July 31, 1965, nytimes.com/1965/07/31/archives /president-signs-medicare-bill-praises-truman-he-flies-to.html.

33 **With President Johnson:** History.com Editors, "President Johnson Signs Medicare into Law."

33 **Only two years:** For more on Medicaid coverage for pregnant women, see Gold et al. 1993 and Gomez et al. 2022. For more on the history of Medicare prescription drug coverage, see Oliver et al. 2004, Center for Medicare Advocacy 2020, CMS 2017, and Cubanski et al. 2022. Rachel Benson Gold, Susheela Singh, and Jennifer Frost, "The Medicaid Eligibility Expansions for Pregnant Women: Evaluating the Strength of State Implementation Efforts," *Family Planning Perspectives* 25, no. 5 (September–October 1993): 196–207; Ivette Gomez, Usha Ranji, Alina Salganicoff, and Brittni Frederiksen, "Medicaid Coverage for Women," KFF, February 17, 2022, kff.org/womens-health-policy/issue-brief/medicaid-coverage-for-women; Thomas R. Oliver, Philip R. Lee, and Helene L. Lipton, "A Political History of Medicare and Prescription Drug Coverage," *Milbank Quarterly* 82, no. 2 (June 2004): 283–354;

Center for Medicare Advocacy, "Part D / Prescription Drug Benefits," Center for Medicare Advocacy, 2020, medicareadvocacy.org/medicare-info/medicare-part-d; Centers for Medicare & Medicaid Services, "Nearly 12 Million People with Medicare Have Saved over $26 Billion on Prescription Drugs Since 2010," press release, January 13, 2017, cms.gov/newsroom/press-releases/nearly-12-million-people -medicare-have-saved-over-26-billion-prescription-drugs-2010; and Juliette Cubanski, Tricia Neuman, Meredith Freed, and Anthony Damico, "How Will the Prescription Drug Provisions in the Inflation Reduction Act Affect Medicare Beneficiaries?," KFF, August 18, 2022, kff.org/medicare/issue-brief/how-will-the -prescription-drug-provisions-in-the-inflation-reduction-act-affect-medicare -beneficiaries.

34 **Laws create coverage for specific:** Examples of disease-specific insurance programs include tuberculosis (Wysolmerski et al. 2015), breast and cervical cancer (Schneider et al. 2002), ALS (Norris 2019 and SSA 2020), ESRD (Norris 2019 and "End-Stage Renal Disease" 2021), HIV/AIDS (Engels 2020), and sickle cell anemia (Elliott 2017 and Fitzgerald 2013); Michael Wysolmerski, Katie Garfield, Amy Rosenberg, and Robert Greenwald, "The Medicaid Tuberculosis Option: An Opportunity for Policy Reform" (issue brief, Center for Health Law and Policy Innovation, Harvard Law School, Jamaica Plain, MA, June 2015), chlpi.org/wp-content/uploads/2014/01 /Issue-Brief-June-2015-The-Medicaid-Tuberculosis-Option.pdf; Andy Schneider, Risa Elias, and Rachel Garfield, "Chapter 1: Medicaid Eligibility" in *The Medicaid Resource Book* (Washington, DC: Kaiser Commission on Medicaid and the Uninsured, July 2002), kff.org/wp-content/uploads/2013/05/mrbeligibility.pdf; Louise Norris, "Medicare Eligibility for ALS and ESRD Patients," Medicareresources .org, January 10, 2019, medicareresources.org/medicare-eligibility-and-enrollment /medicare-eligibility-for-als-and-esrd-patients; Social Security Administration, "President Signs S. 578, the 'ALS Disability Insurance Access Act of 2019,'" *Social Security Legislative Bulletin* no. 116-26, December 28, 2020, ssa.gov/legislation /legis_bulletin_122220.html; Centers for Medicare & Medicaid Services, "End- Stage Renal Disease (ESRD)," CMS.gov, December 1, 2021, cms.gov/Medicare /Coordination-of-Benefits-and-Recovery/Coordination-of-Benefits-and-Recovery -Overview/End-Stage-Renal-Disease-ESRD/ESRD; Tom Engels, "HRSA Celebrates 30 Years of the Ryan White CARE Act," HIV.gov, US Department of Health & Human Services, August 18, 2020, hiv.gov/blog/hrsa-celebrates-30-years-ryan -white-care-act; Victoria L. Elliott, *Maternal and Child Health Services Block Grant: Background and Funding* (Washington, DC: Congressional Research Service, August 28, 2017), fas.org/sgp/crs/misc/R44929.pdf; and D. Fitzgerald, "Q & A: Medicaid Coverage for Sickle Cell Disease," National Health Law Program, July 23, 2013, healthlaw.org/resource/q-a-medicaid-coverage-for-sickle-cell-disease.

34 **children (until they grow up):** Tricia Brooks, Lauren Roygardner, Samantha Artiga, Olivia Pham, and Rachel Dolan, *Medicaid and CHIP Eligibility, Enrollment, and Cost Sharing Policies as of January 2020: Findings from a 50-State Survey,*

KFF, March 26, 2020, kff.org/report-section/medicaid-and-chip-eligibility
-enrollment-and-cost-sharing-policies-as-of-january-2020-findings-from-a-50
-state-survey-tables.

34 **patients experiencing an emergency:** For information on the law, which requires
hospitals to stabilize patients regardless of their ability to pay, see Tiana Mayere
Lee, "An EMTALA Primer: The Impact of Changes in the Emergency Medicine
Landscape on EMTALA Compliance and Enforcement," *Annals of Health Law* 13,
no. 1 (Winter 2004): 145–78.

34 **hostages and their family:** The policy that allowed hostages in Iraq and Kuwait and
their families to receive health coverage took place in the 1990s. See Mike Causey,
"An Umbrella for Hostages," *Washington Post*, December 9, 1990, washingtonpost
.com/archive/local/1990/12/09/an-umbrella-for-hostages/53c8e282-1443-406f
-ba43-f2a77d358f6b.

34 **disabled (after waiting two years):** Katherine N. Bent, *Annual Statistical Report on
the Social Security Disability Insurance Program*, 2019, no. 13-11826 (Washington,
DC: Social Security Administration, October 2020), ssa.gov/policy/docs/statcomps
/di_asr/2019/di_asr19.pdf.

34 **prisoners (until they are:** Douglas C. McDonald, "Medical Care in Prisons," *Crime
and Justice* 26 (1999): 427–78.

34 **The result, as the historian:** Charles E. Rosenberg, "Anticipated Consequences:
Historians, History, and Health Policy," in *History and Health Policy in the United
States: Putting the Past Back In*, ed. Rosemary A. Stevens, Charles E. Rosenberg, and
Lawton R. Burns (New Brunswick, NJ: Rutgers University Press, 2006), 13.

34 **As real estate agents:** "Are Remodeling Costs Cheaper Than a New Build?
(The Answer Might Surprise You)," *Trulia Blog*, October 31, 2016, trulia
.com/blog/renovating-cheaper-teardown-new-build-answer-might-surprise.

35 **In November 1962:** Shana Alexander, "They Decide Who Lives, Who Dies," *Life*,
November 9, 1962.

35 **Most people couldn't afford:** Alexander, "They Decide Who Lives," 104, 106.

36 **Informally referred to:** Alexander, 106.

36 **The public didn't much:** Blagg 2007 and Rettig 2011 both describe how influential
the *Life* magazine story was in shaping debates about bioethics. Childress 1970 and
Rescher 1979 are articles contemporary with the story and are examples of the types
of discussions that were had about the council. Christopher R. Blagg, "The Early
History of Dialysis for Chronic Renal Failure in the United States: A View from
Seattle," *American Journal of Kidney Diseases* 49, no. 3 (March 1, 2007): 482–96;
Richard A. Rettig, "Special Treatment—the Story of Medicare's ESRD Entitlement,"
New England Journal of Medicine 364, no. 7 (February 17, 2011): 596–98; James F.
Childress, "Who Shall Live When Not All Can Live?," *Soundings: An Interdisciplinary
Journal* 53, no. 4 (Winter 1970): 211–17; and Nicholas Rescher, "The Allocation of
Exotic Medical Lifesaving Therapy," in *Biomedical Ethics and the Law*, ed. James M.
Humber and Robert F. Almeder (Boston, MA: Springer, 1979), 525–41.

36 **It also sparked:** These articles more fully detail how the debate about dialysis allocation led to the government programs we currently have: Rettig, "Special Treatment"; and Tamara Estes Savage and Teri Browne, "Dialysis Rationing and the Just Allocation of Resources: An Historical Primer," *Journal of Nephrology Social Work* 36 (Winter 2012): 37–42.

36 **As a result, the same year:** Blagg, "The Early History of Dialysis"; and Rettig, "Special Treatment."

37 **We have already encountered:** There are over five hundred thousand Medicare patients with end-stage renal disease, and Medicare spends $51 billion a year on their care. Half of these patients are under sixty-five and therefore would not be receiving Medicare in the absence of the program. See United States Renal Data System, *2021 Annual Data Report* (Bethesda, MD: National Institutes of Health, 2021), usrds-adr .niddk.nih.gov/2021; and KFF, "Medicare Beneficiaries with End-Stage-Renal Disease (ESRD)," KFF, accessed February 2, 2021, kff.org/medicare/state-indicator /enrollees-with-esrd.

37 **cover patients with tuberculosis:** Wysolmerski et al., "The Medicaid Tuberculosis Option."

37 **breast and cervical cancer:** Schneider, Elias, and Garfield, "Chapter 1: Medicaid Eligibility."

37 **sickle cell anemia:** Elliott, *Maternal and Child Health Services Block Grant*; Health Resources & Services Administration, "Factsheet: Maternal and Child Health," HRSA, May 11, 2017, hrsa.gov/our-stories/maternal-child/factsheet.html; and Fitzgerald, "Q & A: Medicaid Coverage for Sickle Cell Disease."

37 **Lou Gehrig's disease:** Norris, "Medicare Eligibility for ALS and ESRD Patients"; and Social Security Administration, "President Signs S. 578."

37 **HIV/AIDS:** Engels, "HRSA Celebrates 30 Years of the Ryan White CARE Act."

37 **and (most recently) COVID:** Kellie Moss, Lindsey Dawson, Michelle Long, Jennifer Kates, MaryBeth Musumeci, Juliette Cubanski, and Karen Pollitz, "The Families First Coronavirus Response Act: Summary of Key Provisions," KFF, March 23, 2020, kff .org/coronavirus-covid-19/issue-brief/the-families-first-coronavirus-response-act-summary-of-key-provisions.

37 **For example, the 2000:** Nancy C. Lee, Faye L. Wong, Patricia M. Jamison, Sandra F. Jones, Louise Galaska, Kevin T. Brady, Barbara Wethers et al., "Implementation of the National Breast and Cervical Cancer Early Detection Program," in "National Breast and Cervical Cancer Early Detection Program: Two Decades of Service to Underserved Women," supplement, *Cancer* 120, no. S16 (August 15, 2014): 2540–48, doi.org/10.1002/cncr.28820.

37 **Initially, this program:** Both of the following articles give more information on the results and issues from implementing the original breast and cervical cancer screening program: Paula M. Lantz and LE Sever, "Strategies for Providing Follow-Up and Treatment Services in the National Breast and Cervical Cancer Early Detection Program—United States, 1997," *MMWR* 47, no. 11 (March 27, 1998):

215–18, cdc.gov/mmwr/preview/mmwrhtml/00051730.htm; and Herschel W. Lawson, Rosemarie Henson, Janet Kay Bobo, and Mary K. Kaeser, "Implementing Recommendations for the Early Detection of Breast and Cervical Cancer among Low-Income Women," *MMWR Recommendations and Reports* 49, no. RR02 (March 31, 2000): 35–55, ncbi.nlm.nih.gov/pubmed/15580731.

38 **Powerful advocacy groups:** Paula M. Lantz, Carol S. Weisman, and Zena Itani, "A Disease-Specific Medicaid Expansion for Women: The Breast and Cervical Cancer Prevention and Treatment Act of 2000," *Women's Health Issues* 13, no. 3 (May 1, 2003): 79–92.

38 **Eventually the advocates:** The KFF 2019 article summarizes the law that was passed. Roth 2000 details the Senate report for the Breast and Cervical Cancer Treatment Act. KFF, "Coverage of Breast Cancer Screening and Prevention Services," KFF, September 26, 2019, kff.org/womens-health-policy/fact-sheet/coverage-of-breast-cancer-screening-and-prevention-services; William Roth, Senate Comm. on Finance, Breast and Cervical Cancer Treatment Act, S. Rep. No. 106-323 (2000), congress.gov/congressional-report/106th-congress/senate-report/323/1.

39 **On March 9:** Dennis Hevesi wrote a tribute in the *New York Times* in 2012 that tells Katie Beckett's story. Tanenbaum 1995 explains how her story fits into the larger narrative on Medicaid policy. Kavanaugh 2020 explains her story in further detail. Dennis Hevesi, "Katie Beckett, Who Inspired Health Reform, Dies at 34," *New York Times*, May 22, 2012, nytimes.com/2012/05/23/us/katie-beckett-who-inspired-health-reform-dies-at-34.html; Sandra J. Tanenbaum, "Medicaid Eligibility Policy in the 1980s: Medical Utilitarianism and the 'Deserving' Poor," *Journal of Health Politics, Policy and Law* 20, no. 4 (Winter 1995): 933–54; and Connor W. Kavanaugh, "The Katie Beckett Story - How a Young Girl Changed Medicaid Forever," Palladio Consulting, July 27, 2020, palladioplanning.com/palladio-blog/kfqvo8l7iexptxsbg7uq8y8k60n89u.

39 **But her parents:** In case you are wondering how this could happen, it's because of what Medicaid counts as a patient's financial resources in determining whether they are low enough to qualify for Medicaid. In particular, Medicaid says that if a child with disabilities lives at home, the family's income and assets are used to determine her eligibility. However, if she lives in an institution—such as a hospital or nursing home—parental resources are not counted toward eligibility. Thus, a child can be poor enough to qualify for Medicaid if she is in a nursing home, but not if she comes home. For more information, see Tanenbaum, "Medicaid Eligibility Policy in the 1980s."

39 **In November 1981:** Hevesi, "Katie Beckett."

39 **The Reagan administration also:** Katie Beckett's mother wrote a blog post about her experience (Beckett 2017). Hevesi 2012 and Washington State Health Care Authority 2020 give additional context. Julie Beckett, "I Fought for My Daughter to Live at Home, and Congress Wants to Take That Away from People with Disabilities," American Civil Liberties Union, July 24, 2017, aclu.org/blog/disability-rights

/i-fought-my-daughter-live-home-and-congress-wants-take-away-people; Hevesi, "Katie Beckett"; and Washington State Health Care Authority, *Tax Equity and Fiscal Responsibility Act (TEFRA) and Katie Beckett Waivers* (report to the legislature, Olympia, WA, October 15, 2020), hca.wa.gov/assets/program/tax-equity-fiscal -responsibility-act-katie-beckett-waivers-20201015.pdf.

40 **Long enough, in some:** Joseph Shapiro, "Families Fight to Care for Disabled Kids at Home," NPR, November 8, 2010, Home or Nursing Home, npr.org/2010/11/08 /131145660/families-fight-to-care-for-disabled-kids-at-home.

40 **Katie herself ended:** Hevesi, "Katie Beckett."

41 **On May 21, 1974:** Her legal case was reviewed in this article: Dana E. Schaffner, "EMTALA: All Bark and No Bite," *University of Illinois Law Review* 2005, no. 4 (2005): 1021–42; see also Campbell v. Mincey, 413 F. Supp. 16 (N.D. Miss. 1975), No. WC 74-101-S (United States District Court, N.D. Mississippi, W.D. November 28, 1975).

41 **At that time, hospitals:** For more information on this law and the issues surrounding it, see Lee, "An EMTALA Primer."

41 **G. R. Lafon:** Paul Taylor, "Ailing, Uninsured and Turned Away," *Washington Post*, June 30, 1985, washingtonpost.com/archive/politics/1985/06/30/ailing-uninsured -and-turned-away/8d83c59d-15fa-4527-94a7-ef47b6779e50.

41 **Concerns about patient:** Lee, "An EMTALA Primer."

42 **Republican president George:** Former president Bush said this in a 2007 address. For some examples of the response it received, see Krugman 2007, Chron Editorial Board 2007, and Lindeman 2007; White House Office of the Press Secretary, "President Bush Visits Cleveland, Ohio," press release, July 10, 2007, georgewbush -whitehouse.archives.gov/news/releases/2007/07/print/20070710-6.html; Paul Krugman, "The Waiting Game," *New York Times*, July 16, 2007, nytimes.com/2007 /07/16/opinion/16krugman.html; Chron Editorial Board, "That's the Problem: President Bush Suggests Uninsured Children Go to Hospital Emergency Rooms for Their Care," Chron, July 23, 2007, chron.com/opinion/editorials/article/That-s-the -problem-President-Bush-suggests-1814637.php; and Bard Lindeman, "'You Just Go to an Emergency Room' Is No Prescription for Health Care," *Orlando Sentinel*, September 8, 2007, orlandosentinel.com/news/os-xpm-2007-09-09-lbard09-story.html.

42 **But Republicans do:** Haynes Johnson and David S. Broder, *The System: The American Way of Politics at the Breaking Point* (Boston: Little, Brown, 1996), 353, archive.org /details/systemamericanwa00john.

42 **Far from providing:** For the *U.S. News & World Report* article that covered the issue, see Galvin 2019. Venkatesh et al. discuss the issue in their 2019 article; Gaby Galvin, "'Patient Dumping' Still a Problem Despite Law," *U.S. News & World Report*, April 1, 2019, usnews.com/news/health-news/articles/2019-04-01/patient -dumping-still-a-problem-despite-federal-law; and Arjun K. Venkatesh, Shih-Chuan Chou, Shu-Xia Li, Jennie Choi, Joseph S. Ross, Gail D'Onofrio, Harlan M. Krumholz et al., "Association between Insurance Status and Access to Hospital Care in

Emergency Department Disposition," *JAMA Internal Medicine*, 179, no. 5 (April 1, 2019): 686–93.

42 **Congress had tried:** This program is referred to as the Hill-Burton Act. You can find more information about it in these sources: Health Resources & Services Administration, "Hill-Burton Free and Reduced-Cost Health Care," HRSA, April 13, 2017, hrsa.gov/get-health-care/affordable/hill-burton/index.html; and John Henning Schumann, "A Bygone Era: When Bipartisanship Led to Health Care Transformation," NPR, October 2, 2016, npr.org/sections/health-shots/2016/10/02/495775518/a-bygone-era-when-bipartisanship-led-to-health-care-transformation.

42 **That requirement proved:** Karen I. Treiger, "Preventing Patient Dumping: Sharpening the COBRA's Fangs," *New York University Law Review* 61, no. 6 (1986): 1186–223.

43 **In response to this failed:** Treiger, "Preventing Patient Dumping."

43 **The 1986 federal:** Examination and Treatment for Emergency Medical Conditions and Women in Labor, Pub. L. No. 1395dd, § Title 42—The Public Health and Welfare, 2967 (1986), govinfo.gov/content/pkg/USCODE-2010-title42/pdf/USCODE-2010-title42-chap7-subchapXVIII-partE-sec1395dd.pdf.

44 **As one emergency:** Alexander Schmalz and Nicolas T. Sawyer, "The EMTALA Loophole in Psychiatric Care," *Western Journal of Emergency Medicine* 21, no. 2 (March 2020): 244–46.

44 **Another problem with the patch:** Lee, "An EMTALA Primer."

45 **One uninsured man:** David E. Velasquez, "Charity Care Needs to Be Better Than This," *Health Affairs* 40, no. 4 (April 2021): 672–74.

45 **There have been targeted efforts:** KFF, "Health Coverage of Immigrants," KFF, July 15, 2021, kff.org/racial-equity-and-health-policy/fact-sheet/health-coverage-of-immigrants; Elayne J. Heisler and Nancy Leigh Tyler, *Hospital-Based Emergency Departments: Background and Policy Considerations* (Washington, DC: Congressional Research Service, December 8, 2014), fas.org/sgp/crs/misc/R43812.pdf; and [Redacted], *Federal Funding for Unauthorized Aliens' Emergency Medical Expenses* (Washington, DC: Congressional Research Service, October 18, 2004), everycrsreport.com/files/20041018_RL31630_f93644afcce8d94a51a4c0f9cbf1706813e15ee8.pdf.

45 **A 1960 CBS:** You can find the documentary on YouTube, and Blair 2014 discusses the response to the documentary. See Effland 1991 and National Center for Farmworker Health 2014 for further information on the program; *Harvest of Shame*, directed by Fred. W. Friendly, aired November 25, 1960, on CBS, YouTube video, 50:05, November 24, 2010, youtube.com/watch?v=yJTVF_dya7E; Elizabeth Blair, "In Confronting Poverty, 'Harvest of Shame' Reaped Praise and Criticism," NPR, May 31, 2014, npr.org/2014/05/31/317364146/in-confronting-poverty-harvest-of-shame-reaped-praise-and-criticism; Anne B. W. Effland, "The Emergence of Federal Assistance Programs for Migrant and Seasonal Farmworkers in Post-World War II America" (PhD diss., Iowa State University, 1991), doi.org/10.31274/rtd-180813

-9214; and National Center for Farmworker Health, "Migrant Health Program,"
2014, ncfh.org/uploads/3/8/6/8/38685499/mhhistoryandlegislation.pdf.

45 **A young AIDS:** Ryan White's story changed the narrative of the AIDS epidemic.
Johnson 1990 outlines the work and achievements of Ryan White during his short
life. White also coauthored a book about his experiences, which was published after
his death (Katz 1991). In the *Congressional Record*, Ryan's story was one of the
central pieces, and even today, Ryan is given credit for his role in the HIV/AIDS
government program (Engels 2020); Dirk Johnson, "Ryan White Dies of AIDS at 18;
His Struggle Helped Pierce Myths," *New York Times*, April 9, 1990, nytimes.com
/1990/04/09/obituaries/ryan-white-dies-of-aids-at-18-his-struggle-helped-pierce
-myths.html; Jon Katz, review of *My Own Story*, by Ryan White and Ann Marie
Cunningham, *New York Times*, May 12, 1991, Children's Books, nytimes.com/1991
/05/12/books/childrens-books.html; 136 Cong. Rec. S10319 (daily ed. May 15,
1990), congress.gov/bound-congressional-record/1990/05/15/senate-section; and
Engels, "HRSA Celebrates 30 Years of the Ryan White CARE Act."

45 **A global health:** An example of the coverage tuberculosis received is the *Newsweek*
article from 1992. Wysolmerski et al. 2015 explains the resulting policy changes;
Newsweek Staff, "Tuberculosis: A Deadly Return," *Newsweek*, March 15, 1992,
newsweek.com/tuberculosis-deadly-return-195804; Wysolmerski et al., "The
Medicaid Tuberculosis Option."

45 **In 2001, a well-organized:** For information on the Ice Bucket Challenge and the
ALS Association, see ALS Association 2019 and Sifferlin 2014. For information on
some of the MLB's advocacy efforts, see Bloom 2009 and Hjelle 2014. See Norris
2019 for more information on qualifying for Medicare with an ALS diagnosis. ALS
Association, "Ice Bucket Challenge Dramatically Accelerated the Fight against ALS,"
press release, June 4, 2019, als.org/stories-news/ice-bucket-challenge-dramatically
-accelerated-fight-against-als; Alexandra Sifferlin, "Here's How the ALS Ice Bucket
Challenge Actually Started," *Time*, August 18, 2014, time.com/3136507/als-ice
-bucket-challenge-started; Barry M. Bloom, "MLB to Fight '4♦ALS' Awareness,"
MLB.com, February 3, 2009, mlb.com/news/mlb-to-fight-4als-awareness/c
-3792958; Jennifer Hjelle, "Let's Name a Cure in Honor of Lou Gehrig, Instead of a
Disease," *ALS Connections*, ALS Association MN/ND/SD Chapter, July 2014, web
.alsa.org/site/MessageViewer?dlv_id=0&em_id=232467.0; and Norris, "Medicare
Eligibility for ALS and ESRD Patients."

PART II: FORM FOLLOWS FUNCTION

47 **The influential nineteenth century:** Louis H. Sullivan, "The Tall Office Building
Artistically Considered," *Lippincott's Monthly Magazine*, April 1896, 403–9; and
Mervyn D. Kaufman, *Father of Skyscrapers: A Biography of Louis Sullivan* (Boston:
Little, Brown, 1969).

47 **One is that health:** FDR claimed health care was a human right in this speech:
Franklin D. Roosevelt, "1944 State of the Union Message to Congress," January 11,

1944, Franklin D. Roosevelt Presidential Library and Museum, Hyde Park, NY, fdrlibrary.marist.edu/archives/address_text.html.

CHAPTER 4: A UNIVERSAL COMMITMENT

51 **One in ten Americans:** Katherine Keisler-Starkey and Lisa N. Bunch, *Health Insurance Coverage in the United States: 2019*, Current Population Reports, no. P60-271 (Washington, DC: US Government Publishing Office, September 2020), 4.

52 **The evidence from:** For an overview of the results, see: J-PAL Policy Briefcase, "Understanding Medicaid Expansion: The Effects of Insuring Low-Income Adults," J-PAL Policy Briefcase (Cambridge, MA: Abdul Latif Jameel Poverty Action Lab, 2022), povertyactionlab.org/publication/understanding-medicaid-expansion -effects-insuring-low-income-adults.

52 **But it also revealed:** The estimate that the uninsured receive four fifths of the medical care that they would get if they were insured is based on the estimate from the experiment that covering the uninsured with Medicaid increased health-care spending by 25 percent; in other words, the uninsured spend about four fifths (=1/1.25) of what they would spend if they were insured; Amy Finkelstein, Sarah Taubman, Bill Wright, Mira Bernstein, Jonathan Gruber, Joseph Newhouse, Heidi Allen et al., "The Oregon Health Insurance Experiment: Evidence from the First Year," *Quarterly Journal of Economics* 127, no. 3 (August 2012): 1057–1106.

52 **And they pay for only:** Amy Finkelstein, Nathaniel Hendren, and Erzo F. P. Luttmer, "The Value of Medicaid: Interpreting Results from the Oregon Health Insurance Experiment," *Journal of Political Economy* 127, no. 6 (December 2019): 2836–74.

52 **National data corroborate:** Amy Finkelstein, Neale Mahoney, and Matthew J. Notowidigdo, "What Does (Formal) Health Insurance Do, and for Whom?," *Annual Review of Economics* 10, no. 1 (August 2018): 261–86.

53 **Indeed, once the bills:** Neale Mahoney, "Bankruptcy as Implicit Health Insurance," *American Economic Review* 105, no. 2 (February 2015): 710–46.

53 **To understand how these:** Congressional Research Service, *Introduction to the National Flood Insurance Program (NFIP)* (Washington, DC: Congressional Research Service, November 19, 2021), 10, 16–22, sgp.fas.org/crs/homesec /R44593.pdf.

54 **Just as many Americans:** For example, estimates from 2006 suggest that compliance with the mandatory flood insurance requirement was possibly "as low as 43% in some areas of the country (the Midwest), and as high as 88% in others (the West)." Another estimate found the compliance was around 73 percent in New York City in 2016. For more information, see Congressional Research Service, *The National Flood Insurance Program: Selected Issues and Legislation in the 116th Congress* (Washington, DC: Congressional Research Service, December 23, 2019), 17, crsreports.congress.gov /product/pdf/R/R46095/28.

54 **We know what happens:** For some examples, see Eric Lipton and Michael S. Schmidt, "Distribution of Billions in Aid to Storm Victims Will Test FEMA," *New*

York Times, October 30, 2012, nytimes.com/2012/10/31/us/federal-aid-authorized
-for-storm-victims-in-new-york-and-new-jersey.html; Jeremy Diamond and Sophie
Tatum, "Trump Makes Disaster Declaration for Hurricane Harvey," CNN, August
25, 2017, cnn.com/2017/08/25/politics/trump-harvey-declaration/index.html;
Sarah Maslin Nir, "New York and New Jersey Residents to Receive Federal Aid after
Storm," *New York Times*, September 6, 2021, nytimes.com/2021/09/06/nyregion
/new-york-nj-fema-disaster-aid-ida.html; and FEMA, "Declared Disasters," US
Department of Homeland Security, accessed March 17, 2021, fema.gov/disasters
/disaster-declarations.

55 **Stories like these vividly:** Arthur Garson, "Heart of the Uninsured," *Health Affairs*
26, no. 1 (January/February 2007): 230.

55 **That would be like:** Tennessee Williams, *A Streetcar Named Desire: A Play in Three
Acts* (New York: Dramatists Play Service, 1947), 102–3, archive.org/details
/streetcarnamedde0000will_v7x0.

55 **The big potatoes:** Teresa A. Coughlin, Haley Samuel-Jakubos, and Rachel Garfield,
"Sources of Payment for Uncompensated Care for the Uninsured," KFF, April 6,
2021, kff.org/uninsured/issue-brief/sources-of-payment-for-uncompensated-care
-for-the-uninsured.

55 **Yes, every year:** Based on authors' calculations using Centers for Disease Control's
"National Hospital Ambulatory Medical Survey" data from 2019 for emergency room
visits, and from 2014 for Community Health Centers (extrapolated using 2019
community health center visit numbers from KFF 2021, as well as Centers for
Disease Control's "National Ambulatory Medical Care Survey" from 2018 for
physician office visits, and "National Health Interview Survey" from 2018 for
overnight hospital stays). KFF, "Community Health Center Delivery Sites and
Patient Visits," KFF, September 13, 2021, table, 2019 timeframe, kff.org/other
/state-indicator/community-health-center-sites-and-visits.

56 **In dollar terms:** Michael Karpman, Teresa A. Coughlin, and Rachel Garfield,
"Declines in Uncompensated Care Costs for the Uninsured under the ACA
and Implications of Recent Growth in the Uninsured Rate," KFF, April 6, 2021,
kff.org/uninsured/issue-brief/declines-in-uncompensated-care-costs-for
-the-uninsured-under-the-aca-and-implications-of-recent-growth-in-the
-uninsured-rate.

56 **Almost all are required:** American Patient Rights Association, "No Money or
Insurance? Can Hospitals Turn Patients Away?," APRA, June 4, 2019,
americanpatient.org/can-hospitals-turn-patients-away; and Thomas Rice, Pauline
Rosenau, Lynn Y. Unruh, and Andrew J. Barnes, "United States of America: Health
System Review," ed. Richard B. Saltman and Ewout van Ginneken, *Health Systems in
Transition* 15, no. 3 (2013): 243–46.

56 **For-profit hospitals are exempt:** Fredric Blavin and Diane Arnos, "Hospital
Readiness for COVID-19: Analysis of Bed Capacity and How It Varies across the
Country" (Urban Institute, March 2020), urban.org/sites/default/files/publication

/101864/hospital-readiness-for-covid-19_2.pdf; and American Hospital Association, "Fast Facts on U.S. Hospitals, 2019," American Hospital Association, 2019, aha.org /statistics/2020-01-07-archived-fast-facts-us-hospitals-2019.

56 **Aware of medicine's:** Charles Rosenberg, *The Care of Strangers: The Rise of America's Hospital System* (New York: Basic Books, 1987), 71–78; and Paul Starr, *The Social Transformation of American Medicine: The Rise of a Sovereign Profession and the Making of a Vast Industry* (New York: Basic Books, 1982), 32–37.

57 **In this environment:** Rosenberg, *The Care of Strangers*, 18–19.

57 **These early hospitals were funded:** Rosenberg, 102.

57 **This sentiment persists:** Gay Becker, "Deadly Inequality in the Health Care 'Safety Net': Uninsured Ethnic Minorities' Struggle to Live with Life-Threatening Illnesses," *Medical Anthropology Quarterly* 18, no. 2 (June 2004): 260.

57 **Nonprofit hospitals—which account:** Blavin and Arnos, "Hospital Readiness for COVID-19"; and Rebecca Sachs, "How Do Hospitals Set Their Charity Care Policies? Evidence from Nonprofit Tax Returns," 2019, available upon request: rebecca.sachs @cbo.gov.

58 **Publicly owned and:** Blavin and Arnos, "Hospital Readiness for COVID-19"; Douglas Almond, Janet Currie, and Emilia Simeonova, "Public vs. Private Provision of Charity Care? Evidence from the Expiration of Hill-Burton Requirements in Florida," *Journal of Health Economics* 30, no. 1 (January 2011): 189–99; and Rice et al., "United States of America," 243–46.

58 **The government also pays:** Medicaid and CHIP Payment and Access Commission, "Disproportionate Share Hospital Payments," MACPAC, accessed April 21, 2022, macpac.gov/subtopic/disproportionate-share-hospital-payments.

58 **These debts can accrue:** For an evocative description of what this experience was like for one patient—as described by his medical student son—see David E. Velasquez, "Charity Care Needs to Be Better Than This," *Health Affairs* 40, no. 4 (April 2021): 672–74.

58 **Part of the problem is:** David Dranove, Craig Garthwaite, and Christopher Ody, "A Floor-and-Trade Proposal to Improve the Delivery of Charity-Care Services by U.S. Nonprofit Hospitals" (Discussion Paper 2015-07, Hamilton Project, October 2015), hamiltonproject.org/assets/files/floor_and_trade_improve_delivery_of_charity _care_services_dranove.pdf.

58 **For public hospitals:** National Association of Counties, *Counties' Role in Healthcare Delivery and Financing* (Washington, DC: Community Services Division, County Services Department, July 2007), naco.org/sites/default/files/documents /Counties'%20Role%20in%20Healthcare%20Delivery%20and%20Financing.pdf.

58 **Nonprofit hospitals tend:** Susannah Camic Tahk, "Tax-Exempt Hospitals and Their Communities," *Columbia Journal of Tax Law* 6, no. 1 (January 2015): 33; and Dranove, Garthwaite, and Ody, "A Floor-and-Trade Proposal."

58 **In Maryland, for example:** For a summary, see Tozzi 2021. For the legislation, see the Maryland House Bill from 2020. For a report on this information, see the

Maryland Health Services Cost Review Commission 2021. John Tozzi, "Medical Debt Collection Tactics Disproportionately Hit Black Americans," *Bloomberg*, November 22, 2021, bloomberg.com/news/features/2021-11-22/medical-debt -collection-tactics-disproportionately-hit-black-americans; Maryland House Bill 1420 (LegiScan 2020), legiscan.com/MD/bill/HB1420/2020; Maryland Health Services Cost Review Commission, *Analysis of the Impact of Hospital Financial Assistance Policy Options on Uncompensated Care and Costs to Payers* (MSAR no. 12823, Baltimore, MD: Maryland Health Services Cost Review Commission, February 2021), static1.squarespace.com/static/5b05bed59772ae16550f90de/t /6045840486f11518b48230a5/1615168518742/HSCRC+1420+report.pdf.

58 **Throughout the country, it's up:** There is a requirement that nonprofit hospitals "notify" their patients of their charity care policies, but there's no standard—or even guidance—for what constitutes patient "notification"; fine print buried within pages of forms apparently counts as such. For more information and stories about experiences navigating charity care, see Rau 2019 and Wolfson 2020. For more on the requirements hospitals must follow, see Internal Revenue Service 2022; Jordan Rau, "Patients Eligible for Charity Care Instead Get Big Bills," KHN, October 14, 2019, khn.org/news/patients-eligible-for-charity-care-instead-get-big-bills; Bernard J. Wolfson, "Crushed by a Hospital Bill? Stand Up for Yourself," *California Healthline*, March 5, 2020, californiahealthline.org/news/charity-care-tips-crushed-by-a -hospital-bill-stand-up-for-yourself; and Internal Revenue Service, "Financial Assistance Policy and Emergency Medical Care Policy—Section 501(r)(4)," IRS, July 15, 2022, irs.gov/charities-non-profits/financial-assistance-policy-and -emergency-medical-care-policy-section-501r4.

59 **Nonetheless, the existence:** Rosenberg, *The Care of Strangers*, 102.

59 **One of the biggest:** For the number of health center service delivery locations, see National Association of Community Health Centers 2019. Many areas that have been designated as medically underserved do not have a health center (Mickey 2012). And even where they exist, patients may not seek care because they are unaware of their services (Bettigole 2015). National Association of Community Health Centers, "America's Health Centers," August 2019, nachc.org/wp-content /uploads/2019/07/Americas-Health-Centers-Final-8.5.19.pdf; Robert W. Mickey, "Dr. StrangeRove; or, How Conservatives Learned to Stop Worrying and Love Community Health Centers," in *The Health Care Safety Net in a Post-reform World,* ed. Mark A. Hall and Sara Rosenbaum (Ithaca, NY: Rutgers University Press, 2012), 22, doi.org/10.36019/9780813553177-004; and Cheryl Bettigole, "An Uninsured Immigrant Delays Needed Care," *Health Affairs* 34, no. 12 (December 2015): 2192–95.

59 **the clinics offer:** For 2019 statistics on community health centers, see National Association of Community Health Centers 2019. For more information on these centers, see Heisler 2020, Rice et al. 2013, Weiss et al. 2016, and Bureau of Primary Health Care 2018. National Association of Community Health Centers, "America's

Health Centers"; Elayne J. Heisler, *Federal Health Centers and COVID-19* (Washington, DC: Congressional Research Service, April 30, 2020), crsreports .congress.gov/product/pdf/IN/IN11367; Rice et al., "United States of America," 225–27; Adam Weiss, Sharon K. Long, Christal Ramos, and Terri Coughlin, "Federally Qualified Health Centers' Importance in the Safety Net Continues as Affordable Care Act Implementation Moves Ahead," Health Reform Monitoring Survey (Urban Institute, August 26, 2016), http://hrms.urban.org/briefs/fqhc -importance-safety-net.pdf; and Bureau of Primary Health Care, "Sliding Fee Discount Program," in *Health Center Program Compliance Manual* (Health Resources & Services Administration, August 20, 2018), 38–42, bphc.hrsa.gov /sites/default/files/bphc/compliance/hc-compliance-manual.pdf.

59 **These clinics are federally:** National Association of Community Health Centers, "330 Statute," NACHC, accessed March 22, 2022, nachc.org/focus-areas /policy-matters/health-center-funding/330-program-requirements.

60 **Direct federal funding:** For an overall review of these funding sources, see Heisler 2017. For the funding of these centers by source, see Taylor 2010. Elayne J. Heisler, *Federal Health Centers: An Overview* (Washington, DC: Congressional Research Service, May 19, 2017), fas.org/sgp/crs/misc/R43937.pdf; and Jessamyn Taylor, "The Primary Care Safety Net: Strained, Transitioning, Critical" (Background Paper no. 79, George Washington University, Washington, DC, *National Health Policy Forum*, September 28, 2010), hsrc.himmelfarb.gwu.edu/sphhs_centers_nhpf/242.

60 **for Native American:** Indian Health Service, "About IHS," Indian Health Service, accessed March 22, 2022, ihs.gov/aboutihs.

60 **for patients with diseases:** Health Resources & Services Administration, "About the Ryan White HIV/AIDS Program," Ryan White HIV/AIDS Bureau, HRSA, August 3, 2016, hab.hrsa.gov/about-ryan-white-hivaids-program/about-ryan-white-hivaids -program; and Andy Schneider, Risa Elias, and Rachel Garfield, "Chapter 1: Medicaid Eligibility" in *The Medicaid Resource Book* (Washington, DC: Kaiser Commission on Medicaid and the Uninsured, July 2002), kff.org/wp-content/uploads/2013 /05/mrbeligibility.pdf.

60 **another for migrant:** Heisler, *Federal Health Centers*.

60 **prescription drugs:** American Hospital Association, "Fact Sheet: The 340B Drug Pricing Program," American Hospital Association, accessed March 22, 2022, aha .org/fact-sheets/2020-01-28-fact-sheet-340b-drug-pricing-program; and Richard Cauchi, Karmen Hanson, and Steve Landess, "State Pharmaceutical Assistance Programs," National Conference of State Legislatures, June 1, 2018, web.archive.org /web/20200806071906/ncsl.org/research/health/state-pharmaceutical-assistance -programs.aspx.

60 **family planning:** Adrienne Stith Butler and Ellen Wright Clayton, eds., *A Review of the HHS Family Planning Program: Mission, Management, and Measurement of Results* (Washington, DC: National Academies Press, 2009), 487, ncbi.nlm.nih.gov /books/NBK215217/pdf/Bookshelf_NBK215217.pdf.

60 **maternal and child:** Victoria L. Elliott, *Maternal and Child Health Services Block Grant: Background and Funding* (Washington, DC: Congressional Research Service, August 28, 2017), fas.org/sgp/crs/misc/R44929.pdf.

60 **lead screenings:** Centers for Disease Control and Prevention, "About CDC's Childhood Lead Poisoning Prevention Program," CDC, February 3, 2022, cdc.gov /nceh/lead/about/program.htm.

60 **breast and cervical cancer screenings:** Centers for Disease Control and Prevention, "About the National Breast and Cervical Cancer Early Detection Program," CDC, October 18, 2019, cdc.gov/cancer/nbccedp/about.htm.

60 **substance abuse:** Substance Abuse and Mental Health Services Administration, "Community Mental Health Services Block Grant," SAMHSA, 2020, samhsa.gov /grants/block-grants/mhbg.

60 **treatment of sickle:** Health Resources & Services Administration, "Factsheet: Maternal and Child Health," HRSA, accessed July 31, 2020, hrsa.gov/our-stories /maternal-child/factsheet.html.

60 **Health centers can:** Heisler, *Federal Health Centers*, 22–24.

60 **State and local governments have:** For a list of various drug assistance programs, see Asthma and Allergy Foundation of America, "Drug Assistance Programs," AAFA, accessed March 22, 2022, aafa.org/patient-assistance-medicine-drug -programs.

61 **To help navigate:** California Health Care Foundation, "The Clinic's Tale: Chasing FQHC Status Not for the Faint-Hearted," California Health Care Foundation, July 2012, 2, chcf.org/wp-content/uploads/2017/12/PDF-ClinicsTaleChasing FQHCStatus.pdf.

61 **In addition to the consultants:** Laurie E. Felland, Erin Fries Taylor, and Anneliese M. Gerland, "The Community Safety Net and Prescription Drug Access for Low-Income, Uninsured People" (Issue Brief no. 105, Center for Studying Health System Change, April 2006), 1–4.

61 **But in the end:** For example, Rebekah Bernard, a physician who worked at a federally funded center and quit in frustration over this burden, wrote about her experience in a piece titled "Here's Why I No Longer Believe Government Health Care Can Work." She wrote about "extra duties, piles of paperwork," and about "bullying tactics" by a team of office bureaucrats who needed to ensure that her every move complied with federal regulations. See Rebekah Bernard, "I Was a Physician at a Federally Qualified Health Center. Here's Why I No Longer Believe Government Health Care Can Work," Foundation for Economic Education, August 26, 2019, fee.org/articles /i-was-a-physician-at-a-federally-qualified-health-center-heres-why-i-no-longer -believe-government-health-care-can-work.

61 **One physician at a community:** Bettigole, "An Uninsured Immigrant Delays Needed Care," 2192–95.

61 **Sometimes physicians are able:** Kohar Jones, "Asthma and Injustice on Chicago's Southeast Side," *Health Affairs* 35, no. 5 (May 2016): 928–31.

CHAPTER 5: ORIGIN STORIES

63 **The New Testament parable:** Luke 10:30–37 (New Living Translation).

63 **over a dozen hospitals:** Some of the many examples include: Good Samaritan Hospital and ER in San Jose, CA, accessed March 24, 2022, goodsamsanjose.com; MedStar Good Samaritan Hospital in Baltimore, MD, accessed March 24, 2022, medstarhealth.org/locations/medstar-good-samaritan-hospital; Good Samaritan Hospital in Suffern, NY, accessed March 24, 2022, goodsamhosp.org; and Good Samaritan Regional Medical Center in Corvallis, OR, accessed March 24, 2022, samhealth.org/find-a-location/g/good-samaritan-regional-medical-center.

64 **In a famous 1975:** James M. Buchanan, "The Samaritan's Dilemma," in *Altruism, Morality, and Economic Theory*, ed. Edmund S. Phelps (New York: Russell Sage Foundation, 1975), 71–86, http://www.jstor.org /stable/10.7758/9781610446792.10.

64 **How then to protect:** Buchanan, "The Samaritan's Dilemma," 75.

64 **"courage to the sticking place":** William Shakespeare, *Macbeth,* act 1, scene 7, Line 60, 1623.

65 **From the very dawn:** Michele L. Landis, "Fate, Responsibility, and 'Natural' Disaster Relief: Narrating the American Welfare State," *Law & Society Review* 33, no. 2 (1999): 257.

65 **The sociologist and legal:** Michele Landis Dauber, in *The Sympathetic State: Disaster Relief and the Origins of the American Welfare State* (Chicago: University of Chicago Press, 2012), 6.

66 **Thus the end-stage renal disease:** Elisa J. Gordon, Thomas R. Prohaska, and Ashwini R. Sehgal, "The Financial Impact of Immunosuppressant Expenses on New Kidney Transplant Recipients," *Clinical Transplantation* 22, no. 6 (November/December 2008): 738–48.

66 **Such laws reflect our tendency:** Kwame Anthony Appiah, *Experiments in Ethics* (Cambridge, MA: Harvard University Press, 2008), 95–97.

66 **Most people, Unger notes:** Peter K. Unger, *Living High and Letting Die: Our Illusion of Innocence* (New York: Oxford University Press, 1996), 24–36.

67 **The experimental moral:** Joshua Greene, "From Neural 'Is' to Moral 'Ought': What Are the Moral Implications of Neuroscientific Moral Psychology?," *Nature Reviews Neuroscience* 4, no. 10 (October 2003): 848–49; and Appiah, *Experiments in Ethics*, 93–100.

67 **Dauber describes how:** Dauber, *The Sympathetic State*, 15.

68 **This recategorization, however:** Dauber, 15.

68 **Perhaps no example:** Cornell University, School of Industrial and Labor Relations, *Disaster Relief Medicaid Evaluation Project*, December 2005, health.ny.gov/health _care/medicaid/related/docs/drm_report.pdf; Centers for Medicare & Medicaid Services, "1135 Waiver - at a Glance," Department of Health and Human Services, accessed May 5, 2022, cms.gov/Medicare/Provider-Enrollment-and-Certification /SurveyCertEmergPrep/Downloads/1135-Waivers-At-A-Glance.pdf; and Centers for Medicare & Medicaid Services, "About Section 1115 Demonstrations," Medicaid

.gov, accessed May 5, 2022, medicaid.gov/medicaid/section-1115-demonstrations /about-section-1115-demonstrations/index.html.

69 **The answer lies in part:** Michael B. Katz, in *The Undeserving Poor: America's Enduring Confrontation with Poverty,* 2nd ed. (New York: Oxford University Press, 2013), 1.

69 **As the sociologist, Theda:** For a discussion of the policy forces behind veterans' pension and cash welfare for the indigent, see Skocpol 1995. For a discussion of the policy forces affecting natural disaster relief and unemployment insurance, see Dauber 1982. Or as the historian David Rosner has put it, "One need only recall President Reagan's use of the notion of the 'truly needy,' or the distinctions between Medicare and Medicaid, Social Security and Welfare, to realize the centrality of popular conceptions of human worth in determining entitlement. In earlier periods of American history, the terms 'deserving' and 'undeserving,' 'worthy' and 'unworthy,' were used to define who was to be cared for and what services were to be provided through a variety of charitable public programs" (Rosner 1982). Theda Skocpol, *Protecting Soldiers and Mothers: The Political Origins of Social Policy in the United States* (Cambridge, MA: Belknap Press, 1995), 149; Dauber, *The Sympathetic State*; and David Rosner, "Health Care for the 'Truly Needy': Nineteenth-Century Origins of the Concept," *Milbank Memorial Fund Quarterly* 60, no. 3 (September 1982): 355.

69 **In the Victorian:** For more discussion on the ideas of deserving and undeserving poor, see Katz, *The Undeserving Poor,* 1–9, 25; Michael B. Katz, *In the Shadow of the Poorhouse: A Social History of Welfare in America* (New York: Basic Books, 1986), 25, 34, 95–96, 128; Charles Rosenberg, *The Care of Strangers: The Rise of America's Hospital System* (New York: Basic Books, 1987), 19, 103; and Rosner, "Health Care for the 'Truly Needy,'" 355.

70 **Illness in the nineteenth:** George A. Akerlof, "The Economics of 'Tagging' as Applied to the Optimal Income Tax, Welfare Programs, and Manpower Planning," *American Economic Review* 68, no. 1 (March 1978): 8–19.

70 **Patients who applied:** Rosenberg, *The Care of Strangers,* 24–25.

70 **An excerpt from:** Rosenberg, 25.

70 **All told, the admissions:** Rosenberg, 24.

71 **So too did the pricing:** Rosenberg, 29.

71 **The legacy of this:** H. W. Brands, *Reagan: The Life* (New York: Doubleday, 2015), 155–56.

71 **Medicaid itself was:** Sandra J. Tanenbaum, "Medicaid Eligibility Policy in the 1980s: Medical Utilitarianism and the 'Deserving' Poor," *Journal of Health Politics, Policy and Law* 20, no. 4 (Winter 1995): 933–34.

71 **This was why Medicaid:** Tanenbaum, "Medicaid Eligibility Policy in the 1980s," 933–54; Ezekiel J. Emanuel, *Which Country Has the World's Best Health Care?* (New York: PublicAffairs, 2020), 23.

71 **Likewise, President Richard Nixon:** Richard M. Nixon, "Statement on Signing the Social Security Amendments of 1972," October 30, 1972, American Presidency

Project, University of California, Santa Barbara, presidency.ucsb.edu/documents
/statement-signing-the-social-security-amendments-1972.

CHAPTER 6: WHAT IS TO BE DONE

74 **from a scholar at the conservative:** Robert E. Moffit, "Personal Freedom,
Responsibility, and Mandates," *Health Affairs* 13, no. 2 (Spring 1994): 101–3.

74 **to a moderate:** Martha Bebinger, "Personal Responsibility: How Mitt Romney
Embraced the Individual Mandate in Massachusetts Health Reform," *Health Affairs*
31, no. 9 (September 2012): 2105–13.

74 **to a notorious:** J. Ruth Bader Ginsburg, National Federation of Independent
Business v. Sebelius, 567 U.S. 519 (2012), Justia Opinion Summary and
Annotations, Justia Law, accessed March 15, 2022, supreme.justia.com/cases
/federal/us/567/519.

74 **In an era in which:** John E. Ransom, "The Beginnings of Hospitals in the United
States," *Bulletin of the History of Medicine* 13, no. 5 (May 1943): 514–39.

74 **The problem was that seamen:** Robert Straus, *Medical Care for Seamen: The
Origin of Public Medical Service in the United States*, Merchant Seaman Studies 1
(New Haven, CT: Yale University Press, 1950), 25–26.

74 **Alexander Hamilton had**: Straus, *Medical Care for Seamen*, 23.

75 **Here's how it worked**: Straus, 32–34.

75 **Requiring that sailors**: Straus, 33.

75 **The medical sociologist:** For Straus's PhD thesis that was turned into this book, see
Straus, *Medical Care for Seamen*.

76 **The entire text:** Straus, 32–34.

76 **The 2010 Patient Protection:** If you would like to read the legislation, you can find it
on HealthCare.gov. To read some of the discussion that the length of the ACA
sparked among politicians, see Kessler 2013; Centers for Medicare & Medicaid
Services, "Read the Affordable Care Act, Health Care Law," HealthCare.gov, 2010,
healthcare.gov/where-can-i-read-the-affordable-care-act; and Glenn Kessler, "How
Many Pages of Regulations for Obamacare?," *Washington Post*, May 15, 2013,
washingtonpost.com/blogs/fact-checker/post/how-many-pages-of-regulations-for
-obamacare/2013/05/14/61eec914-bcf9-11e2-9b09-1638acc3942e_blog.html.

76 **Both coupled the insurance:** For information on the Marine-Hospital dues, see
"Abolition" 1884. For Obamacare, see Jost 2017. "Abolition of Marine-Hospital
Dues," *Journal of the American Medical Association* 3, no. 5 (August 2, 1884): 130; and
Timothy Jost, "The Tax Bill and the Individual Mandate: What Happened, and What
Does It Mean?," *Health Affairs Forefront* (blog), *Health Affairs*, December 20, 2017,
healthaffairs.org/do/10.1377/forefront.20171220.323429/full.

76 **Economic theorists arrived:** For an example of the economic theory argument for
compulsory insurance based on the Samaritan's dilemma, see Stephen Coate,
"Altruism, the Samaritan's Dilemma, and Government Transfer Policy," *American
Economic Review* 85, no. 1 (March 1995): 46–57.

76 **We can see it at:** Carlo De Pietro, Paul Camenzind, Isabelle Sturny, Luca Crivelli, Suzanne Edwards-Garavoglia, Anne Spranger, Friedrich Wittenbecher et al., "Switzerland: Health System Review," ed. Wilm Quentin, Friedrich Wittenbecher, Anne Spranger, Suzanne Edwards-Garavoglia, *Health Systems in Transition* 17, no. 4 (2015): 23.

77 **We will not let:** Thomas Zeltner, "Understanding the 'Swiss Watch' Function of Switzerland's Health System," interview by Tsung-Mei Cheng, *Health Affairs* 29, no. 8 (August 2010): 1443.

77 **United States Supreme Court justice:** Ginsburg, National Federation of Independent Business v. Sebelius, 567 U.S. 519.

77 **The famously free-market:** F. A. Hayek, *The Constitution of Liberty* (Chicago: University of Chicago Press, 1960), 299–300.

78 **Yet he nonetheless embraced:** Hayek, *The Constitution of Liberty,* 286.

78 **the entire moral and cultural:** Moffit, "Personal Freedom, Responsibility, and Mandates," 101–3.

78 **Two decades after:** Sarah Kliff, "Romney's Law, ACA Very Similar," *Politico,* May 12, 2011, politico.com/story/2011/05/romneys-law-aca-very-similar-054853; and Jessica Taylor, "Mitt Romney Finally Takes Credit for Obamacare," NPR, October 23, 2015, npr.org/sections/itsallpolitics/2015/10/23/451200436/mitt-romney-finally -takes-credit-for-obamacare.

78 **Romney's argument for:** Bebinger, "Personal Responsibility."

79 **A striking illustration:** J. E. King and John Marangos, "Two Arguments for Basic Income: Thomas Paine (1737-1809) and Thomas Spence (1750-1814)," *History of Economic Ideas* 14, no. 1 (2006): 55–71; and Annie Lowrey, *Give People Money: How a Universal Basic Income Would End Poverty, Revolutionize Work, and Remake the World* (New York: Crown, 2018), 5, 29–31.

79 **Also like compulsory health insurance:** Ezra Klein, "Bernie Sanders," *Vox,* July 28, 2015, vox.com/2015/7/28/9014491/bernie-sanders-vox-conversation; and Charles Murray, *In Our Hands: A Plan to Replace the Welfare State* (Washington, DC: AEI Press, 2016), 5.

79 **Murray, who has argued:** Murray, *In Our Hands,* 3.

80 **Murray's UBI proposal:** Murray, 7.

80 **There's also a rich philosophical:** Norman Daniels, *Just Health Care* (Cambridge: Cambridge University Press, 1985), 56.

CHAPTER 7: ADEQUACY, NOT EQUALITY

81 **Of all the inequalities:** King was speaking in March 1966, a few months before the enactment of Medicare, which—in a little-known part of its history—required Southern hospitals to desegregate as a condition for receiving the new federal funding. See Vann R. Newkirk II, "The Fight for Health Care Has Always Been about Civil Rights," *The Atlantic,* June 27, 2017, theatlantic.com/politics/archive/2017/06 /the-fight-for-health-care-is-really-all-about-civil-rights/531855.

81 **Richer Americans and White:** Adriana Lleras-Muney, "Mind the Gap: A Review of *The Health Gap: The Challenge of an Unequal World*," by Sir Michael Marmot, *Journal of Economic Literature* 56, no. 3 (September 2018): 1080–101; and Raj Chetty, Michael Stepner, Sarah Abraham, Shelby Lin, Benjamin Scuderi, Nicholas Turner, Augustin Bergeron et al., "The Association between Income and Life Expectancy in the United States, 2001-2014," *JAMA* 315, no. 16 (April 26, 2016): 1750–66.

81 **Black children who live:** Schwandt et al. document this in their article. Additionally, Kennedy-Moulton et al. linked birth records in California to government income tax records and found that infant and maternal health in Black families from the top of the income distribution was worse than that of White families from the bottom of the income distribution. Hannes Schwandt, Janet Currie, Marlies Bär, James Banks, Paola Bertoli, Aline Bütikofer, Sarah Cattan, et al., "Inequality in Mortality between Black and White Americans by Age, Place, and Cause and in Comparison to Europe, 1990 to 2018," *Proceedings of the National Academy of Sciences* 118, no. 40 (September 28, 2021): e2104684118; and Kate Kennedy-Moulton, Sarah Miller, Petra Persson, Maya Rossin-Slater, Laura R. Wherry, and Gloria Aldana, "Maternal and Infant Health Inequality: New Evidence from Linked Administrative Data" (Summer Institute 2022, National Bureau of Economic Research, July 20, 2022), conference .nber.org/conf_papers/f170399.pdf.

81 **Maternal mortality is 2.5:** Eugene Declercq and Laurie Zephyrin, "Maternal Mortality in the United States: A Primer," *Commonwealth Fund*, December 16, 2020, doi.org/10.26099/ta1q-mw24.

82 **Uwe Reinhardt, the late:** Uwe E. Reinhardt, "Wanted: A Clearly Articulated Social Ethic for American Health Care," *JAMA* 278, no. 17 (November 5, 1997):1446–47.

82 **"In the western United States":** Victor R. Fuchs, *Who Shall Live? Health, Economics, and Social Choice*, 2nd ed. (New York: Basic Books, 1974), 52.

82 **In one state, the people:** Fuchs, *Who Shall Live?*, 52–55.

82 **Fuchs famously attributed:** Fuchs, 52–54.

83 **a team of researchers conducted:** Chetty et al., "The Association between Income and Life Expectancy."

84 **The experiences of the elderly:** Amy Finkelstein, Matthew Gentzkow, and Heidi Williams, "Place-Based Drivers of Mortality: Evidence from Migration," *American Economic Review* 111, no. 8 (August 2021): 2697–735.

84 **A team of economists:** Elliott S. Fisher, David E. Wennberg, Therese A. Stukel, Daniel J. Gottlieb, F. L. Lucas, and Étoile L. Pinder, "The Implications of Regional Variations in Medicare Spending. Part 1: The Content, Quality, and Accessibility of Care," *Annals of Internal Medicine* 138, no. 4 (February 18, 2003): 273–87; Elliott S. Fisher, David E. Wennberg, Therese A. Stukel, Daniel J. Gottlieb, F. L. Lucas, and Étoile L. Pinder, "The Implications of Regional Variations in Medicare Spending. Part 2: Health Outcomes and Satisfaction with Care," *Annals of Internal Medicine* 138, no. 4 (February 18, 2003): 288–98; and Jonathan Skinner, "Causes and Consequences of Regional Variations in Health Care," in *Handbook of Health Economics*, ed. Mark V. Pauly, Thomas G. McGuire, and Pedro P. Barros, vol. 2 (Amsterdam: Elsevier, 2011), 45–93.

84 **The surgeon and author:** Atul Gawande, "The Cost Conundrum," *New Yorker*, May 25, 2009, newyorker.com/magazine/2009/06/01/the-cost-conundrum.

85 **These different practice patterns:** David Cutler, Jonathan S. Skinner, Ariel Dora Stern, and David Wennberg, "Physician Beliefs and Patient Preferences: A New Look at Regional Variation in Health Care Spending," *American Economic Journal: Economic Policy* 11, no. 1 (February 2019): 192–221.

85 **Amy and her collaborators realized:** Finkelstein, Gentzkow, and Williams, "Place-Based Drivers of Mortality"; Amy Finkelstein, Matthew Gentzkow, and Heidi Williams, "Sources of Geographic Variation in Health Care: Evidence from Patient Migration," *Quarterly Journal of Economics* 131, no. 4 (November 2016): 1681–726.

86 **Indeed, evidence from Sweden:** The finding that gaps in life expectancy between the top and bottom of the national income distribution are similar in Sweden and Norway to that in the US is even more striking when we remember that income inequality itself is substantially lower in Sweden and Norway than in the United States. Yet, despite Sweden and Norway exhibiting smaller differences in income between those at the top and those at the bottom, differences in life expectancy between those at the top and those at the bottom of the income distribution are similar to those in the US. For more information on Sweden and Norway respectively, see Yiqun Chen, Petra Persson, and Maria Polyakova, "The Roots of Health Inequality and the Value of Intrafamily Expertise," *American Economic Journal: Applied Economics* 14, no. 3 (July 3, 2022): 185–223; and Jonas Minet Kinge, Jørgen Heibø Modalsli, Simon Øverland, Håkon Kristian Gjessing, Mette Christophersen Tollånes, Ann Kristin Knudsen, Vegard Skirbekk et al., "Association of Household Income with Life Expectancy and Cause-Specific Mortality in Norway, 2005–2015," *JAMA* 321, no. 19 (May 13, 2019): 1916–25.

86 **Today, there is widespread:** Laura McGovern, G. Miller, and P. Hughes-Cromwick, "The Relative Contribution of Multiple Determinants to Health" (health policy brief, *Health Affairs*, August 21, 2014); J. Michael McGinnis, Pamela Williams-Russo, and James R. Knickman, "The Case for More Active Policy Attention to Health Promotion," *Health Affairs* 21, no. 2 (March/April 2002): 78–93; and Bridget C. Booske, Jessica K. Athens, David A. Kindig, Hyojun Park, and Patrick L. Remington, "Different Perspectives for Assigning Weights to Determinants of Health" (*County Health Rankings Working Paper*, University of Wisconsin Population Health Institute, Madison, WI, February 2010).

87 **Indeed, there is now increasing:** U.S. Department of Health and Human Services, "Social Determinants of Health," Healthy People 2030, accessed January 25, 2022, health.gov/healthypeople/objectives-and-data/social-determinants-health.

87 **As the physicians:** David Stuckler and Sanjay Basu, in *The Body Economic: Why Austerity Kills* (New York: Basic Books, 2013), xi.

87 **They also smoked less:** Chen, Persson, and Polyakova, "The Roots of Health Inequality."

87 **In other words, as the:** Lleras-Muney, "Mind the Gap", 1081.

89 **Rawls insisted that:** John Rawls, *A Theory of Justice* (Cambridge, MA: Belknap Press, 1971), 83–84, 93; and Samuel Freeman, *Rawls* (New York: Routledge, 2007), 88.

89 **The philosopher and medical:** O'Neill and Bidadanure 2014 explains how Rawls influenced Daniels. Freeman 2007 notes that Rawls has cited Daniels when discussing health care. Martin O'Neill and Juliana Bidadanure, "Daniels, Norman," in *The Cambridge Rawls Lexicon*, ed. Jon Mandle and David A. Reidy (Cambridge: Cambridge University Press, 2014), 179–81; and Freeman, *Rawls*, 231.

89 **Daniels emphasized that:** Norman Daniels, *Just Health Care* (Cambridge: Cambridge University Press, 1985), 56.

89 **"great strategic importance for opportunity":** Daniels, *Just Health Care*, 46–47.

89 **"maintain normal species functioning":** Daniels, 57.

90 **"attain their *full potential*":** World Health Organization, "Health Equity," WHO, accessed March 8, 2022, who.int/westernpacific/health-topics/health-equity.

90 **The Centers for Disease:** Centers for Disease Control and Prevention, "Health Equity," National Center for Chronic Disease Prevention and Health Promotion, March 3, 2022, cdc.gov/chronicdisease/healthequity/index.htm.

90 **Nevertheless, in the end:** Daniels, *Just Health Care*, 79.

90 **Indeed, Daniels goes:** Daniels, 78–79.

90 **Daniels recognizes that:** Norman Daniels, "Symposium on the Rationing of Health Care: 2 Rationing Medical Care—a Philosopher's Perspective on Outcomes and Process," *Economics & Philosophy* 14, no. 1 (April 1998): 36.

90 **Consider the media:** Rex Weiner, "Keeping the Wealthy Healthy—and Everyone Else Waiting," Inequality.org, July 11, 2017, inequality.org/research/keeping-wealthy-healthy-everyone-else-waiting.

91 **In the aughts:** Colleen M. Flood and Tom Archibald, "The Illegality of Private Health Care in Canada," *Canadian Medical Association Journal* 164, no. 6 (March 20, 2001): 825–30; "Unsocialized Medicine," editorial, *Wall Street Journal*, June 13, 2005, wsj.com/articles/SB111862181968257580; and Susan Pinker, "The Chaoulli Case: One-Tier Medicine Goes on Trial in Quebec," *Canadian Medical Association Journal* 161, no. 10 (November 16, 1999): 1305–6.

91 **More recently, one:** Zachary B. Wolf, Tami Luhby, and Curt Merrill, "Here's What Bernie Sanders' 'Medicare for All' Proposal Actually Says," CNN, March 2, 2020, cnn.com/interactive/2020/03/politics/medicare-for-all-annotated; and Sierra Dean, "Canada's Landmark Chaoulli Decision: A Vital Blueprint for Change in the Canadian Health Care System," *Law and Business Review of the Americas* 13, no. 2 (2007): 417.

92 **The nineteenth-century philanthropists:** Charles E. Rosenberg, *Our Present Complaint: American Medicine, Then and Now* (Baltimore: Johns Hopkins University Press, 2007), 170.

92 **The US was a leader:** Cristobal de Brey, Thomas D. Snyder, Anlan Zhang, and Sally A. Dillow, *Digest of Education Statistics: 2019* (NCES 2021-009, National Center for Education Statistics, Institute of Education Sciences, US Department of Education, Washington, DC, February 2021), tables 203.10 and 205.20, nces.ed.gov

/pubs2021/2021009.pdf; and Claudia Goldin and Lawrence F. Katz, *The Race between Education and Technology* (Cambridge, MA: Harvard University Press, 2008), 5–7, 142–43.

92 **Indigent criminal defendants:** Caroline Wolf Harlow, Defense Counsel in Criminal Cases (Bureau of Justice Statistics Special Report, no. NCJ 179023, US Department of Justice, Office of Justice Programs, US Department of Justice, November 2000).

93 **The national government:** Raemeka Mayo, Randy Moore, and Kristen Ricks, *Annual State and Local Government Finances Summary: 2019* (G19-ALFIN, U.S. Census Bureau, July 30, 2021), 3; Vlad Khaustovich, "Security Services in the US," Industry Report 56161 (IBIS World, August 2021), my.ibisworld.com/download/us/en /industry/1487/9/0/pdf; and Gabriel Schulman, "Security Alarm Services in the US" (IBIS World, 2021), my.ibisworld.com/download/us/en/industry/1491/1/0/pdf.

93 **The dearth of:** In particular, for dissatisfaction with the US health system, see the two mentioned figures in Gallup 2022 and McCarthy 2019. For dissatisfaction relative to that in other countries, see Skinner et al. 2020, Schoen et al. 2007, and Roehr 2007; Gallup, "Healthcare System," Gallup, 2022, fig. "Views of Healthcare Industry," news .gallup.com/poll/4708/Healthcare-System.aspx; Justin McCarthy, "Fewer in U.S. See Health System as Having Major Problems," Gallup, December 2, 2019, news .gallup.com/poll/268850/fewer-health-system-having-major-problems.aspx; Gideon Skinner, James Stannard, and Imogen Drew, *Perils of Perception 2020: Causes of Death* (Ipsos MORI, 2020), 48, ipsos.com/sites/default/files/ct/news/documents /2020-02/ipsos-mori-perils-of-perception-2020-causes-of-death.pdf; Cathy Schoen, Robin Osborn, Michelle M. Doty, Meghan Bishop, Jordon Peugh, and Nandita Murukutla, "Toward Higher-Performance Health Systems: Adults' Health Care Experiences in Seven Countries, 2007," *Health Affairs* 26, no. Supplement 2 (January 2007): w717–34, doi.org/10.1377/hlthaff.26.6.w717; and Bob Roehr, "US Has Highest Dissatisfaction with Health Care," *BMJ* 335, no. 7627 (November 10, 2007): 956.

94 **The health-care sector:** Anne B. Martin, Micah Hartman, David Lassman, and Aaron Catlin, "National Health Care Spending in 2019: Steady Growth for the Fourth Consecutive Year," *Health Affairs* 40, no. 1 (January 2021): 14–24.

PART III: THE BLUEPRINT

95 **Proponents of universal:** The phrase has been used by many politicians but is perhaps most associated with former president Barack Obama. Barack Obama, "United States Health Care Reform: Progress to Date and Next Steps," *JAMA* 316, no. 5 (August 2, 2016): 525–32; Barack Obama, "Remarks by the President on the Affordable Care Act," Miami Dade College, Miami, FL, October 20, 2016, transcript, obamawhitehouse.archives.gov/the-press-office/2016/10/20/remarks-president -affordable-care-act; and Scott Wilson and Ovetta Wiggins, "Obama Defends Health-Care Law, Calling Health Insurance 'a Right,'" *Washington Post*, September 26, 2013, washingtonpost.com/politics/obama-defends-health-care-law-calling

-health-insurance-a-right/2013/09/26/9e1d946e-26b8-11e3-b75d-5b7f66349852
_story.html.

95 **This right exists:** Douglas C. McDonald, "Medical Care in Prisons," *Crime and Justice*
26 (1999): 427–78; Craig A. Conway, "A Right of Access to Medical and Mental
Health Care for the Incarcerated," June 10, 2009, Health Law & Policy Institute,
University of Houston Law Center, law.uh.edu/healthlaw/perspectives/2009
/%28CC%29%20Prison%20Health.pdf; and Estelle v. Gamble, 429 U.S. 97 (1976),
Oyez, oyez.org/cases/1976/75-929.

96 **The decision didn't:** See Estelle v. Gamble (429 U.S. 97 (1976)). For the aftermath of
this case, see Philip Genty, "Confusing Punishment with Custodial Care: The
Troublesome Legacy of Estelle v. Gamble," *Vermont Law Review* 21, no. 379 (1996):
379–407; and McDonald, "Medical Care in Prisons," 430.

96 **Most states allow:** Wendy Sawyer, "The Steep Cost of Medical Co-pays in Prison
Puts Health at Risk," *Prison Policy Initiative*, April 19, 2017, prisonpolicy.org/blog
/2017/04/19/copays; and Lauren-Brooke Eisen, *Charging Inmates Perpetuates Mass
Incarceration* (New York: Brennan Center for Justice at New York University School
of Law, 2015).

96 **Even FDR implicitly:** Franklin D. Roosevelt, "State of the Union Message to
Congress," January 11, 1944, Franklin D. Roosevelt Presidential Library and
Museum, Hyde Park, NY, fdrlibrary.marist.edu/archives/address_text.html.

96 **The economist Arthur:** Arthur M. Okun, *Equality and Efficiency: The Big Tradeoff*,
(Washington, DC: Brookings Institution, 1975; Washington, DC: Brookings
Institution Press, 2015), 16. Citation refers to the 2015 edition.

CHAPTER 8: THE FOUNDATION

101 **Republican governor Mitt Romney led:** Pam Belluck and Katie Zezima,
"Massachusetts Legislation on Insurance Becomes Law," *New York Times*, April 13,
2006, nytimes.com/2006/04/13/us/massachusetts-legislation-on-insurance
-becomes-law.html.

102 **But unlike its:** Ewout van Ginneken and Thomas Rice, "Enforcing Enrollment in
Health Insurance Exchanges: Evidence from the Netherlands, Switzerland, and
Germany," *Medical Care Research and Review* 72, no. 4 (August 2015): 496–509; and
Kevin Williamson, "Another Way to Universal Health Care," *National Review*, February
6, 2019, nationalreview.com/2019/02/another-way-to-universal-health-care.

102 **Thanks to this ruthless:** Federico Toth, "Going Universal? The Problem of the
Uninsured in Europe and in OECD Countries," *International Journal of Health
Planning and Management* 35, no. 5 (September 2020): 1193–1204.

102 **The Dutch subsequently copied:** van Ginneken and Rice, "Enforcing Enrollment in
Health Insurance Exchanges"; and Toth, "Going Universal?"

102 **In the US, by contrast:** Dan Mangan, "Trump Touts Repeal of Key Part in
'Disastrous Obamacare'—the Individual Mandate," CNBC, January 31, 2018, cnbc
.com/2018/01/30/trump-touts-repeal-of-obamacare-individual-mandate.html.

102 **The most intimidating:** "Cops (Live)," live at the Metropolitan Opera House, from *A Night at the Met*, 1986, YouTube video, 2:50, January 30, 2017, https://www.youtube .com/watch?v=fhmS9KD_jGw&list=PL2MtElzTEi6lx1EpGPKDAQwUWoDMu9 beu&index=10.

102 **Even when the US briefly:** Congressional Budget Office, "Payments of Penalties for Being Uninsured under the Affordable Care Act: 2014 Update," June 5, 2014, cbo .gov/publication/45397; and Christine Eibner and Sarah Nowak, "The Effect of Eliminating the Individual Mandate Penalty and the Role of Behavioral Factors," July 2018, doi.org/10.26099/SWQZ-5G92.

103 **There were also numerous:** For details on the US exemptions, see Congressional Budget Office, "Payments of Penalties for Being Uninsured." For information on the Dutch system, see van Genneken and Rice, "Enforcing Enrollment in Health Insurance Exchanges."

103 **basic coverage to be automatic:** "Basic Coverage to Be Automatic," *New York Times*, July 31, 1965, timesmachine.nytimes.com/timesmachine/1965/07/31 /issue.html.

103 **Almost all of the elderly:** Robert M. Ball, "The First 60 Days of Medicare," *Journal of the National Medical Association* 58, no. 6 (November 1966): 475–79.

103 **In modern times, Medicare coverage:** Centers for Medicare & Medicaid Services, *Enrolling in Medicare Part A & Part B* (Baltimore: US Department of Health and Human Services, January 2018), medicare.gov/Pubs/pdf/11036-Enrolling -Medicare-Part-A-Part-B.pdf.

104 **The result: virtually all:** Both in 2018 and 2020, only 1 percent of individuals sixty-five and older were uninsured. See Katherine Keisler-Starkey and Lisa N. Bunch, *Health Insurance Coverage in the United States: 2020*, Current Population Reports, no. P60-274 (Washington, DC: US Census Bureau, September 2021), 3, fig. 2, census.gov/content/dam/Census/library/publications/2021/demo/p60-274.pdf.

104 **Not so with Medicare:** US Centers for Medicare & Medicaid Services, "How to Get Prescription Drug Coverage," Medicare.gov, accessed February 18, 2022, medicare .gov/drug-coverage-part-d/how-to-get-prescription-drug-coverage; Juliette Cubanski, Anthony Damico, and Tricia Neuman, "10 Things to Know about Medicare Part D Coverage and Costs in 2019," KFF, June 4, 2019, kff.org/medicare /issue-brief/10-things-to-know-about-medicare-part-d-coverage-and-costs-in-2019; and Medicare Payment Advisory Commission, "The Medicare Prescription Drug Program (Part D): Status Report," in *Report to the Congress: Medicare Payment Policy* (Washington, DC: MedPAC, March 2020), 403–53, medpac.gov/wp-content /uploads/import_data/scrape_files/docs/default-source/reports/mar20_medpac _ch14_sec.pdf.

CHAPTER 9: FREE AND CLEAR

105 **An exasperated President Truman:** Steven Weisman, "Edwin Nourse, 90, Dies; Truman's Economic Aide," *New York Times*, April 10, 1974, nytimes.com/1974/04

/10/archives/edwin-nourse-90-dies-trumans-economic-aide-sought-anonymity
-top.html.

106 **In the Senate, Massachusetts:** 117 Cong. Rec. (Bound) Senate (daily ed.
January 25, 1971) (statement of Sen. Edward Kennedy), 284–88.

106 **President Nixon's Republican:** *Health Care Crisis in America, 1971: Hearings
Ninety-Second Congress, First Session on Examination of the Health Care Crisis in
America,* vol. 1 (Washington, DC: US Government Printing Office, 1971), 18,
healthcare-now.org/wp-content/uploads/2017/10/Health-Care-Crisis-Hearings
-1971-Part-1.pdf.

106 **The Nixon administration saw:** United States Congress Senate Committee on Labor
and Public Welfare—Subcommittee on Health, 1:64–65.

106 **Physicians and insurers:** Beatrix Hoffman, "Restraining the Health Care Consumer:
The History of Deductibles and Co-payments in U.S. Health Insurance," *Social
Science History* 30, no. 4 (Winter 2006): 507.

107 **A similar debate:** For the final decisions, see Act to Provide Hospital Insurance
Program for the Aged under the Social Security Act with a Supplementary Health
Benefits Program and an Expanded Program of Medical Assistance, to Increase
Benefits under the Old-Age, Survivors, and Disability Insurance System, to Improve
the Federal-State Public Assistance Programs, and for Other Purposes, H.R. 6675,
89th Cong. (1965). For a summary of arguments from all sides of the discussion, see
Wilbur J. Cohen, "Reflections on the Enactment of Medicare and Medicaid," supp.
Health Care Financing Review 1985 (December 1985): 3–11; and Wilbur J. Cohen and
Robert M. Ball, "Social Security Amendments of 1965: Summary and Legislative
History," *Social Security Bulletin* 28, no. 9 (September 1965), ssa.gov/policy/docs
/ssb/v28n9/v28n9p3.pdf.

107 **"Like ants at a picnic":** For the original article, see Pauly 1968. His points are also
summarized in the interview; Mark V. Pauly, "The Economics of Moral Hazard:
Comment," *American Economic Review* 58, no. 3 (June 1968): 531–37; and Mark
Pauly, "Behaving Badly? How Current Tax Policy Spurs Inefficient Health Insurance,
Medical Spending," interview, On My Mind: Conversations with Economists,
Economic Research Initiative on the Uninsured, University of Michigan, accessed
February 24, 2022, rwjf-eriu.org/forthemedia/interviews_mark_pauly.html.

107 **Some economists had produced:** See, for example, Martin S. Feldstein, "Hospital
Cost Inflation: A Study of Nonprofit Price Dynamics," *American Economic Review* 61,
no. 5 (December 1971): 853–72.

107 **"I don't think we have":** United States Congress Senate Committee on Labor and
Public Welfare—Subcommittee on Health, *Health Care Crisis in America, 1971:
Hearings, Ninety-Second Congress, First Session on Examination of the Health Care
Crisis in America,* vol. 1 (Washington: U.S. Government Printing Office, 1971), 146,
https://www.healthcare-now.org/wp-content/uploads/2017/10/Health-Care
-Crisis-Hearings-1971-Part-1.pdf.

107 **Health-care spending was fixed:** United States Congress Senate Committee on
Labor and Public Welfare—Subcommittee on Health, 1:140–41.

108 **"No one *wants* to receive"**: Deborah Stone, "Moral Hazard," *Journal of Health Politics, Policy and Law* 36, no. 5 (October 2011): 889.

108 **Only one thing was sure:** One economist who—in that era—set out to determine "whether or not the contention [that deductibles reduce the frequency of claims] is valid in the field of health insurance" summarized the inconclusive results of his literature review under a section titled "Problems." There he wrote, "Researchers are often frustrated in their work and find that definitive answers are impossible to obtain. From the beginning, great interest in the study has been expressed by all those who have been contacted. Unfortunately, however, very little useful or reliable data have been located." We felt a certain pang of envy for the apparent ability of researchers of a bygone era to be able to publish their exercises in frustration. For the full article, see Charles P. Hall Jr., "Deductibles in Health Insurance: An Evaluation," *Journal of Risk and Insurance* 33, no. 2 (June 1966): 255.

108 **To settle the debate:** For a comprehensive description of the RAND health insurance experiment, see Newhouse 1993. For a description of its origins as an attempt to "answer" the Kennedy-Nixon debate, see Newhouse 2020. For the cost of the experiment and comparison to other social experiments, see Greenberg and Shroder 2004. Joseph P. Newhouse, *Free for All? Lessons from the RAND Health Insurance Experiment* (Cambridge, MA: Harvard University Press, 1993); Joseph P. Newhouse, "The Design of the RAND Health Insurance Experiment: A Retrospective," in "Multiarm Randomized Control Trials in Evaluation and Policy Analysis," ed. Andrew. P. Jaciw, special issue, *Evaluation Review* (December 2020), 1–32, doi.org/10.1177 /0193841X20976520; and David Greenberg and Mark Shroder, *Digest of Social Experiments,* 3rd ed. (Washington, DC: Urban Institute Press, 2004).

109 **We've done some of this:** For an overview, see Liran Einav and Amy Finkelstein, "Moral Hazard in Health Insurance: What We Know and How We Know It," *Journal of the European Economic Association* 16, no. 4 (August 2018): 957–82.

109 **Co-pays and deductibles didn't:** Newhouse, *Free for All?*

110 **As Joe Newhouse:** Newhouse, 351.

110 **Rather, by the time the:** Paul Starr, *Remedy and Reaction: The Peculiar American Struggle over Health Care Reform* (New Haven, CT: Yale University Press, 2011), 63–72.

110 **Its fingerprints are:** For trends in deductible amounts in medical plans between 1980 and 1988, see figure 2.2 in the United States General Accounting Office 1990 report. For changes in the average annual deductibles in employer-based plans in later years, see the Kaiser Family Foundation's annual *Employer Health Benefits Survey* reports. In particular, for the change between 1988 and 1999, see Exhibit 7.16 in Levitt et al. 1999; for 2001–2005, see Exhibit 7.2 in Claxton et al. 2005; for 2006–2008, see Exhibit 7.5 in Claxton et al. 2008; for 2009–2018, see figure 7.8 in Claxton et al. 2018; United States General Accounting Office, "Health Insurance: Cost Increases Lead to Coverage Limitations and Cost Shifting" (Report to Congressional Requesters, no. HRD-90-068, United States General Accounting Office, Washington, DC, May 1990), fig. 2.2, gao.gov/assets/hrd-90-68.pdf; Larry Levitt, Janet Lundy, Catherine

Hoffman, Jon Gabel, Heidi Whitmore, Jeremy Pickreign, and Kimberly Hurst, *Employer Health Benefits: 1999 Annual Survey* (Menlo Park, CA: Henry J. Kaiser Family Foundation, Health Research and Educational Unit, 1999), 72, Exhibit 7.16; Gary Claxton, Isadora Gil, Benjamin Finder, Jon Gabel, Jeremy Pickreign, Heidi Whitmore, and Samantha Hawkins, *Employer Health Benefits: 2005 Annual Survey* (Menlo Park, CA: Henry J. Kaiser Family Foundation, Health Research and Educational Unit, 2005), 79, Exhibit 7.2; Gary Claxton et al., *Employer Health Benefits: 2008 Annual Survey* (Menlo Park, CA: Henry J. Kaiser Family Foundation; Health Research and Educational Unit, 2008), 100, Exhibit 7.5; and Gary Claxton, Matthew Rae, Michelle Long, Heidi Whitmore, and Anthony Damico, *Employer Health Benefits: 2018 Annual Survey* (Menlo Park, CA: Henry J. Kaiser Family Foundation; Health Research and Educational Unit, 2018), 104, fig. 7.8.

110 **The government subsequently:** Allan B. Hubbard, "The Health of a Nation," *New York Times*, April 3, 2006, nytimes.com/2006/04/03/opinion/the-health-of-a -nation.html; and John A. Nyman, "American Health Policy: Cracks in the Foundation," *Journal of Health Politics, Policy and Law* 32, no. 5 (October 2007): 759–83.

111 **Every major proposal:** For Kennedy's proposal, Carter's proposal, and the ACA, see Starr 2011. For Nixon's proposal, see Nixon 1974. For Clinton's proposal, see Davis and Stremikis 2009. Starr, *Remedy and Reaction*, 56, 60–61, 244–46; Richard Nixon, "Special Message to the Congress Proposing a Comprehensive Health Insurance Plan," February 6, 1974, American Presidency Project, University of California, Santa Barbara, presidency.ucsb.edu/documents/special-message-the-congress-proposing -comprehensive-health-insurance-plan; and Karen Davis and Kristof Stremikis, "The Costs of Failure: Economic Consequences of Failure to Enact Nixon, Carter, and Clinton Health Reforms," Commonwealth Fund, December 21, 2009, commonwealthfund.org/blog/2009/costs-failure-economic-consequences -failure-enact-nixon-carter-and-clinton-health-reforms.

111 **Even health insurance:** Office of Inspector General, Medicaid Cost Sharing (no. OEI-03-91-018, Department of Health and Human Services, July 1993), oig.hhs .gov/oei/reports/oei-03-91-01800.pdf; and Medicaid and CHIP Payment and Access Commission, "Federal Legislative Milestones in Medicaid and CHIP," MACPAC, accessed January 14, 2022, macpac.gov/reference-materials/federal-legislative -milestones-in-medicaid-and-chip.

111 **In all of these cases:** For examples of the Congressional Budget Office using results from the RAND experiment in its decisions (including encouraging high-deductible health plans), see Congressional Budget Office 1983, 1996, and 2006. For how the RAND experiment was connected to and directly preceded increases or the introduction of cost sharing in private insurance, Medicare, and Medicaid, see Hoffman 2006. For an example of how the RAND experiment is still referenced today in explaining cost sharing, see Healthcare Triage 2014. Newhouse has also noted that there are examples of corporations such as Xerox increasing its deductible with explicit reference to the study's results. Yet he fittingly cautioned that "whether these

changes were a direct effect of the Experiment's results must remain a largely speculative issue" (Newhouse 1993). Congressional Budget Office, *Changing the Structure of Medicare Benefits: Issues and Options* (CBO Study, Congressional Budget Office, Washington, DC, March 1983), cbo.gov/sites/default/files/98th -congress-1983-1984/reports/doc16a_0.pdf; Congressional Budget Office, *The High-Deductible/MSA Option under Medicare: Exploring the Implications of the Balanced Budget Act of 1995* (CBO Memorandum, Congressional Budget Office, Washington, DC, March 1996), cbo.gov/sites/default/files/104th-congress-1995 -1996/reports/1996doc24.pdf; Congressional Budget Office, *Consumer-Directed Health Plans: Potential Effects on Health Care Spending and Outcomes* (CBO Study, no. 2585, Congressional Budget Office, Washington, DC, December 2006), 32, cbo .gov/sites/default/files/109th-congress-2005-2006/reports/12-21-healthplans.pdf; Beatrix Hoffman, "Restraining the Health Care Consumer: The History of Deductibles and Co-payments in US Health Insurance," in "The Persistence of the Health Insurance Dilemma," ed. John E. Murray, special issue, *Social Science History* 30, no. 4 (Winter 2006): 501–28; Healthcare Triage, "RAND and the Moral Hazard: Healthcare Triage #10," January 7, 2014, YouTube video, 6:52, youtube.com/watch ?v=q0OtUbDYdxw; and Newhouse, *Free for All?*, 341.

111 **Its influence has:** Roosa Tikkanen, Robin Osborn, Elias Mossialos, Ana Djordjevic, and George A. Wharton, "International Health Care System Profiles: Canada," Commonwealth Fund, June 5, 2020, commonwealthfund.org/international-health -policy-center/countries/canada; Roosa Tikkanen, Robin Osborn, Elias Mossialos, Ana Djordjevic, and George A. Wharton, "International Health Care System Profiles: England," Commonwealth Fund, June 5, 2020, commonwealthfund.org /international-health-policy-center/countries/england; and Roosa Tikkanen, Robin Osborn, Elias Mossialos, Ana Djordjevic, and George A. Wharton, "International Health Care System Profiles: France," Commonwealth Fund, June 5, 2020, commonwealthfund.org/international-health-policy-center/countries/france.

111 **Japan began requiring:** Shuichi Nakamura, "Japan's Welfare for the Elderly—Past, Present, and Future," *Asia Health and Wellbeing Initiative*, December 2018, ahwin .org/japans-welfare-for-the-elderly-past-present-and-future.

111 **France, Switzerland, and:** Marzena Tambor, Milena Pavlova, Piotr Woch, and Wim Groot, "Diversity and Dynamics of Patient Cost-Sharing for Physicians' and Hospital Services in the 27 European Union Countries," *European Journal of Public Health* 21, no. 5 (October 2011): 585–90; Thomas Rice, Wilm Quentin, Anders Anell, Andrew J. Barnes, Pauline Rosenau, Lynn Y. Unruh, and Ewout Van Ginneken, "Revisiting Out-of-Pocket Requirements: Trends in Spending, Financial Access Barriers, and Policy in Ten High-Income Countries," *BMC Health Services Research* 18, no. 1 (May 18, 2018): 371; and Hossein Zare and Gerard Anderson, "Trends in Cost Sharing among Selected High Income Countries—2000–2010," *Health Policy* 112, no. 1–2 (September 2013): 35–44.

112 **That's presumably why:** Roosa Tikkanen, Robin Osborn, Elias Mossialos, Ana Djordjevic, and George A. Wharton, "International Health Care System Profiles:

Germany," Commonwealth Fund, June 5, 2020, commonwealthfund.org/international-health-policy-center/countries/germany; Roosa Tikkanen, Robin Osborn, Elias Mossialos, Ana Djordjevic, and George A. Wharton, "International Health Care System Profiles: Australia," Commonwealth Fund, June 5, 2020, commonwealthfund.org/international-health-policy-center/countries/australia; Roosa Tikkanen, Robin Osborn, Elias Mossialos, Ana Djordjevic, and George A. Wharton, "International Health Care System Profiles: Netherlands," Commonwealth Fund, June 5, 2020, commonwealthfund.org/international-health-policy-center/countries/netherlands; and Roosa Tikkanen, Robin Osborn, Elias Mossialos, Ana Djordjevic, and George A. Wharton, "International Health Care System Profiles: Switzerland," Commonwealth Fund, June 5, 2020, commonwealthfund.org/international-health-policy-center/countries/switzerland.

113 **There will always be people:** For evidence of the impacts that even very small co-pays can have on health-care use, see, for example, Tal Gross, Timothy J. Layton, and Daniel Prinz, "The Liquidity Sensitivity of Healthcare Consumption: Evidence from Social Security Payments," *American Economic Review: Insights* 4, no. 2 (June 2022): 175–90.

113 **In fact, we were stunned:** Zare and Anderson, "Trends in Cost Sharing."

113 **Consider, for example, the UK:** Geoffrey Rivett, *The History of the NHS*, Nuffield Trust, November 11, 2019, nuffieldtrust.org.uk/health-and-social-care-explained/the-history-of-the-nhs; and "Origins of the NHS," Cabinet Papers, National Archives, Kew, Surrey, UK, accessed November 9, 2021, nationalarchives.gov.uk/cabinetpapers/alevelstudies/origins-nhs.htm.

113 **In 1951, patient:** "Great Britain: The Beginning of the End?," *Time*, April 30, 1951, content.time.com/time/subscriber/article/0,33009,814773,00.html.

113 **Co-pays for prescription:** Tony Delamothe, "A Centrally Funded Health Service, Free at the Point of Delivery," *BMJ* 336, no. 7658 (June 21, 2008): 1410–12.

113 **Today in Britain:** Aaron Kulakiewicz, Elizabeth Parkin, and Tom Powell, "NHS Charges" (Commons Library Research Briefing, no. 7227, House of Commons Library, January 6, 2022), 9, researchbriefings.files.parliament.uk/documents/CBP-7227/CBP-7227.pdf.

114 **Exemptions from cost sharing:** Rivett, *The History of the NHS*; and Kulakiewicz, Parkin, and Powell, "NHS Charges," 9.

114 **A list of Israel's:** "שירותים בתשלום" ["Paid services"], Clalit Health Fund, 2021, clalit.co.il/he/info/about_site/Pages/sherutim_betashlum.aspx.

114 **In a similarly short-sighted:** 387 Parl. Deb. (June 19, 2002) cols. 279–81.

115 **One single mother took her:** Anna Tims, "Call for Action, as NHS Accuses Patients of Prescription 'Fraud,'" *The Guardian*, February 3, 2019, theguardian.com/money/2019/feb/03/nhs-prescriptions-free-fraud-penalty-charge.

115 **This became apparent:** Ian Gilmore, *Prescription Charges Review Implementing Exemption from Prescription Charges for People with Long Term Conditions: A Report for the Secretary of State* (Department of Health and Social Care, November 2009),

assets.publishing.service.gov.uk/government/uploads/system/uploads/attachment
_data/file/213884/dh_116367.pdf.

115 **US states that tried:** Lucy Johns and Gerald S. Adler, "Evaluation of Recent Changes
in Medicaid," *Health Affairs* 8, no. 1 (Spring 1989): 171–81; and Office of Inspector
General, *Medicaid Cost Sharing* (no. OEI-03-91-018, Department of Health and
Human Services, July 1993), oig.hhs.gov/oei/reports/oei-03-91-01800.pdf.

116 **In several European:** Three examples of governments abandoning cost sharing after
introducing it are Germany, the Netherlands, and Hungary. For information on
Germany, see "Bundestag" 2012. For information on the Netherlands and Hungary
(as well as information on cost sharing throughout the EU), see Tambor et al. 2011.
"Bundestag schafft einstimmig die Praxisgebühr ab" [Bundestag unanimously
abolishes the practice fee], Deutscher Bundestag, 2012, bundestag.de/webarchiv
/textarchiv/2012/41447099_kw45_de_praxisgebuehr-209922; and Tambor,
Pavlova, Woch, and Groot, "Diversity and Dynamics of Patient Cost-Sharing."

116 **In 2004, for example:** Martin Siegel and Reinhard Busse, *Can People Afford to Pay for
Health Care? New Evidence on Financial Protection in Germany* (Copenhagen: World
Health Organization, 2018), 12–27.

116 **Eight years later:** "Bundestag schafft einstimmig die Praxisgebühr ab," Deutscher
Bundestag.

116 **The practice fees:** Nikolaus Nützel, "Bürokratische Eigenbeteiligung an der
Gesundheit" [Bureaucratic contribution to health], Deutschlandfunk, August 9,
2012, deutschlandfunk.de/buerokratische-eigenbeteiligung-an-der-gesundheit.862
.de.html?dram:article_id=217042; and Falk Osterloh, "Praxisgebühr: Das Ende
eines Irrtums" [Practice fee: End of a mistake], *Deutsches Ärzteblatt* 9, no. 26
(November 16, 2012): aerzteblatt.de/archiv/132637/Praxisgebuehr-Das-Ende-eines
-Irrtums.

116 **The French experience:** Tikkanen et al., "International Health Care System Profiles:
France"; and Anna Sagan and Sarah Thomson, eds., *Voluntary Health Insurance in
Europe: Country Experience*, Observatory Studies Series 42 (Copenhagen: World
Health Organization, 2016), 51–53.

116 **As it increased:** Zare and Anderson, "Trends in Cost Sharing."

117 **But it enacted:** Karine Chevreul, Karen Berg Brigham, Isabelle Durand-Zaleski, and
Cristina Hernández-Quevedo, "France: Health System Review," *Health Systems in
Transition* 17, no. 5 (2015): 87–90; and Sagan and Thomson, *Voluntary Health
Insurance in Europe*, 51–53.

117 **The end result: almost:** Tikkanen et al., "International Health Care System Profiles:
France."

117 **A similar story:** Centers for Medicare & Medicaid Services, "2019 Medicare Parts
A & B Premiums and Deductibles," CMS.gov, October 12, 2018, cms.gov/newsroom
/fact-sheets/2019-medicare-parts-b-premiums-and-deductibles.

117 **Which may be why, after:** Hoffman, "Restraining the Health Care Consumer"; and
Charles R. Morris, *The AARP: America's Most Powerful Lobby and the Clash of
Generations* (New York: Times Books, 1996), 9–15.

117 **These days, only:** Wyatt Koma, Juliette Cubanski, and Tricia Neuman, "A Snapshot of Sources of Coverage among Medicare Beneficiaries in 2018," KFF, March 23, 2021, kff.org/medicare/issue-brief/a-snapshot-of-sources-of-coverage-among-medicare -beneficiaries-in-2018.

118 **Another unusual aspect:** The original article that launched the field of health economics is Arrow 1963. His rejoinder to Pauly can be found in Arrow 1968; Kenneth J. Arrow, "Uncertainty and the Welfare Economics of Medical Care," *American Economic Review* 53, no. 5 (December 1963): 941–73; and Kenneth Arrow, "The Economics of Moral Hazard: Further Comment," *American Economic Review* 58, no. 3 (June 1968): 531–37.

119 **There's also a much:** Steven B. Cohen, "The Concentration of Health Care Expenditures and Related Expenses for Costly Medical Conditions, 2012" (Statistical Brief, no. 455, Agency for Healthcare Research and Quality, Rockville, MD, 2014).

119 **Indeed, most likely:** Most employer-provided insurance has caps; see Koma et al. 2021. Similarly, most Medicare Part B cost sharing is uncapped, but 90 percent of the people have supplemental coverage; see Claxon et al. 2019. Koma, Cubanski, and Neuman, "A Snapshot of Sources of Coverage"; and Gary Claxton, Matthew Rae, Anthony Damico, Gregory Young, Daniel McDermott, and Heidi Whitmore, "Section 7: Employee Cost Sharing," in *2019 Employer Health Benefits Survey* (San Francisco: KFF [Kaiser Family Foundation], September 25, 2019), kff.org /report-section/ehbs-2019-section-7-employee-cost-sharing.

CHAPTER 10: A SHACK, NOT A CHATEAU

121 **Over two thousand:** Arthur Lubow, "Terra Cotta Soldiers on the March," *Smithsonian,* July 2009, smithsonianmag.com/history/terra-cotta-soldiers -on-the-march-30942673.

122 **They might also want:** History.com Editors, "Pilot Sully Sullenberger Performs 'Miracle on the Hudson,'" History, January 25, 2022, history.com/this-day-in -history/sully-sullenberger-performs-miracle-on-the-hudson.

123 **In Singapore, hospitals:** Khoo Teck Puat Hospital, "Hospital Charges," Khoo Teck Puat Hospital, May 18, 2021, ktph.com.sg/patients/hospital-charges.

123 **Patients can pay:** Roosa Tikkanen, Robin Osborn, Elias Mossialos, Ana Djordjevic, and George A. Wharton, "International Health Care System Profiles: Singapore," Commonwealth Fund, June 5, 2020, commonwealthfund.org/international -health-policy-center/countries/singapore.

123 **Australia's system is similar:** Australian Institute of Health and Welfare, "Private Health Insurance," Australian Institute of Health and Welfare, July 23, 2020, aihw .gov.au/reports/australias-health/private-health-insurance; and "The Public and Private Hospital Systems," Healthdirect, October 15, 2021, healthdirect.gov.au /understanding-the-public-and-private-hospital-systems.

123 **The private insurance primarily:** Accounts and details about the varying experiences mothers can have on public and private health insurance in Australia can

be found in the following articles: Dylan Scott, "Two Sisters. Two Different Journeys through Australia's Health Care System," *Vox*, January 15, 2020, vox.com/2020/1 /15/21030568/australia-health-insurance-medicare; Uta Mihm, "Do You Need Health Insurance to Have a Baby?," CHOICE, October 14, 2019, choice.com.au /babies-and-kids/getting-ready-for-baby/planning-for-baby/articles/health -insurance-for-pregnancy-and-birth; Gemma Bath, "100 Mums on Their Experience Giving Birth in a Public or Private Hospital," Mamamia, April 26, 2021, mamamia .com.au/difference-private-public-birth; Karen Willis and Sophie Lewis, "Which Are Better, Public or Private Hospitals?," The Conversation, March 17, 2016, theconversation.com/which-are-better-public-or-private-hospitals-54338; Gary L. Freed, Erin Turbitt, and Amy Allen, "Public or Private Care: Where Do Specialists Spend Their Time?," *Australian Health Review* 41, no. 5 (2017): 541–45; and "Luxury Post-birth 'Staycation' for Parents," Ramsay Health Care, June 24, 2021, ramsayhealth.com.au/News/General-News/Luxury-post-birth-staycation-for -parents.

124 **Far from offering:** Priyanka Dayal McCluskey, "Patients Want Private Rooms, and Hospitals Are Accommodating Them," *Boston Globe*, February 16, 2019, bostonglobe .com/metro/2019/02/16/hospitals-face-pressure-provide-private-rooms-for -patients/EO1dIbbu3dxGiyOuHPEhfN/story.html; Michigan Department of Community Health, *The 2007 Minimum Design Standards for Health Care Facilities in Michigan* (Michigan Department of Community Health, 2007), michigan.gov /documents/mdch/bhs_2007_Minimum_Design_Standards_Final_PDF _Doc._198958_7.pdf.

124 **The twenty-seven-year-old:** Julia Kollewe, "Private Hospitals Profit from NHS Waiting Lists as People without Insurance Pay Out," *The Guardian*, September 18, 2021, theguardian.com/society/2021/sep/18/private-hospitals-profit-from-nhs -waiting-lists-as-people-without-insurance-pay-out.

125 **The middle-aged Englishwoman:** Robert Booth, "'I Didn't Matter': The Long Wait for Mental Health Treatment," *The Guardian*, January 25, 2016, theguardian.com /society/2016/jan/25/nhs-mental-health-crisis-long-wait-for-treatment.

125 **The forty-year-old Canadian:** Sonja Puzic, "'It's Insane': Ont. Patient Told She'd Have to Wait 4.5 Years to See Neurologist," CTVNews, November 2, 2017, ctvnews .ca/health/it-s-insane-ont-patient-told-she-d-have-to-wait-4-5-years-to-see- neurologist-1.3661114.

125 **When surveyed, about:** OECD, *Waiting Times for Health Services: Next in Line* (Paris: Organisation for Economic Co-operation and Development, 2020), 16, fig. 2.2, oecd-ilibrary.org/social-issues-migration-health/waiting-times-for-health-services _242e3c8c-en.

125 **Nor is the US itself:** OECD, *Waiting Times for Health Services*, 15, fig. 2.1.

125 **Within the US, wait:** For a meta-analysis of thirty-four such audit studies, see Hsiang et al. 2019. Saloner et al. 2019 is an audit study that compares community health centers and private offices in terms of patients' ability to get an appointment with Medicaid or no insurance, whereas Cama et al. 2017 is an audit study that looks at the

availability of pediatric care for those with private insurance vs. Medicaid or no insurance. Lee et al. 2018 and Nguyen et al. 2019 are examples of other studies that compare outcomes for private insurance and Medicaid. Walter R. Hsiang, Adam Lukasiewicz, Mark Gentry, Chang-Yeon Kim, Michael P. Leslie, Richard Pelker, Howard P. Forman et al., "Medicaid Patients Have Greater Difficulty Scheduling Health Care Appointments Compared with Private Insurance Patients: A Meta-analysis," *Inquiry: The Journal of Health Care Organization, Provision, and Financing* 56 (January–December 2019), doi.org/10.1177/0046958019838118; Brendan Saloner, Adam S. Wilk, Douglas Wissoker, Molly Candon, Katherine Hempstead, Karin V. Rhodes, Daniel E. Polsky et al., "Changes in Primary Care Access at Community Health Centers between 2012/2013 and 2016," *Health Services Research* 54, no. 1 (February 2019): 181; Shireen Cama, Monica Malowney, Anna Jo Bodurtha Smith, Margaret Spottswood, Elisa Cheng, Louis Ostrowsky, Jose Rengifo et al., "Availability of Outpatient Mental Health Care by Pediatricians and Child Psychiatrists in Five US Cities," *International Journal of Health Services* 47, no. 4 (October 2017): 621–35; Yoon H. Lee, Andrew X. Chen, Varshini Varadaraj, Gloria H. Hong, Yimin Chen, David S. Friedman, Joshua D. Stein et al., "Comparison of Access to Eye Care Appointments between Patients with Medicaid and Those with Private Health Care Insurance," *JAMA Ophthalmology* 136, no. 6 (June 2018): 622–29; and Jenny Nguyen, Nidharshan S. Anandasivam, Daniel Cooperman, Richard Pelker, and Daniel H. Wiznia, "Does Medicaid Insurance Provide Sufficient Access to Pediatric Orthopedic Care under the Affordable Care Act?," *Global Pediatric Health* 6 (February 19, 2019), doi.org/10.1177 /2333794X19831299.

126 **We know this because the:** Congressional Budget Office, "The Veterans Community Care Program: Background and Early Effects," October 2021, cbo.gov/system/files /2021-10/57257-VCCP.pdf.

126 **In 2014, a series:** German Lopez, "The VA Scandal of 2014, Explained," *Vox*, May 13, 2015, vox.com/2014/9/26/18080592/va-scandal-explained; and Scott Bronstein and Drew Griffin, "A Fatal Wait: Veterans Languish and Die on a VA Hospital's Secret List," April 23, 2014, cnn.com/2014/04/23/health/veterans-dying-health-care -delays.

126 **The outcry prompted:** Lopez, "The VA Scandal of 2014"; and 115th Congress, Act to Amend the Veterans Access, Choice, and Accountability Act of 2014, Pub. L. No. 115-26, 131 Stat. 130 (2017), govinfo.gov/content/pkg/PLAW-115publ26/pdf /PLAW-115publ26.pdf.

126 **Subsequently, it tightened:** US Department of Veterans Affairs, "VA Launches New Health Care Options under MISSION Act," news release, June 6, 2019, news.va.gov /61286/va-launches-new-health-care-options-mission-act/.

126 **Typical wait times:** Measured wait times for Medicaid patients include only data for patients who are offered an appointment; as noted, the set of physicians who will accept Medicaid patients is narrower than for privately insured patients; Daniel R. Levinson, *Access to Care: Provider Availability in Medicaid Managed Care*

(Washington, DC: Office of Inspector General, Department of Health and Human Services, December 2014); and Saloner et al., "Changes in Primary Care Access."

127 **The VA standards in turn:** OECD, *Waiting Times for Health Services*, 25–27; Luigi Siciliani, Michael Borowitz, and Valerie Moran, eds., *Waiting Time Policies in the Health Sector: What Works?* (Paris: Organisation for Economic Co-operation and Development, 2013), 52–54, oecd-ilibrary.org/social-issues-migration-health /waiting-times-for-elective-surgery-what-works_9789264179080-en.

127 **To enforce the VA:** US Department of Veterans Affairs, "VA Launches New Health Care Options."

127 **Likewise, a number:** For Denmark, see Denmark Ministry 2008. For Norway, see "Your Rights" 2019. For Portugal, see Denmark Ministry of Health and Prevention, *Health Care in Denmark* (Copenhagen: Ministry of Health and Prevention, 2008), 15, ilo.org/dyn/travail/docs/2047/health%20in%20Denmark.pdf; "Your Rights in Case of Exceeded Waiting Time," Helsenorge, September 23, 2019, helsenorge.no/en /health-rights-in-norway/Your-rights-in-case-of-exceeded-waiting-time; Pedro Gomes, "Integrated Management System of the Waiting List for Elective Surgery: The Portuguese Case" (UEMS European Union of Medical Specialists, Lisbon, Portugal, October 1, 2016), uems.eu/__data/assets/pdf_file/0011/39863/Gomes -P.-SIGIC-Integrated-Management-System-of-the-Waiting-List-for-Elective -Surgery.-The-Portuguese-Case.pdf; and Pedro Pita Barros, Rita Cristivao, and Pedro Andrade Gomes, "Portugal," in *Waiting Time Policies*, 19, read.oecd-ilibrary.org /social-issues-migration-health/waiting-time-policies-in-the-health-sector/portugal _9789264179080-16-en.

127 **Portugal even prophylactically:** Gomes, "Integrated Management System of the Waiting List"; and Barros, Cristivao, and Gomes, "Portugal."

127 **In 2010, in Denmark:** Siciliani, Borowitz, and Moran, *Waiting Time Policies*, 128.

128 **Patients with Medicare:** Robert A. Berenson and Dean M. Harris, "Using Managed Care Tools in Traditional Medicare: Should We? Could We?," *Law and Contemporary Problems* 65, no. 4 (Autumn 2002): 139–67; and US Centers for Medicare & Medicaid Services, "How Original Medicare Works," Medicaid.gov, accessed February 23, 2022, medicare.gov/what-medicare-covers/your-medicare-coverage -choices/how-original-medicare-works.

128 **The originating statute:** Berenson and Harris, "Using Managed Care Tools in Traditional Medicare"; Robert M. Ball, "Perspectives on Medicare," *Health Affairs* 14, no. 4 (Winter 1995): 62–72.

128 **By contrast, in most other:** Nadine Reibling and Claus Wendt, "Gatekeeping and Provider Choice in OECD Healthcare Systems," *Current Sociology* 60, no. 4 (July 2012): 489–505.

129 **"There are so many specialty":** Jamie Koufman, "The Specialists' Stranglehold on Medicine," *New York Times*, June 3, 2017, nytimes.com/2017/06/03/opinion /sunday/the-specialists-stranglehold-on-medicine.html.

129 **And there's certainly:** Donald A. Barr, "The Ethics of Withholding Care," in *The Picture of Health: Medical Ethics and the Movies*, ed. Henri Colt, Silvia Quadrelli, and

Friedman Lester (New York: Oxford University Press, 2011), 225–29; Ellen Goodman, "The HMO Horror Show," *Boston Globe*, March 29, 1998; and Matthew Rees, "Will Helen Hunt Save US Health Care?," *Ottawa Citizen*, July 2, 1998.

130 **We see this in the:** Geruso et al. (forthcoming) describes the study. For other evidence on the impact of gatekeeping, see, for example, Eliason et al. 2021 and Brot-Goldberg et al. 2023; Michael Geruso, Timothy J. Layton, and Jacob Wallace, "What Difference Does a Health Plan Make? Evidence from Random Plan Assignment in Medicaid," *American Economic Journal: Applied Economics* (forthcoming), doi.org/10.1257/app.20210843; Paul J. Eliason, Riley J. League, Jetson Leder-Luis, Ryan C. McDevitt, and James W. Roberts, "Ambulance Taxis: The Impact of Regulation and Litigation on Health Care Fraud" (NBER Working Paper Series, no. 29491, National Bureau of Economic Research, Cambridge, MA, November 2021), doi.org/10.3386/w29491; and Zarek Brot-Goldberg, Samantha Burn, Timothy Layton, and Boris Vabson, "Rationing Medicine through Bureaucracy: Authorization Restrictions in Medicare" (NBER Working Paper Series, no. 30878, National Bureau of Economic Research, Cambridge, MA, January 2023), https://www.nber.org/papers/w30878.

CHAPTER 11: TRUST THE PROCESS

133 **One early autumn:** "The Life and Death Game," episode of *Where There's Life* (Yorkshire, UK: ITV Studios, October 1986), Y18750091, ITV Archive; Malcolm Ashmore, Michael Joseph Mulkay, and Trevor J. Pinch, *Health & Efficiency: A Sociology of Health Economics* (Milton Keynes, UK: Open University Press, 1989), 72; Eleanor MacKillop and Sally Sheard, "The Politics of Health Policy Knowledge Transfer: The Evolution of the Role of British Health Economics Academic Units," *Evidence & Policy* 15, no. 4 (November 2019): 489–507.

134 **Primary care is cheap:** Ann Kempski and Ann Greiner, *Primary Care Spending: High Stakes, Low Investment* (Washington, DC: Primary Care Collaborative, December 2020), pcpcc.org/sites/default/files/resources/PCC_Primary_Care_Spending_2020.pdf; and Sara Martin, Robert L. Phillips, Stephen Petterson, Zachary Levin, and Andrew W. Bazemore, "Primary Care Spending in the United States, 2002-2016," *JAMA Internal Medicine* 180, no. 7 (July 2020): 1019–20.

135 **Indeed, most countries':** Valérie Paris, Emily Hewlett, Ane Auraaen, Jan Alexa, and Lisa Simon, "Health Care Coverage in OECD Countries in 2012" (OECD Health Working Papers, no. 88, OECD, May 27, 2016), doi.org/10.1787/18152015.

135 **Costa Rica, for example:** Atul Gawande, "Costa Ricans Live Longer Than We Do. What's the Secret?," August 23, 2021, *New Yorker*, newyorker.com/magazine/2021/08/30/costa-ricans-live-longer-than-we-do-whats-the-secret.

137 **New antihypertensives and statins:** David M. Cutler and Srikanth Kadiyala, "The Return to Biomedical Research: Treatment and Behavioral Effects," in *Measuring the Gains from Medical Research: An Economic Approach*, ed. Kevin M. Murphy and Robert H. Topel (Chicago: University of Chicago Press, 2003), 110–62.

137 **Since 2000, countries:** Richard Layard, David Clark, Martin Knapp, and Guy Mayraz, "Cost-Benefit Analysis of Psychological Therapy," *National Institute Economic Review* 202, no. 1 (October 2007): 90–98; Laurence Pollock, "Rise of a Treatment That Works," *The Guardian*, April 22, 2008, theguardian.com/society /2008/apr/23/health.mentalhealth; Benjamin Ly Serena, "Revisiting Offsets of Psychotherapy Coverage" (CEBI Working Paper Series, no. 05/21, February 2021), papers.ssrn.com/sol3/papers.cfm?abstract_id=3797764; Lyn Littlefield, "Ten Years of Better Access," *InPsych* 39, no. 1 (February 2017): 7.

137 **Medicare coverage in the US:** For example, see the following: Kaiser Family Foundation, "Timeline: History of Health Reform in the U.S.," 2013, kff.org /wp-content/uploads/2011/03/5-02-13-history-of-health-reform.pdf; Ann Bittinger, Thomas D. Bixby, Clay J. Countryman, Christopher P. Dean, Anne W. Hance, Brian Kalver, Matthew R. Keuten et al., "The Medicare Improvements for Patients and Providers Act," American Health Lawyers Association, August 2008, 22; Judith Graham, "Medicare to Cover More Mental Health Costs," *New Old Age* (blog), December 27, 2013, newoldage.blogs.nytimes.com/2013/12/27/medicare-to-cover -more-mental-health-costs; Louis Jacques, Tamara Syrek Jensen, Jyme Schafer, Stuart Caplan, and Lawrence Schott, "Final Coverage Decision Memorandum for Screening for Depression in Adults," Medicare Coverage Database, Centers for Medicare & Medicaid Services, October 14, 2011, cms.gov/medicare-coverage-database/view /ncacal-decision-memo.aspx?proposed=N&NCAId=251; Beth McGinty, "Medicare's Mental Health Coverage: How COVID-19 Highlights Gaps and Opportunities for Improvement," Commonwealth Fund, July 9, 2020, doi.org /10.26099/sp60-3p16; and Louise Norris, "Medicare and the Affordable Care Act," Medicareresources.org, accessed September 15, 2021, medicareresources.org/basic -medicare-information/health-reform-and-medicare.

137 **This is why most countries:** Ane Auraaen, Rie Fujisawa, Gregoire de Lagasnerie, and Valérie Paris, "How OECD Health Systems Define the Range of Good and Services to Be Financed Collectively" (OECD Health Working Papers, no. 90, OECD, November 3, 2016), 14–19, doi.org/10.1787/5jlnb59ll80x-en.

138 **Health economist Alan:** "The Life and Death Game."

138 **In 1987, Coby Howard:** US Congress, Office of Technology Assessment, *Evaluation of the Oregon Medicaid Proposal* (Washington, DC: Government Printing Office, May 1992), ota.fas.org/reports/9213.pdf.

138 **Coby's story—and that:** Gina Kolata, "Increasingly, Life and Death Issues Become Money Matters," *New York Times*, March 20, 1988, nytimes.com/1988/03/20 /weekinreview/ideas-trends-increasingly-life-and-death-issues-become-money -matters.html.

138 **So too did Oregon's:** Thomas Bodenheimer, "The Oregon Health Plan—Lessons for the Nation," *New England Journal of Medicine* 337, no. 9 (August 28, 1997): 651–56; and Lindsay M. Sabik and Reidar K. Lie, "Priority Setting in Health Care: Lessons from the Experiences of Eight Countries," *International Journal for Equity in Health* 7, no. 1 (January 21, 2008): 1–13.

139 **The eleven-member commission:** Bob DiPrete and Darren Coffman, "A Brief History of Health Services Prioritization in Oregon" (Oregon Health Services Commission, March 2007), 7.

139 **The commissioners worked:** Bodenheimer, "The Oregon Health Plan," 651–56.

139 **Aided by hundreds:** US Congress, Office of Technology Assessment, *Evaluation of the Oregon Medicaid Proposal*.

139 **The first version:** Timothy Egan, "New Health Test: The Oregon Plan," *New York Times*, May 6, 1990, nytimes.com/1990/05/06/us/new-health-test-the-oregon-plan.html.

139 **Critics quickly pointed:** DiPrete and Coffman, "Health Services Prioritization in Oregon," 7.

139 **The committee had:** David C. Hadorn, "Setting Health Care Priorities in Oregon: Cost-Effectiveness Meets the Rule of Rescue," *JAMA* 265, no. 17 (May 1991): 2219.

140 **Even the commissioners:** US Congress, Office of Technology Assessment, *Evaluation of the Oregon Medicaid Proposal*.

140 **Effective care for acute:** Hadorn, "Setting Health Care Priorities in Oregon," 2219.

140 **Each of their original:** US Congress, Office of Technology Assessment, *Evaluation of the Oregon Medicaid Proposal*.

140 **At this final stage:** Hadorn, "Setting Health Care Priorities in Oregon," 2219.

140 **In moral philosophy:** Norman Daniels, "Reflective Equilibrium," in *Stanford Encyclopedia of Philosophy*, ed. Edward N. Zalta (Stanford University, 1997, article published April 28, 2003, revised October 14, 2016), plato.stanford.edu/archives/sum2020/entries/reflective-equilibrium.

141 **We think of it:** Peter Lattman, "The Origins of Justice Stewart's 'I Know It When I See It,'" *Wall Street Journal*, September 27, 2007, Law Blog, wsj.com/articles/BL-LB-4558.

141 **And it's the same approach:** Nicholas Timmins, Michael Rawlins, and John Appleby, *A Terrible Beauty: A Short History of NICE—The National Institute of Health and Care Excellence* (Nonthaburi, Thailand: Health Intervention and Technology Assessment Program, January 2016), hitap.net/en/documents/164742.

141 **When London hosted the 2012:** "British Celebrate National Health Care in Olympics Opening Ceremony," MSNBC, July 30, 2012, msnbc.com/msnbc/british-celebrate-national-health-care-i-msna27791.

141 **The next year it:** Sunder Katwala, "The NHS: Even More Cherished Than the Monarchy and the Army," *New Statesman* (London), January 14, 2013, newstatesman.com/politics/2013/01/nhs-even-more-cherished-monarchy-and-army.

141 **"The NHS is the closest":** Lauren Frayer, "U.K. Hospitals Are Overburdened, but the British Love Their Universal Health Care," NPR, March 7, 2018, npr.org/sections/parallels/2018/03/07/591128836/u-k-hospitals-are-overburdened-but-the-british-love-their-universal-health-care.

141 **In response to these issues:** Karl Claxton, Steve Martin, Marta Soares, Nigel Rice, Eldon Spackman, Sebastian Hinde, Nancy Devlin et al., "Methods for the Estimation of the National Institute for Health and Care Excellence Cost-Effectiveness Threshold," *Health Technology Assessment* 19, no. 14 (February 2015): 1.

142 **One of its first decisions:** National Institute for Health and Care Excellence, "20 Years of NICE," NICE: In Depth, accessed February 10, 2022, indepth.nice.org.uk /20-years-of-NICE/index.html.

142 **NICE was controversial:** NICE, "20 Years of NICE."

142 **Drugs approved for a small:** While an exact threshold was not set, new guidance was given for when to approve medications with high costs, relative to benefits, for certain terminal patients. In practice, researchers have found the cost-effectiveness threshold for approval of these drugs to be close to £50,000. For more information, see the following: National Institute for Health and Clinical Excellence, "Appraising Life-Extending, End of Life Treatments," July 2009, nice.org.uk/guidance/gid-tag387 /documents/appraising-life-extending-end-of-life-treatments-paper2; Josien Bovenberg, Hannah Penton, and Nasuh Buyukkaramikli, "10 Years of End-of-Life Criteria in the United Kingdom," *Value in Health* 24, no. 5 (May 1, 2021): 691–98; and L. Hamerslag, S. Haynes, J. Kusel, and S. Costello, "RS2 Cost-Effectiveness of End-of-Life, Life-Extending Interventions: NICE's Cost-Effectiveness Threshold Explored," *Value in Health* 14, no. 7 (November 1, 2011): A243, doi.org/10.1016/j .jval.2011.08.070.

142 **The cost-effectiveness limit:** "Changes to NICE Drug Appraisals: What You Need to Know," National Institute for Health and Care Excellence, April 4, 2017, nice.org.uk /news/feature/changes-to-nice-drug-appraisals-what-you-need-to-know.

142 **One of the more telling:** Helen Pidd, "Avastin Prolongs Life but Drug Is Too Expensive for NHS Patients, Says Nice," *The Guardian*, August 23, 2010, theguardian .com/society/2010/aug/24/avastin-too-expensive-for-patients; and Centers for Medicare & Medicaid Services, "National Coverage Determination—Anti-Cancer Chemotherapy for Colorectal Cancer," no. 13-3, sec. 110.17, Medicare Coverage Database, January 28, 2005, cms.gov/medicare-coverage-database/view/ncd.aspx ?NCDId=291&ncdver=1&bc=BAABAAAAAAAA&.

142 **The NHS therefore:** "Gran Loses Cancer Drug Appeal," BBC News, March 26, 2007, news.bbc.co.uk/1/hi/england/6496279.stm; and Robert Winnett and Rebecca Smith, "NHS Watchdog to Tell Patients How to Buy Medicine Unavailable on Health Service," *The Telegraph* (London), August 11, 2008, telegraph.co.uk/news/uknews /2541644/NHS-watchdog-to-tell-patients-how-to-buy-medicine-unavailable-on -health-service.html.

142 **This provoked a storm:** T. R. Reid, *The Healing of America: A Global Quest for Better, Cheaper, and Fairer Health Care* (New York: Penguin Books, 2010), 116; and "Gran Loses Cancer Drug Appeal," BBC News.

142 **along with dramatic:** Sarah Lyall, "Paying Patients Test British Health Care System," *New York Times*, February 21, 2008, nytimes.com/2008/02/21/world/europe /21britain.html.

142 **Facing public and political:** Laura Donnelly, "Cameron Pledges to Lift Restrictions on Cancer Drugs Available on NHS," *The Telegraph* (London), April 3, 2010, telegraph .co.uk/news/election-2010/7549678/Cameron-pledges-to-lift-restrictions-on -cancer-drugs-available-on-NHS.html; and Karl Claxton, "The UK's Cancer Drugs

Fund Does More Harm Than Good," *New Scientist*, January 13, 2015, newscientist
.com/article/dn26785-the-uks-cancer-drugs-fund-does-more-harm-than-good.

143 **When it came to power:** Randeep Ramesh, "Emergency Fund to Pay for 'Too
Expensive' Cancer Drugs," *The Guardian*, July 27, 2010, theguardian.com/society
/2010/jul/27/cancer-patients-fund-drugs-nice.

143 **Ultimately, a tenuous:** For examples of some expensive drugs receiving NICE
approval in this period, see Sarah Boseley, "Skin Cancer Drug Zelboraf Gets NHS
Go-Ahead," *The Guardian*, November 2, 2012, theguardian.com/society/2012/nov
/02/skin-cancer-drug-nhs; Press Association, "Prostate Cancer: Health Watchdog
Reverses NHS Guidance on Drug," *The Guardian*, May 16, 2012, theguardian.com
/society/2012/may/16/prostate-cancer-nhs-drug-abiterone; and Sarah Boseley,
"NHS Plan to Reassess Value of Cancer Drugs Alarms Patient Groups," *The
Guardian*, February 25, 2016, theguardian.com/society/2016/feb/25/patient
-groups-alarmed-by-nhs-plan-to-reassess-value-of-cancer-drugs.

143 **Most other high-income countries now:** Auraaen et al., "How OECD Health
Systems Define the Range," 14–19.

143 **Sweden made this:** Lars Bernfort, "Decisions on Inclusion in the Swedish Basic
Health Care Package—Roles of Cost-Effectiveness and Need," *Health Care Analysis*
11, no. 4 (December 2003): 301–8.

143 **That's why Sweden:** Bernfort, "Swedish Basic Health Care Package," 301–8; Elly A.
Stolk, Werner B. F. Brouwer, and Jan J. V. Busschbach, "Rationalising Rationing:
Economic and Other Considerations in the Debate about Funding of Viagra," *Health
Policy* 59, no. 1 (January 2002): 53–63; "Prioritized List, Guidelines, Interventions &
Services for Non-Coverage," Health Evidence Review Commission, Oregon Health
Authority, accessed February 10, 2022, oregon.gov/oha/HPA/DSI-HERC/Pages
/Searchable-List.aspx; and "Medicijnkosten—Viagra," Zorginstituut Nederland,
accessed February 10, 2022, medicijnkosten.nl/zoeken?trefwoord=viagra.

143 **But Sweden does cover:** Jean Georges, "The Availability of Antidementia Drugs in
Europe," *European Neurological Review*, no. 1 (2007): 40–44; Mohammed Fakhro,
Richard Ingemansson, Ingrid Skog, Lars Algotsson, Lennart Hansson, Bansi Koul,
Ronny Gustafsson et al., "25-Year Follow-Up after Lung Transplantation at Lund
University Hospital in Sweden: Superior Results Obtained for Patients with Cystic
Fibrosis," *Interactive Cardiovascular and Thoracic Surgery* 23, no. 1 (July 2016): 65–73.

143 **The Swedes' "principle of need":** Sabik and Lie, "Priority Setting in Health
Care," 1–13; and Bernfort, "Swedish Basic Health Care Package," 301–8.

143 **"priority to the worse off":** World Health Organization, *Making Fair Choices on the
Path to Universal Health Coverage: Final Report of the WHO Consultative Group on
Equity and Universal Health Coverage* (Geneva: World Health Organization, 2014),
apps.who.int/iris/handle/10665/112671.

144 **We also saw it:** Chris P. Lee, Glenn M. Chertow, and Stefanos A. Zenios, "An Empiric
Estimate of the Value of Life: Updating the Renal Dialysis Cost-Effectiveness
Standard," *Value in Health* 12, no. 1 (January 2009): 80–87; and World Health
Organization, *Making Fair Choices*.

CHAPTER 12: BUDGET MATTERS

145 **Once upon a time:** Keith Fontenot, Caitlin Brandt, and Mark B. McClellan, "A Primer on Medicare Physician Payment Reform and the SGR," Brookings Institution, February 2, 2015, brookings.edu/blog/usc-brookings-schaeffer-on-health-policy /2015/02/02/a-primer-on-medicare-physician-payment-reform-and-the-sgr; Billy Wynne, "May the Era of Medicare's Doc Fix (1997-2015) Rest in Peace: Now What," *Health Affairs Blog,* April 15, 2015, healthaffairs.org/blog/2015/04/14/may-the-era -of-medicares-doc-fix-1997-2015-rest-in-peace-now-what; and Terence Samuel, "Doc Fix Deal Produces Rare Bipartisan Celebration at the White House," *Washington Post,* April 21, 2015, washingtonpost.com/news/post-politics/wp/2015/04/21/doc -fix-deal-produces-rare-bipartisan-celebration-at-the-white-house.

146 **Every year, Congress:** Jonathan Skinner, Eli Cahan, and Victor R. Fuchs, "Stabilizing Health Care's Share of the GDP," *New England Journal of Medicine* 386, no. 8 (February 24, 2022): 709–11.

147 **In essentially every:** See, for example, Joseph White, *Competing Solutions: American Health Care Proposals and International Experience* (Washington, DC: Brookings Institution, 1995); Jacob S. Hacker, "The New Push for American Health Security," in *Health at Risk: America's Ailing Health System—and How to Heal It* (New York: Columbia University Press, 2008), 106–36; and Ezekiel J. Emanuel, *Which Country Has the World's Best Health Care?* (New York: PublicAffairs, 2020).

147 **In the UK, for example:** UK Parliament, "The Budget and Parliament," UK Parliament, accessed January 19, 2023, www.parliament.uk/about/how/role/check -and-approve-government-spending-and-taxation/the-budget-and-parliament; Emanuel, *Which Country Has the World's Best Health Care?,* 61–63; and Emanuel, 118–121.

147 **These budgets put:** Ane Auraaen, Rie Fujisawa, Gregoire De Lagasnerie, and Valérie Paris, "How OECD Health Systems Define the Range of Good and Services to Be Financed Collectively" (OECD Health Working Papers, no. 90, OECD, November 3, 2016), 18–19, doi.org/10.1787/5jlnb59ll80x-en.

147 **In Israel, for example:** Shadmi, "המחדל הלאומי של אי הרחבת סל הבריאות" ["The national neglect of not expanding the health basket"], *Haaretz,* February 5, 2002.

147 **In Canada, political parties:** Rachel Browne, "Explainer: Where the Major Federal Parties Stand on Health Care—National," Global News, October 4, 2019, globalnews.ca/news/5961823/explainer-where-the-major-federal-parties-stand-on -health-care.

148 **In the UK, any increased:** Louise Dalingwater, "The NHS at the Heart of the Election Campaign," *Revue française de civilisation britannique* 20, no. 3 (October 16, 2015), doi.org/10.4000/rfcb.568; and Theresa May, "PM Speech on the NHS: 18 June 2018," Royal Free Hospital, London, June 18, 2018, transcript, gov.uk /government/speeches/pm-speech-on-the-nhs-18-june-2018.

148 **Fifty years ago, the health-care:** OECD, "Health Spending, Total, % of GDP, 1970–2020," March 2, 2022, Canada, France, Germany United Kingdom, United

States, data.oecd.org/chart/6DeG; and Skinner, Cahan, and Fuchs, "Stabilizing Health Care's Share of the GDP," 709–11, online appendix.

148 **The development and adoption:** See, for example, Burton A. Weisbrod, "The Health Care Quadrilemma: An Essay on Technological Change, Insurance, Quality of Care, and Cost Containment," *Journal of Economic Literature* 29, no. 2 (June 1991): 523–52; Amitabh Chandra and Jonathan Skinner, "Technology Growth and Expenditure Growth in Health Care," *Journal of Economic Literature* 50, no. 3 (September 2012): 645–80; David M. Cutler and Srikanth Kadiyala, "The Return to Biomedical Research: Treatment and Behavioral Effects," in *Measuring the Gains from Medical Research: An Economic Approach*, ed. Kevin M. Murphy and Robert H. Topel, (Chicago: University of Chicago Press, 2003), 110-62; David M. Cutler, *Your Money or Your Life: Strong Medicine for America's Healthcare System* (New York: Oxford University Press, 2005); and Joseph P. Newhouse, "Medical Care Costs: How Much Welfare Loss?," *Journal of Economic Perspectives* 6, no. 3 (Summer 1992): 3–21.

149 **Some economists have argued:** This theoretical argument has been made in Hall and Jones 2007. Empirical evidence as to whether this is the case is not conclusive. See Acemoglu et al. 2013. Robert E. Hall and Charles I. Jones, "The Value of Life and the Rise in Health Spending," *Quarterly Journal of Economics* 122, no. 1 (February 2007): 39–72; and Daron Acemoglu, Amy Finkelstein, and Matthew J. Notowidigdo, "Income and Health Spending: Evidence from Oil Price Shocks," *Review of Economics and Statistics* 95, no. 4 (October 2013): 1079–95.

149 **One clear example:** Kim Rueben and Megan Randall, *Balanced Budget Requirements: How States Limit Deficit Spending* (Washington, DC: Urban Institute, November 2017), urban.org/research/publication/balanced-budget -requirements.

149 **As a result, states have:** Carrie H. Colla and Jonathan Skinner, "Has the ACA Made Health Care More Affordable?," in *The Trillion Dollar Revolution: How the Affordable Care Act Transformed Politics, Law, and Health Care in America*, ed. Ezekiel J. Emanuel and Abbe R. Gluck (New York: PublicAffairs, 2020), 257.

150 **The state of Maryland:** Centers for Medicare & Medicaid Services, "Maryland All-Payer Model," January 24, 2022, innovation.cms.gov/innovation-models /maryland-all-payer-model; and Tara Golshan, "The Answer to America's Health Care Cost Problem Might Be in Maryland," *Vox*, January 22, 2020, vox.com/policy -and-politics/2020/1/22/21055118/maryland-health-care-global-hospital-budget.

150 **As the philosopher:** Norman Daniels, "Symposium on the Rationing of Health Care: 2 Rationing Medical Care—a Philosopher's Perspective on Outcomes and Process," *Economics & Philosophy* 14, no. 1 (April 1998): 31.

150 **To see this, consider:** We define taxpayer spending as a share of GDP by the variable "Domestic General Government Health Expenditure as a % of Gross Domestic Product." See World Health Organization, "Global Health Expenditure Database," WHO, 2019, apps.who.int/nha/database/Select/Indicators/en.

151 **To be clear, total spending:** World Health Organization, "Global Health Expenditure Database."

152 **We realize of course:** See, for example, Michael L. Millenson, "Half a Century
        of the Health Care Crisis (and Still Going Strong)," *Health Affairs Forefront*,
        September 12, 2018, healthaffairs.org/do/10.1377/forefront.20180904.457305;
        and David U. Himmelstein, Steffie Woolhandler, Mark Almberg, and Clare
        Fauke, "The U.S. Health Care Crisis Continues: A Data Snapshot," *International
        Journal of Social Determinants of Health and Health Services* 48, no. 1
        (January 2018): 28–41.

152 **"In recent years":** Victor R. Fuchs, *Who Shall Live? Health, Economics, and Social
        Choice*, 2nd ed. (New York: Basic Books, 1974), 9.

153 **When US health-care spending:** Nisha Kurani, Jared Ortaliza, Emma Wager, Lucas
        Fox, and Krutika Amin, "How Has U.S. Spending on Healthcare Changed over
        Time?," Peterson-KFF Health System Tracker, February 25, 2022, healthsystemtracker
        .org/chart-collection/u-s-spending-healthcare-changed-time.

153 **If we listen:** Indeed, as early as 1949, President Truman—in his message to Congress
        proposing national health insurance—warned, "As treatment has become more
        expensive, families have found it more and more difficult to meet the extraordinary
        costs of accidents, serious illness or major surgery. . . . It is no longer just the poor who
        are unable to pay for all the medical care they need—such care is now beyond the
        means of all but the upper income groups" (Truman 1949). For some other examples
        of the steady stream of pronouncements over the last half century about the alarming
        level of health-care spending, see Millenson 2018. Harry S. Truman, "Special
        Message to the Congress on the Nation's Health Care Needs," April 22, 1949,
        trumanlibrary.gov/library/public-papers/85/special-message-congress-nations
        -health-needs; and Michael L. Millenson, "Half a Century of the Health Care Crisis
        (and Still Going Strong)," *Health Affairs Forefront*, September 12, 2018, healthaffairs
        .org/do/10.1377/forefront.20180904.457305.

153 **The real crisis is not:** Katherine Baicker and Jonathan Skinner, "Health Care
        Spending Growth and the Future of U.S. Tax Rates," *Tax Policy and the Economy* 25,
        no. 1 (September 2011): 39–68.

153 **From Nixon, to Clinton:** Shanoor Seervai and David Blumenthal, "Lessons on
        Universal Coverage from an Unexpected Advocate: Richard Nixon," Commonwealth
        Fund, *To the Point* (blog), November 2, 2017, commonwealthfund.org/blog/2017
        /lessons-universal-coverage-unexpected-advocate-richard-nixon; Barack Obama,
        "Remarks of Senator Barack Obama: Health Care Town Hall," Bristol, VA, June 5,
        2008, Vote Smart, justfacts.votesmart.org/public-statement/346763/remarks-of
        -senator-barack-obama-health-care-town-hall; and Alison P. Galvani, Alyssa S.
        Parpia, Eric M. Foster, Burton H. Singer, and Meagan C. Fitzpatrick, "Improving the
        Prognosis of Health Care in the USA," *The Lancet* 395, no. 10223 (February 15,
        2020): 524–33.

154 **You'd have to be:** OECD, *Health at a Glance 2019: OECD Indicators* (Paris:
        Organisation for Economic Co-operation and Development, November 7, 2019),
        Executive Summary, Indicator Overview, oecd-ilibrary.org/social-issues-migration
        -health/health-at-a-glance-2019_4dd50c09-en.

154 **Lower the prices:** Gerard F. Anderson, Peter Hussey, and Varduhi Petrosyan, "It's Still the Prices, Stupid: Why the US Spends So Much on Health Care, and a Tribute to Uwe Reinhardt," *Health Affairs* 38, no. 1 (January 2019): 87–95; David Squires and Chloe Anderson, "US Health Care from a Global Perspective: Spending, Use of Services, Prices, and Health in 13 Countries" (Commonwealth Fund pub. 1819, vol. 15, October 2015), 1–16; and Nicolas Shanosky, Daniel McDermott, and Nisha Kurani, "How Do U.S. Healthcare Resources Compare to Other Countries?," Peterson-KFF Health System Tracker, August 12, 2020, healthsystemtracker.org/chart-collection /u-s-health-care-resources-compare-countries.

154 **Slash administrative costs:** David M. Cutler, "Reducing Administrative Costs in U.S. Health Care" (policy proposal 2020-09, Hamilton Project, Brookings Institution, March 2020), hamiltonproject.org/assets/files/Cutler_PP_LO.pdf; and David M. Cutler and Dan P. Ly, "The (Paper) Work of Medicine: Understanding International Medical Costs," *Journal of Economic Perspectives* 25, no. 2 (Spring 2011): 3–25.

155 **And behind door number three:** William H. Shrank, Teresa L. Rogstad, and Natasha Parekh, "Waste in the US Health Care System: Estimated Costs and Potential for Savings," *JAMA* 322, no. 15 (October 7, 2019): 1501–9.

155 **But so too is the:** Lakdawalla 2018 summarizes some of the research on the responsiveness of pharmaceutical innovation to prices and profits. Examples of papers showing physician responses to payments include Clemens and Gottlieb 2014, Alexander and Schnell 2019, Cabral et al. 2021, and Brekke et al. 2017. Darius N. Lakdawalla, "Economics of the Pharmaceutical Industry," *Journal of Economic Literature* 56, no. 2 (June 2018): 397–449; Jeffrey Clemens and Joshua D. Gottlieb, "Do Physicians' Financial Incentives Affect Medical Treatment and Patient Health?," *American Economic Review* 104, no. 4 (April 2014): 1320–49; Diane Alexander and Molly Schnell, "The Impacts of Physician Payments on Patient Access, Use, and Health" (NBER Working Paper no. 26095, National Bureau of Economic Research, Cambridge, MA, July 2019); Marika Cabral, Colleen Carey, and Sarah Miller, "The Impact of Provider Payments on Health Care Utilization of Low-Income Individuals: Evidence from Medicare and Medicaid" (NBER Working Paper, no. 29471, National Bureau of Economic Research, Cambridge, MA, November 2021), doi.org/10.3386 /w29471; and Kurt R. Brekke, Tor Helge Holmås, Karin Monstad, and Odd Rune Straume, "Do Treatment Decisions Depend on Physicians' Financial Incentives?," *Journal of Public Economics* 155 (November 2017): 74–92.

155 **Proponents of "Medicare for all":** Manuela Tobias, "Comparing Administrative Costs for Private Insurance and Medicare," PolitiFact, September 20, 2017, politifact .com/factchecks/2017/sep/20/bernie-sanders/comparing-administrative-costs -private-insurance-a; and Boards of Trustees, Federal Hospital Insurance and Federal Supplementary Medical Insurance Trust Funds, *2017 Annual Report of the Boards of Trustees of the Federal Hospital Insurance and Federal Supplementary Medical Insurance Trust Funds* (Washington, DC: Centers for Medicare & Medicaid Services, 2017), 10, cms.gov/Research-Statistics-Data-and-Systems/Statistics-Trends-and-Reports /ReportsTrustFunds/Downloads/TR2017.pdf.

155 **Unfortunately, a large body:** See, for example, Zarek C. Brot-Goldberg, Amitabh Chandra, Benjamin R. Handel, and Jonathan T. Kolstad, "What Does a Deductible Do? The Impact of Cost-Sharing on Health Care Prices, Quantities, and Spending Dynamics," *Quarterly Journal of Economics* 132, no. 3 (August 2017): 1261–318; Vilsa Curto, Liran Einav, Amy Finkelstein, Jonathan Levin, and Jay Bhattacharya, "Health Care Spending and Utilization in Public and Private Medicare," *American Economic Journal: Applied Economics* 11, no. 2 (April 2019): 302–32; Michael Geruso, Timothy J. Layton, and Jacob Wallace, "What Difference Does a Health Plan Make? Evidence from Random Plan Assignment in Medicaid" (NBER Working Paper, no. 27762, National Bureau of Economic Research, Cambridge, MA, August 2020); Marika Cabral and Mark R. Cullen, "The Effect of Insurance Coverage on Preventive Care," *Economic Inquiry* 55, no. 3 (July 2017): 1452–67; and Sarah L. Taubman, Heidi L. Allen, Bill J. Wright, Katherine Baicker, and Amy N. Finkelstein, "Medicaid Increases Emergency-Department Use: Evidence from Oregon's Health Insurance Experiment," *Science* 343, no. 6168 (January 17, 2014): 263–68.

156 **It's also likely why:** Emanuel, *Which Country Has the World's Best Health Care?*, 377–81.

156 **One study estimated that:** OECD, *Tackling Wasteful Spending on Health* (Paris: OECD Publishing, 2017), oecd.org/els/health-systems/Tackling-Wasteful -Spending-on-Health-Highlights-revised.pdf; and Matthew Limb, "A Fifth of Healthcare Spending Is Wasted, Says OECD Report," *BMJ* 356 (January 13, 2017): j215.

156 **While we wait:** Esther Duflo, "The Economist as Plumber," *American Economic Review* 107, no. 5 (May 2017): 1–26.

157 **Indeed, we've discovered:** Liran Einav, Amy Finkelstein, and Neale Mahoney, "Long-Term Care Hospitals: A Case Study in Waste," *Review of Economics and Statistics* (August 9, 2021), doi.org/10.1162/rest_a_01092.

157 **A collection of health economists:** "About the Project," 1% Steps for Health Care Reform, accessed March 3, 2022, onepercentsteps.com/about.

158 **Still, let's not kid ourselves:** KFF, "Total Number of Medicare Beneficiaries by Type of Coverage," KFF, accessed Januray 18, 2023, Timeframe 2019, kff.org/medicare /state-indicator/total-medicare-beneficiaries; and Gary Claxton, Matthew Rae, Anthony Damico, Gregory Young, Daniel McDermott, and Heidi Whitmore, "Summary of Findings," in *2019 Employer Health Benefits Survey* (San Francisco: Kaiser Family Foundation, September 25, 2019), kff.org/report-section/ehbs-2019 -summary-of-findings.

CHAPTER 13: BEYOND BASIC

162 **Consider the contrasting:** Roosa Tikkanen, Robin Osborn, Elias Mossialos, Ana Djordjevic, and George A. Wharton, "International Health Care System Profiles: England," Commonwealth Fund, June 5, 2020, commonwealthfund.org /international-health-policy-center/countries/england; and Singapore Ministry of Health, "About Integrated Shield Plans," Singapore Ministry of Health, accessed

February 22, 2022, moh.gov.sg/cost-financing/healthcare-schemes-subsidies
/medishield-life/about-integrated-shield-plans.

163 **In Singapore, the upgrade:** Singapore Ministry of Health, "About Integrated
Shield Plans."

163 **In the UK, however:** NHS, "If I Pay for Private Treatment, How Will My NHS
Care Be Affected?," NHS, June 26, 2018, nhs.uk/common-health-questions/nhs
-services-and-treatments/if-i-pay-for-private-treatment-how-will-my-nhs-care-be
-affected.

163 **It's the disease that President:** Multiple Sclerosis Trust UK, "Types of MS," MS
Trust UK, October 1, 2020, mstrust.org.uk/about-ms/what-ms/types-ms; and West
Wing Wiki, "Multiple Sclerosis," accessed February 18, 2022, westwing.fandom
.com/wiki/Multiple_Sclerosis.

163 **There are a number of:** Multiple Sclerosis Association of America, "Long-Term
Treatments for Multiple Sclerosis," MSAA, December 17, 2015, mymsaa.org
/ms-information/treatments/long-term.

164 **But the NHS doesn't cover:** Multiple Sclerosis Trust UK, "Ozanimod (Zeposia)—
NICE Says No in Final Decision," MS Trust UK, May 13, 2021, mstrust.org.uk
/news/ozanimod-zeposia-nice-says-no-final-decision; NICE, "Ozanimod for
Treating Relapsing–Remitting Multiple Sclerosis" (technology appraisal guidance,
no. TA706, NICE, February 12, 2021), nice.org.uk/consultations/1204/2
/information-about-ozanimod; and NICE, "Beta Interferons and Glatiramer Acetate
for Treating Multiple Sclerosis" (technology appraisal guidance, no. TA527, NICE,
June 27, 2018), nice.org.uk/guidance/ta527/chapter/2-Information-about-the
-beta-interferons-and-glatiramer-acetate.

164 **By law, individuals cannot:** New York American College of Emergency Physicians,
"Medicaid Beneficiaries Cannot Be Billed," New York ACEP, accessed February 18,
2022, nyacep.org/practice-resources-2/resources/practice-management-resources
/medicaid/222-medicaid-beneficiaries-cannot-be-billed.

165 **But, second, something:** Jonathan Gruber and Kosali Simon, "Crowd-Out 10 Years
Later: Have Recent Public Insurance Expansions Crowded Out Private Health
Insurance?," *Journal of Health Economics* 27, no. 2 (March 2008): 201–17; and Thomas
Buchmueller, John C. Ham, and Lara D. Shore-Sheppard, "The Medicaid Program,"
in *Economics of Means-Tested Transfer Programs in the United States,* vol. 1, ed. Robert
A. Moffitt (Chicago: University of Chicago Press: 2016), 21–136.

166 **Medicare has already:** Meredith Freed, Jeannie Fuglesten Biniek, Anthony Damico,
and Tricia Neuman, "Medicare Advantage in 2021: Enrollment Update and Key
Trends," KFF, June 21, 2021, web.archive.org/web/20220307202453/http://www
.kff.org/medicare/issue-brief/medicare-advantage-in-2021-enrollment-update-and
-key-trends.

166 **The Medicare eligible:** US Centers for Medicare & Medicaid Services, "How Do
Medicare Advantage Plans Work?," Medicare.gov, accessed February 18, 2022,
medicare.gov/sign-up-change-plans/types-of-medicare-health-plans/medicare
-advantage-plans/how-do-medicare-advantage-plans-work.

166 **This private Medicare:** Yash M. Patel and Stuart Guterman, "The Evolution of Private Plans in Medicare," Commonwealth Fund, December 8, 2017, commonwealthfund.org/publications/issue-briefs/2017/dec/evolution-private-plans-medicare.

167 **The result is that we:** Vilsa Curto, Liran Einav, Jonathan Levin, and Jay Bhattacharya, "Can Health Insurance Competition Work? Evidence from Medicare Advantage," *Journal of Political Economy* 129, no. 2 (February 2021): 570–606; Liran Einav and Jonathan Levin, "Managed Competition in Health Insurance," *Journal of the European Economic Association* 13, no. 6 (December 2015): 998–1021; and Thomas G. McGuire, Joseph P. Newhouse, and Anna D. Sinaiko, "An Economic History of Medicare Part C," *Milbank Quarterly* 89, no. 2 (June 2011): 28–332.

167 **Over sixty million:** "CMS Program Statistics—Medicare Total Enrollment," Centers for Medicare & Medicaid Services, August 31, 2022, data.cms.gov/summary-statistics-on-beneficiary-enrollment/medicare-and-medicaid-reports/cms-program-statistics-medicare-total-enrollment.

167 **As a result, the government:** Alicia L. Cooper and Amal N. Trivedi, "Fitness Memberships and Favorable Selection in Medicare Advantage Plans," *New England Journal of Medicine* 366, no. 2 (January 12, 2012): 150–57; and Stephanie L. Shimada, Alan M. Zaslavsky, Lawrence B. Zaborski, A. James O'Malley, Amy Heller, and Paul D. Cleary, "Market and Beneficiary Characteristics Associated with Enrollment in Medicare Managed Care Plans and Fee-for-Service," *Medical Care* 47, no. 5 (May 2009): 517–23.

169 **Fortunately, there are other:** For more detail on what the government has done and what effects it may have had, see Joseph P. Newhouse and Thomas G. McGuire, "How Successful Is Medicare Advantage?," *Milbank Quarterly* 92, no. 2 (June 2014): 351–94; Thomas G. McGuire and Joseph P. Newhouse, "Medicare Advantage: Regulated Competition in the Shadow of a Public Option," in *Risk Adjustment, Risk Sharing and Premium Regulation in Health Insurance Markets: Theory and Practice* (London: Academic Press, 2018), 563–98; and Cooper and Trivedi, "Fitness Memberships and Favorable Selection," 150–57.

171 **Liran and his collaborators have:** Curto et al., "Can Health Insurance Competition Work?," 570–606.

171 **And it is why about:** Elias Mossialos, Martin Wenzl, Robin Osborn, and Chloe Anderson, eds., *International Profiles of Health Care Systems, 2014: Australia, Canada, Denmark, England, France, Germany, Italy, Japan, The Netherlands, New Zealand, Norway, Singapore, Sweden, Switzerland, and the United States* (New York: Commonwealth Fund, January 23, 2015), commonwealthfund.org/publications/fund-reports/2015/jan/international-profiles-health-care-systems-2014-australia-canada; and "Room Options and Billing under OHIP at GRH," Grand River Hospital, August 1, 2021, grhosp.on.ca/care/visitors/billing/room-options.

172 **Canadians have no issue:** Roosa Tikkanen, Robin Osborn, Elias Mossialos, Ana Djordjevic, and George A. Wharton, "International Health Care System Profiles: Canada," Commonwealth Fund, June 5, 2020, commonwealthfund.org

/international-health-policy-center/countries/canada; Marthe Cloutier and Bruno
Gagnon, "Taxation of Employee Benefits (Group Insurance) in Canada,"
Canadian Institute of Actuaries, 2017, cia-ica.ca/docs/default-source/pec-2018
/g10-5---taxation-of-ee-benefits-2017-clean-(e).pdf; and Amy Finkelstein, "The Effect
of Tax Subsidies to Employer-Provided Supplementary Health Insurance: Evidence
from Canada," *Journal of Public Economics* 84, no. 3 (June 2002): 305–39.

172 **Many of these countries:** Rifat Atun, Luiz Odorico Monteiro de Andrade, Gisele
Almeida, Daniel Cotlear, Tania Dmytraczenko, Patricia Frenz, Patrícia Garcia, et al.,
"Health-System Reform and Universal Health Coverage in Latin America," *The
Lancet* 385, no. 9974 (March 28, 2015): 1234.

173 **The supplementary system may pay:** Jeffrey Clemens and Joshua D. Gottlieb,
"Do Physicians' Financial Incentives Affect Medical Treatment and Patient Health?,"
American Economic Review 104, no. 4 (April 2014): 1320–49; and Diane Alexander
and Molly Schnell, "The Impacts of Physician Payments on Patient Access, Use, and
Health" (NBER Working Paper no. 26095, National Bureau of Economic Research,
Cambridge, MA, July 2019).

173 **Such concerns loomed:** Sierra Dean, "Canada's Landmark Chaoulli Decision: A
Vital Blueprint for Change in the Canadian Health Care System," *Law & Business
Review of the Americas* 13, no. 2 (2007): 417.

174 **The Quebec government argued:** Amélie Quesnel-Vallée, Richard A. McKay, and
Noushon Farmanara, "*Chaoulli v Quebec:* Cause or Symptom of Quebec Health
System Privatization?," in *Is Two-Tier Health Care the Future?,* ed. Colleen M. Flood
and Bryan Thomas (Ottawa, ON: University of Ottawa Press, 2020), 93–122; and
Christopher P. Manfredi and Antonia Maioni, "The Last Line of Defence for Citizens:
Litigating Private Health Insurance in *Chaoulli v. Québec,*" in "Symposium on
Chaoulli," ed. Bruce Ryder, special issue, *Osgoode Hall Law Journal* 44, no. 2
(Summer 2006): 249.

174 **The Supreme Court:** Manfredi and Maioni, "The Last Line of Defence for Citizens,"
249; Dean, "Canada's Landmark Chaoulli Decision," 417; and Quesnel-Vallée,
McKay, and Farmanara, "*Chaoulli v Quebec,*" 93–122.

174 **It did not specify:** Colleen M. Flood and Terrence Sullivan, "Supreme Disagreement:
The Highest Court Affirms an Empty Right," *CMAJ* 173, no. 2 (July 19, 2005):
142–43; and Quesnel-Vallée, McKay, and Farmanara, "*Chaoulli v Quebec,*" 93–122.

175 **Quebec lost its case:** Yanick Labrie, "The Chaoulli Decision and Health Care Reform:
A Missed Opportunity?" (Viewpoint, Health Care Series, Montreal Economic
Institute, June 2015), iedm.org/sites/default/files/pub_files/lepoint0415_en.pdf.

175 **Indeed, duplicative private:** CBC News, "No One Wants Quebec's Limited Private
Health Insurance," CBC, March 30, 2009, cbc.ca/news/canada/montreal/no-one
-wants-quebec-s-limited-private-health-insurance-1.853098; Montreal Economic
Institute, "Ten Years after the Chaoulli Decision, Quebec Patients Are Still
Waiting as Long as Ever," Cision, June 4, 2015, newswire.ca/news-releases/ten
-years-after-the-chaoulli-decision-quebec-patients-are-still-waiting-as-long-as
-ever-517852131.html.

175 **In Australia, about half:** Francesca Colombo and Nicole Tapay, "Private Health Insurance in Australia: A Case Study" (OECD Health Working Papers, no. 8, OECD, October 30, 2003), doi.org/10.1787/478608584171.

175 **In Singapore, two thirds:** Singapore Ministry of Health, "Admissions and Outpatient Attendances," Singapore Ministry of Health, accessed January 18, 2023, moh.gov.sg/resources-statistics/singapore-health-facts/admissions-and-outpatient-attendances.

175 **Far from:** Colombo and Tapay, "Private Health Insurance in Australia."

175 **Likewise, government policy:** Patel and Guterman, "The Evolution of Private Plans in Medicare"; and McGuire, Newhouse, and Sinaiko, "An Economic History of Medicare Part C," 289–332.

175 **Indeed, a common:** Craig Garthwaite, Tal Gross, and Matthew J. Notowidigdo, "Hospitals as Insurers of Last Resort," *American Economic Journal: Applied Economics* 10, no. 1 (January 2018): 1–39.

176 **Recent experiences:** State of Israel, 2014, "הוועדה המייעצת לחיזוק מערכת הבריאות הציבורית" ["The Advisory Committee for strengthening the public health system"], health.gov .il/PublicationsFiles/publichealth2014.pdf.

177 **One is to increase funding:** Sally Williams and James Buchan, "Assessing the New NHS Consultant Contract," *King's Fund* (May 2006), kingsfund.org.uk /sites/default/files/field/field_publication_file/assessing-new-nhs-consultant -contract-sally-williams-james-buchan-10-may-2006.pdf; and State of Israel, "הוועדה המייעצת לחיזוק מערכת הבריאות הציבורית" ["Advisory Committee"].

HOME INSPECTION: TAKING STOCK

182 **But that, as Kipling:** Rudyard Kipling, *Soldiers Three: A Collection of Stories Setting Forth Certain Passages in the Lives and Adventures of Privates Terence Mulvaney, Stanley Ortheris, and John Learoyd* (Chicago: Rand, McNally, n.d., ca. 1896–1899), 133, archive.org/details/soldiersthreecol00kipl2.

EPILOGUE: CAN IT BE BUILT?

185 **In 1916, the president:** Sarah Richardson, "How Surgeon General Rupert Blue Became America's Heroic Microbe Hunter," Historynet, September 3, 2020, historynet.com/americas-heroic-microbe-hunter; and Irving Fisher, "The Need for Health Insurance," *American Labor Legislation Review* 7, no. 1 (March 1917): 9.

185 **In the early 1970s:** Godfrey Hodgson, "The Politics of American Health Care: What Is It Costing You?," *The Atlantic*, October 1973, theatlantic.com/past/docs/politics /healthca/hodgson.htm.

185 **"the feeling among experts":** George D. Lundberg, "National Health Care Reform: An Aura of Inevitability Is Upon Us," *JAMA* 265, no. 19 (May 15, 1991): 2566–67.

187 **"No country has acquired":** Jacob S. Hacker, "The Historical Logic of National Health Insurance: Structure and Sequence in the Development of British, Canadian,

and U.S. Medical Policy," *Studies in American Political Development* 12, no. 1 (April 1998): 57.

187 **But there's also another:** Paul Starr, *Remedy and Reaction: The Peculiar American Struggle over Health Care Reform* (New Haven, CT: Yale University Press, 2011), 281.

187 **This narrative starts:** Starr, *Remedy and Reaction*, 29–35; Hacker, "The Historical Logic of National Health Insurance," 107–13; and Isadore S. Falk, "Proposals for National Health Insurance in the USA: Origins and Evolution, and Some Perceptions for the Future," *Milbank Memorial Fund Quarterly: Health and Society* 55, no. 2 (Spring 1977): 161–91.

188 **More near misses came:** Starr, *Remedy and Reaction*, 40; Hacker, "The Historical Logic of National Health Insurance," 116; Theodore Marmor, *The Politics of Medicare,* 2nd ed. (Hawthorne, NY: Aldine de Gruyter, 2000), 6–10.

188 **His failed attempts:** Hacker, "The Historical Logic of National Health Insurance," 97.

188 **The British Medical Association:** Howard Glennerster, *British Social Policy: 1945 to the Present,* 3rd ed.(Malden, MA: Blackwell, 2007), 53.

188 **One physician member:** "British Physicians Defy Health Plan," *New York Times,* March 18, 1948, timesmachine.nytimes.com/timesmachine/1948/03/18/85199829 .html?pageNumber=29.

188 **In the UK case:** Cal Flyn, "The Birth of Britain's National Health Service," in *The History of the NHS,* part 1, Wellcome Collection, June 21, 2018, wellcomecollection .org/articles/WyjHUicAACvGnmJI.

189 **Winston Churchill—the Tory:** Glennerster, *British Social Policy,* 53.

189 **The Tories voted against:** Lily Foster, "What Resistance Was There to the Formation of the NHS?," West End at War, January 17, 2019, westendatwar.org.uk/page/what _resistance_was_there_to_the_formation_of_the_nhs.

189 **The enactment was:** Anthony Broxton, "Lower Than Vermin: The Story of Bevan's Quote That Lives On," *Tides of History* (blog), July 3, 2018, tidesofhistory.com /2018/07/03/lower-than-vermin-the-story-of-bevans-quote-that-lives-on.

189 **As one leading scholar:** Glennerster, *British Social Policy,* 53.

189 **Universal coverage in Canada:** Hacker, "The Historical Logic of National Health Insurance," 101.

189 **A few years later:** Hacker, 99–104; and Alvin Finkel, *Social Policy and Practice in Canada: A History* (Waterloo, ON: Wilfrid Laurier University Press, 2006), 177–80.

190 **Nixon made a concerted:** David Blumenthal and James A. Morone, "Presidential Scandal: Bad Medicine for Health Care Reform," Commonwealth Fund, June 21, 2017, doi.org/10.26099/v4qy-x770; and Starr, *Remedy and Reaction,* 72–76.

190 **There are various theories:** Hacker, "The Historical Logic of National Health Insurance," 121; and Starr, *Remedy and Reaction,* 72–76.

191 **Like "surfers waiting":** John W. Kingdon, *Agendas, Alternatives, and Public Policies,* (Boston: Little, Brown, 1984), 173.

191 **"Chance only favors":** Louis Pasteur said this at a lecture at the University of Lille on December 7, 1854. His exact words (in French) were: "Le hasard ne favorise

que les esprits préparés." See René Vallery-Radot, *The Life of Pasteur* (New York: Garden City, 1926), 79.

192 **In 1953, a British:** Stan Brock and Amanda Wilson, "Remote Area Medical: Pioneers of No-Cost Health Care," in *Healthcare Disparities at the Crossroads with Healthcare Reform*, ed. Richard Allen Williams (New York: Springer, 2011), 413–20.

192 **Decades later—after:** Remote Area Medical, "Our Founder," Remote Area Medical, accessed March 8, 2022, ramusa.org/our-founder; and Brock and Wilson, "Remote Area Medical," 413–20.

192 **By this time, Brock:** Brock and Wilson, 413–20; "Free Pop-up Clinic Schedule," Remote Area Medical, accessed March 8, 2022, ramusa.org/clinic-schedule.

192 **In 1910, at the wee:** T. C. Douglas, *The Making of a Socialist: The Recollections of T.C. Douglas*, ed. Lewis H. Thomas (Edmonton, AB: University of Alberta Press, 1982), 6–7, archive.org/details/makingofsocialis00doug.

193 **Like Stan Brock, Tommy Douglas:** Douglas, *The Making of a Socialist*, 6–7.

193 **In 1947, as premier:** Finkel, *Social Policy and Practice in Canada*, 171; and T. R. Reid, *The Healing of America: A Global Quest for Better, Cheaper, and Fairer Health Care* (New York: Penguin Books, 2010), 126–34.

INDEX